THE
University
AND THE
State

Other books published in cooperation with the University Centers for Rational Alternatives:

THE IDEA OF A MODERN UNIVERSITY (1974)

THE PHILOSOPHY OF THE CURRICULUM (1975)

THE ETHICS OF TEACHING AND SCIENTIFIC RESEARCH (1977)

THE
University
AND THE
State:
WHAT ROLE FOR GOVERNMENT IN HIGHER EDUCATION ?

edited by
Sidney Hook
Paul Kurtz
Miro Todorovich

ℙ *Prometheus Books*
Buffalo, New York 14215

THE
University
AND THE
State

Published by Prometheus Books
1203 Kensington Avenue, Buffalo, New York 14215

Library of Congress Catalog Card Number 77–26375
ISBN 0–87975–098–7

Contents

Contents

Introduction

The essays published in this volume were originally delivered at the Fourth General Meeting of University Centers for Rational Alternatives held at George Washington University, Washington D.C. in December, 1976. The meeting was devoted to the exploration of one of the most important themes in the educational life of our times. Indeed, next to the question of what the idea of a modern university is or should be, the most fateful of the issues that concern educators and their fellow citizens is: what should the university's relationship be to the state and government?

This issue possesses more than a perennial relevance. Its topicality was reinforced at the time of the Conference by the fact that the political guard of the nation was about to change amid widespread uncertainty as to the direction of its educational policy. Since then the pronouncements of some of its spokesmen have been disquieting to those who recognize the necessity of some state support and yet seek jealously to preserve institutional autonomy with respect to the fulfillment of the academic mission.

Regardless of whether a university considers itself private or public, it cannot be indifferent to the educational policies of the state if it wishes to survive in an era of mounting inflationary costs. Private institutions face the additional hazard that under some specious interpretation of what constitutes discrimination, and of arbitrary ill-founded notions of what constitutes evidence, their tax-exempt status might be challenged and cancelled. All universities must be even more concerned with trends in the educational policies formulated by government if they wish to pre-serve the relative autonomy of their academic mission. Unless one regards the university purely as a business proposition or as a service appendage to a governmental bureau, what happens to its academic mission is of far greater importance than whether it survives or not.

Our primary concern here as elsewhere is to explore the rational alternatives to educational programs in dispute in the academy that affect the life of the academy in important ways; and therewith to spark fruitful debate or discussion. University Centers for Rational Alternatives is happy to observe that, hard upon its Conference on the Philosophy of the Curriculum two years ago where the question of the role of general education in liberal arts colleges was made the focus of the discussion, a lively renaissance of interest in the theme developed in prestigious educational institutions across the country from Harvard to Stanford. The outcome of these renewed discussions seems to run counter to the indiscriminate and undiscriminating elective curriculum that came in the wake of the student disorders of the late sixties and early seventies. It bids fair to redirect the main currents of curricular reform in present-day American undergraduate education.

To the theme of the Conference on the State and the University, University Centers for Rational Alternatives as an organization brings no partisan ideological commitments. As individuals, the participants have different commitments, and our task is to examine all of them. We believe that before proposing desirable policies to regulate the tangled relations between state or government and higher education, it is an intelligent procedure to examine the existing policies and their costs. The efficacy or relative efficiency of a policy when it is implemented may have a bearing on its equity. This will explain the strategy and organiza-tion of the sessions. They were planned to terminate with an analysis of normative questions based on an accurate picture of the current scene.

That ideas, even of the most abstract character, concerning equality, excellence, discrimination and democracy have practical consequences, especially in the field of education, can hardly be disputed. The more significant questions, however, are whether ideas should be justified by their consequences, and if so by what consequences? Or should our leading ideas be accepted as indisputable first principles or axioms and applied regardless of their consequences? In the latter case we face the difficulty of distinguishing between "prejudices"—as we call the first

2

principles of those who disagree with us—and "truths" which our own first principles seem to so clearly express. It is not unreasonable, however, to hold that in a community whose educational agencies depend upon public support, the actual impact of policies underwritten by government on the quality of education will have to be critically assessed. Even though the assessment may be skewed by the principles one brings to the evaluations, there is usually sufficient agreement on the facts in the case to provide a basis for further reflection on the validity of the policies.

With cordial thanks and appreciation, University Centers for Rational Alternatives wishes to acknowledge support for its projects from: The National Endowment for the Humanities, the Alfred P. Sloan Foundation, and the Andrew W. Mellon Foundation.

Sidney Hook

THE GOVERNMENT AS
A PATRON OF
HIGHER EDUCATION

Federal Patronage of the Universities: A Rose by Many Other Names?

Chester E. Finn, Jr.
Brookings Institution

The federal reservoir annually pours almost $15 billion into the nation's higher education system, a princely sum, equivalent to $1,500 for every college and university student in the land, nearly $24,000 per faculty member, and enough money to replace Harvard's celebrated endowment ten times over.

Yet, that money flows through so many channels, twists and turns so many times between its source and its destinations, is so uneven in its impact, so cramped in the uses to which it can be put, and requires of its recipients so much in return, that one hesitates to describe Washington as a patron of the higher learning. Perhaps the only form of financing that *cannot* be found among the more than four hundred separate federal legislative provisions bearing on higher education is unrestricted support for such learning.

Several historical reasons suggest themselves. The most important is constitutional, for among the responsibilities the founding fathers reserved to the states was education. The colleges of the seventeenth and eighteenth centuries had been chartered by the individual colonies (or by the king) and were generally paid for with a blend of private and local public funds. Presidents Washington, Jefferson, Madison, and John Quincy Adams urged Congress to alter this pattern by establishing a national university, and in 1816 a committee of the House of Representatives reported favorably on the idea; but Congress rejected the proposal and, save for the military academies—West Point was established in 1802—and a few other highly specialized institutions under direct federal auspices, postsecondary education remained in state and private hands.

The Morrill Act of 1862 marked the first serious encroachment on this tradition and set a precedent for the use of federal resources to strengthen and enlarge the nation's higher education system, but it set other precedents as well. It showed that these resources need not flow directly from Washington to existing institutions, there to be used for whatever the college desired, but could instead go to intermediaries for specific purposes linked to other objectives of the national government. In this case, the intermediaries were the states, the avowed purpose was the endowment and support of colleges teaching "agricultural and mechanic arts," and the larger federal interest was the promotion of migration through the orderly disposition of federal lands. Congress was later to vote annual appropriations for support of the "land grant colleges" which resulted, and it happens that these small sums, now totalling about $12 million per annum, are perhaps the least cramped of the myriad provisions through which Washington puts money into higher education. Nevertheless, most subsequent enactments held to the course charted in 1862, and attempts to stray in other directions have generally been successfully opposed by those whose constitutional, fiscal, or educational principles did not countenance overt federal financing of higher education per se.

Issues of academic and religious freedom were also involved. The sectarian character of many of the nation's institutions of higher education touches on the First Amendment as well as the Tenth. While the federal government could plausibly "purchase" a particular service or activity from a church-related college, any allocation of unrestricted funds to such a school would pose questions about the separation of church and state, while any allocation of general support that excluded such institutions would be unfair and politically vulnerable. A further set of political and philosophical obstacles to federal patronage of the university is symbolized by the phrase "federal control of education," which has echoed across the decades. The academic community is jealous of its freedom, and conservative politicians and "small government" groups have exploited that sensitivity by encouraging the idea that federal funds would tie federal strings to the institutions receiving the money. All too often that threat has come true, but there is some irony in the fact that many of today's irksome controls follow from the narrowness and specificity of the numerous "categorical" programs that arose in lieu of general support.

Except for the land-grant legislation and a handful of other elderly programs, most of the arrangements for channeling federal funds to the nation's campuses are creations of the postwar period. Many, though not all, can be traced to a quartet of purposes that the academy seemed well suited to accomplish: the re-entry of servicemen into civilian life; the production of new scientific knowledge and technological capacity; the training of skilled manpower in particular fields; and the abolition of poverty and inequality. Each of these impulses gave rise to a number of discrete programs, and, since it is rare for a program to be abolished, the number of provisions on the federal statute books has grown quite large, as has the total amount of money that passes through them. Many colleges and universities now derive a sizable fraction of their income from Washington but, because none of these programs supplies a consequential amount of "unrestricted" money to the generality of American postsecondary institutions, it is still a misnomer to speak of federal patronage. Indeed, perhaps the central conflict between the academy and the national government is the enduring tension between Washington's desire to use its money to steer the universities in directions of its choosing, and the determination of the campuses to garner sufficient funds to chart their own course.

ACCOUNTING FOR FIFTEEN BILLION DOLLARS

> "With respect to higher education, the federal government has made no decision. It has made bits and pieces of decisions about specific and limited issues."
>
> James A. Perkins, 1973[1]

So numerous are the programs, so varied their goals, so fragmented is the government's administration of them, and so uneven their impact on the academy, that one has difficulty grasping their entirety. Discussions of federal higher education programs often confine themselves to the programs administered by the U.S. Office of Education, yet these total but a few billion dollars, a sizable sum to be sure, but a different order of magnitude from $15 billion.

Definitional problems abound, further bedeviled by attempts to read the collective mind of Congress in order to ascertain the government's motive in establishing a given program. What is one to say, for example, about the G.I. Bill, which for the past several years has been the broadest channel of federal funds into higher education, but which could scarcely be termed a program meant to strengthen the higher education system? What about research programs created to further the mission of a single federal agency and apt to benefit some universities quite handsomely while conferring little or nothing on the average college? How is one to count aid to students, some of which ends up in the university checking account but some of which purchases beer and textbooks? What should be done with the so-called "tax expenditures," which are not direct federal outlays at all but, rather, revenues that are never collected because the taxpayer avails himself of provisions in the tax code that may—but need not—be thought of as meant to foster higher education?

In its annual compilations accompanying the president's budget message, the Office of Management and Budget (OMB) tries to corral these programmatic mustangs, and by examining three separate "summary tables" (one for tax expenditures, one for research and development, one for all the rest), one can glimpse their totality. These analyses are invaluable, there being few alternatives, but they do not lack uncertainties of their own. First, the budget figures are prospective, not retrospective, and thus tend to reflect what the president wants Congress to appropriate, rather than the amounts actually spent in a particular year.

Second, the OMB corrals are sometimes too large and too confining. The cost of operating West Point and Annapolis, for example, would not ordinarily be regarded as a "higher education" expense, but it is included here. On the other hand, vast federal outlays that may yield sizable sums for colleges and universities—programs such as General Revenue Sharing, and the Comprehensive Employment and Training activities of the Labor Department—are omitted, because the money flows through intermediaries, because it is not necessarily spent on higher education, and because it is extremely hard to determine what portion is and what is not.

Third, there are technical problems. Some programs are "forward funded," meaning that funds appropriated in one year actually arrive on campus the following year. In other instances, particularly in the realm of federally sponsored research, one must distinguish between "obligations'' and ''outlays,'' for money that is promised one year may actually be spent in later years.

Fourth, ''higher'' education is itself an elusive category so far as federal programs are concerned. Veteran and Social Security beneficiaries may be in high school. Other recipients of federal student aid may attend vocational schools. Research funds may be awarded to a legal entity called a university but in fact be intended for, and spent by, a self-contained laboratory that is only loosely tied to the campus.

Such considerations impede any attempt to tally the aggregate federal financial involvement with the higher education industry. Nevertheless, for all its shortcomings, the annual OMB analysis remains the most ambitious and comprehensive effort to make such a tally on a regular basis.

A deeper truth lurks in that claim: so scattered and decentralized are Washington's sources of funds for higher education that nowhere, short of the Executive Office of the President, is anyone in a position to add them all up. Mechanical though that may sound, it symbolizes the difficulty of grasping federal higher education policy in its entirety. Simply stated, James Perkins was correct: there is no such thing. Instead, there is an aggregation of programs and activities that lack coherence and central direction and have little in common with each other save that each somehow affects the academy.

STUDENT AID

Today the fastest growing and by far the largest mode of federal expenditure in the realm of higher education is assistance to individuals. Increased support for students accounts for five of the six billion dollars added to overall federal higher education outlays in the brief period from (fiscal) 1968 to 1975. From one-third of the total a decade ago, student aid now constitutes two-thirds.

Many partial explanations suggest themselves, but three stand out. First, since the heyday of the civil rights and anti-poverty movements in the early sixties, both the executive branch and the Congress have pursued a ''student aid strategy,'' preferring to add resources to programs that help needy students pay for college rather than those that help colleges balance their budgets. This emphasis on stuents generally, and impoverished students particularly, has many expressions in the federal statutes but is perhaps best symbolized by the Higher Education Act of

Table I
Federal Funds for Higher Education:
Actual Outlays in Fiscal Year 1976[a]

	Millions of U.S. Dollars
I. Assistance to Students	
Department of Health, Education, and Welfare	
U. S. Office of Education	
Basic Opportunity Grants[b]	$ 905
"Campus-based" aid and SSIG program[c]	947
Guaranteed loans[d]	318
Other Office of Education[e]	18
Social Security—dependents and survivors education benefits[f]	998
Health training and other HEW[g]	278
Veterans Education Benefits[h]	4,301
Department of Defense[i]	300
Other[j]	113
Total	$ 8,178
II. Payments to Institutions	
Research and development conducted in colleges and universities[k]	$ 2,675
Programs for disadvantaged students and developing institutions[l]	224
Vocational education[m]	163
Other Office of Education[n]	84
Special institutions[o]	84
Health resources[p]	759
Department of Defense[q]	297
Other[r]	112
Total	$ 4,398
III. Tax Expenditures[s]	
Exclusion of scholarships and fellowships	$ 195
Parental personal exemptions for students aged nineteen and over	720
Deductibility of contributions—personal	510
Deductibility of contributions—corporate	190
Exclusion of veterans education benefits	305
Total[t]	$ 1,920
Grand Total	$14,496

NOTES:

a. Figures in this table represent actual outlays in fiscal year 1976, which corresponds to school year 1975–76. Since several student aid programs are "forward-funded," some of these outlays represent appropriations actually made for fiscal year 1975, but not available to students until 1975–76. All figures are derived from the Office of Management and Budget, *Special Analyses: Budget of the United States Government, Fiscal Year 1978* (Washington, D.C.: U.S. Government Printing Office, January 1977), indicated in subsequent table notes simply as *Budget*.

b. *Budget*, Table I–2. This is a "forward-funded" program. Hence the figure corresponds to Fiscal 1975 appropriations, plus an additional sum "drawn down" from the 1976 appropriation when funds proved inadequate to meet student demand. It may be noted that this program has been growing very rapidly. President Carter's budget request for Fiscal 1978 (school year 1978–79) asked $2.3 billion for this program. See *Higher Education Daily*, vol. 5, no. 36, February 23, 1977, p. 1.

c. *Budget*, Table I–2. This figure includes the line marked "Work-Study, supplementary grants and student supplementary incentive grants" and also that for "Direct student loans." These programs are also forward-funded.

d. *Budget*, Table I–2. This figure includes the line marked "Guaranteed student loans" and also that for "Student loan insurance fund." Actual outlays tend to understate the true cost of this program. The Fiscal 1976 appropriation totalled $654 million, and "obligations" that year came to $450 million. See *Higher Education Daily*, loc. cit., p. 6.

e. Author's estimate, derived by taking the Office of Education student aid totals shown in *Budget*, Table I–9 and subtracting the outlays for specific programs named above.

f. *Budget*, Table I–2. This is the entry for "Student grants (OASDI)."

g. *Budget*, Table I–9. This figure represents the sum of "Health Agencies and other," "National Institutes of Health," and "Other HEW," minus $31 million for Social Security student grants at the graduate level already accounted for.

h. *Budget*, Table I–3. This is the higher education entry for "Veterans readjustment." It may be noted that veterans readjustment (i.e., G.I. Bill) payments shown in Table I–3 also include an additional $140 million at the elementary and secondary level, and $786 million for "adult and continuing education." Thus the figure shown in the text table considerably understates the full cost of the G.I. Bill. On the other hand, it should be noted that this program has been diminishing. The Carter budget for Fiscal 1978 projected total outlays of $3.7 billion, down from $5.2 billion (at all levels) in Fiscal 1976. See *Higher Education and National Affairs*, vol. XXVI, no. 8 (February 25, 1977), p. 5.

i. *Budget*, Table I–9. This represents the sum of the Defense entries for undergraduate and graduate student support.

j. *Budget*, Table I–9. This represents the sum of "Justice," "Other" (both places the entry appears), and "National Science Foundation."

k. *Budget*, Table P–6. The corresponding figure for "Obligations" in Fiscal 1976 (which is probably a more accurate gauge of the level of federal spending for this purpose) is $2,690 million.

l. *Budget*, Table I–2.

m. *Budget*, Table I–2. It may be noted that only a small portion of federal outlays for vocational and occupational education take place at the higher education level. Elementary and secondary schools account for another $423 million, and adult and continuing education for an additional $142 million.

Notes to Table I (Continued)

n. *Budget*, Table I–2. This represents the entry for "Other Office of Education" minus the amount entered above for "Other Office of Education" student assistance.

o. *Budget*, Table I–2. This figure includes only the higher educational institutions such as Howard University and Gallaudet College and omits an additional $28 million for "other institutions" such as the American Printing House for the Blind.

p. *Budget*, Tables I–2 and I–3. This figure represents the sum of "Other HEW" (Table I–2), "Health professions training, Research training (NIH) and Alcohol, Drug, and Mental Health Administration" (all from Table I–3) minus the amount entered above for "Health Training and other HEW" student assistance.

q. *Budget*, Table I–3. This represents the sum of "Military service academies, Reserve Officers Training Corps and Other DOD" minus the amount assigned to Defense for student assistance above.

r. *Budget*, Tables I–2 and I–3. This represents the sum of "National Science Foundation" and "Other" (both from Table I–2) and "Other" from I–3, minus the amount entered above for "Other" student assistance.

s. All of these figures are from *Budget* Table F–1.

t. This total is understated, because the special analyses do not include all tax expenditures on behalf of higher education. Sunley estimates that in Fiscal year 1977 "direct" tax expenditures for higher education totalled $2,360 million, which he derived by including the deductibility of bequests, unrealized capital gains on gifts and bequests, and the exclusion from taxation of student Social Security benefits, as well as those tax expenditures noted in the table. He also estimates an "indirect" federal tax expenditure for higher education of $1,480 million, resulting from the deductibility of state and local taxes (a portion of which underwrites colleges and universities) and the exemption of interest on state and local debt (including certain capital expenses of state colleges and universities). See Emil Sunley, "Federal and State Tax Policies," prepared for a Brookings Institution conference on Public Policy and Private Higher Education, revised draft, March 1977.

1965, the thoroughgoing amendments approved in 1972, and the refinements added in 1976.

Second, the decision to revive the G.I. Bill in 1966, combined with the vast increase in the veterans' rolls after the Vietnam War, meant a mushrooming of the outlays needed to honor the government's commitment to pay so much per month to every veteran pursuing an approved course of study.

Third, the 1965 amendments to the Social Security Act extended benefits to young persons—the dependents and survivors of Social Security recipients—enrolled in school or college who previously lost such benefits upon attaining their eighteenth birthday. This provision now costs about one billion dollars a year, although these monies come from the Social Security trust fund rather than from ordinary appropriations.

As these explanations suggest, federal student aid does not extend to every college student. In every instance, eligibility for such assistance depends both on being a student *and* on satisfying one or more essentially unrelated conditions. This is a far cry from the old idea of a "scholarship," a concept which, as the name suggests, meant a payment to an individual because he was a student and, perhaps, also because he was a very good student, but which did not require him to be something else, too. One still encounters vestiges of the scholarship based on merit in some university campuses and in a few state programs, but merit has never had much to do with federal student aid, and those few postgraduate programs where it did have shrunk and been eclipsed by vast enterprises that pay no attention whatever to intellectual prowess or academic promise.

A wide array of circumstances today qualifies a person for federal student aid. Among the smaller programs, one encounters assistance for students who are native Americans, for those who are Cuban refugees, for those who are blind, for those planning to become nurses, and for those who propose to improve their skills as prison guards. But the major categories of recipients are those who are poor (more precisely, those who are unable to pay for college), those who have recently worn military uniforms, and those whose parents are (or were) Social Security beneficiaries.

From the campus perspective, these restrictions matter greatly, for they have the effect of altering the (net) cost of attendance for some students but not for others, and that variation is related to factors over which neither the college, nor for practical purposes, the student himself, has any control.

The traditional approach to student aid in American universities empowers the admissions-and-scholarship office to evaluate applicants' financial situations and then to allot available aid resources in accord with the institution's general admissions strategy. This process has both objective and subjective features: while scholarship officers strive for even-handedness in their appraisal of individuals' ability to pay for college, they also attend to unique family circumstances: how many children are being supported, how many are enrolled in college, and whether the parents have heavy medical bills, aged relatives, or other extenuating

15

conditions which affect their ability to pay for tuition, room, and board? Is the candidate able to help himself with summer or term-time employment? Is he able to borrow some of the funds he needs?

Since a college's own financial aid resources are always limited, other factors are also weighed. How important is it to the institution to ensure that a particular student actually matriculates there? It is not unknown to use financial aid as an inducement, offering more of it to an applicant whose talents mesh with the college's aspirations and relatively less to other candidates. Broad social considerations also enter into these awards: a college handing out its own money can decide whether to concentrate on very poor, or not quite so poor, individuals, and whether to encourage minority students, older students, or whatever. In addition, the college can package its student aid offerings in ways that reflect its overall resources, the particular circumstances of the individual, and the institution's own enrollment priorities. One student may get mostly grant aid, while another is given a job, and still another takes out a loan.

The federal programs curb this flexibility. While the inventive financial aid officer can sometimes make use of federal student assistance in constructing individualized aid packages for his students, he must contend with the variegated requirements and complex procedures of a dozen separate programs.

The less prosperous the college, the more its financial aid—and potentially also its admissions—are molded by these programs. An institution with sizable student aid resources of its own can fill in the missing pieces in the federal jigsaw puzzle. After using whatever government assistance it and its students are eligible for, it can then deploy its own money to help individuals it deems worthy of assistance and whose needs are not adequately met by the federal programs. But an impoverished college has no such ability. If its students do not qualify for federal aid (or other external aid schemes) it may simply not be able to enroll those who cannot afford to come on their own.

Perversely, it is usually the least prosperous institutions, particularly in the private sector, that depend most heavily on tuitions for their income. If they cannot attract students willing and able to pay the cost of attendance, they cannot endure. So they have two options: to enroll wealthy students, if enough are interested in attending; or to enroll those eligible for federal aid on terms set by the government. Either strategy obviously menaces the college's ability to contour its own enrollment according to its educational and social philosophies.

16

Moreover, the federal student aid programs that confer the most discretion on the campuses have barely held their own in Washington since 1972, while those that offer the least flexibility to the colleges have expanded greatly.

FEDERAL STUDENT AID IN 1977

Eight programs account for the lion's share of federal aid to students at the present time. They have little in common; each arose for particular reasons found compelling at the time; they all work somewhat differently; and they do not fit together very well. All are aimed primarily at undergraduates, though several assist graduate students as well. This list does not, however, include most fellowships and traineeships for graduate and professional students; nor does it include a number of lesser undergraduate programs.

A. Basic Educational Opportunity Grants (BEOG). Enacted in 1972, this program is now the foundation of federal aid to needy undergraduates. In 1976—77, it will expend approximately $1.3 billion via individual grants ranging between $200 and $1,400. (Amendments passed in 1976 increase the maximum to $1,800 in Fiscal 1978.) A student's stipend is calculated by taking the estimated total annual costs of attendance at the college of his choice and subtracting the amount that he (and his family) are deemed able to contribute. That determination is based on a national "family contribution schedule" published by the U.S. Office of Education, and different from those ordinarily used by college scholarship officers. In practice, eligibility for a Basic Grant ordinarily vanishes as family income nears $12,000.

Two other important limitations are contained in this program. First, the government will not pay more than one-half of a student's total cost of attendance, meaning that if he selects an inexpensive college he may get less than he would otherwise be entitled to. (This provision loses its force when the cost of attendance rises above $2,800, for there the $1,400 limit takes over.) Public college spokesmen generally protest this limitation, arguing that it penalizes low income students seeking low tuition institutions. Private sector leaders tend to favor it, arguing that by making public campuses less of a "free ride" for BEOG recipients, it encourages them to matriculate at private institutions.

Second, the Basic Grants program is not a true "entitlement" scheme. Though the formula tells a student what portion of $1,400 (if

17

any) his own circumstances and his choice of college would qualify him for, the funds needed to realize that promise are subject to the normal process of federal budget-and-appropriations. If insufficient money is voted, individual grants may be scaled down. In the first two years of the program, this posed no problem, since more money was appropriated than proved necessary, but in 1975–76 and 1976–77, student participation exceeded government predictions, and additional funds had to be supplied in order to "fully fund" the program and honor its implicit pledge.

B. Veterans Education Benefits. Revived in 1966, for the past several years the G.I. Bill has bulked the largest of all federal student aid programs. To qualify, an individual must have served in the armed forces since 1954 and must be enrolled in an institution or course of study approved by the Veterans Administration. Various provisions (whether the veteran is single or married, the number of his dependents, the amount of time he spent in uniform, etc.) govern the size of an individual's stipend and the number of months it is due him, but two key variables commonly found in other student aid programs are conspicuously absent from these calculations: financial need (i.e., the recipient's ability to pay for college himself) and the cost of attending a particular college or university. Two veterans with the same number of dependents and identical service records will receive exactly the same stipend, even if one is rich and the other poor, and even if one enrolls in a low-cost community college and the other in an expensive private university. For single persons in 1975–76, those stipends (for full-time study) came to $270 a month, or $2,700 over a ten-month school year.

The G.I. Bill is in flux. The end of the Vietnam War and the advent of the volunteer army brought conflicting pressures to repeal, extend, or alter the program, and in the final days of the 94th Congress, sweeping amendments were approved for veterans enlisting after December 31, 1976. It is too soon to evaluate the new program, which will require a "contribution" from enlistees that the government will match on a ratio of two-to-one. It may be noted, however, that again neither "need" nor cost-of-education will affect the size of a veteran's award.

C. Social Security Education Benefits. Prior to 1965, the additional benefits paid to the children of Social Security recipients ended when they reached their eighteenth birthday. Since that year, these benefits have been continued until the twenty-second birthday for those who remain in school on a full-time basis and do not marry. The money actually accrues to the family unit, and there is no requirement that it be used for educational expenses but is generally assumed to serve that purpose. The size of an individual's "student benefits," dependent on a number of variables built into the Social Security Act and regulations, averages (according to the particular category of recipient) $84 to $154 a month. As with the G.I. Bill, neither "ability to pay" nor the cost of a particular college enters into these calculations.

This program is a "true entitlement," in that no funds need to be appropriated to carry out its provisions. The Social Security trust fund pays whatever is required.

It may also be noted that in January, 1976 and again in 1977 the Ford administration proposed to phase out these student benefits, arguing that students needing aid could be served by BEOG and other straightforward assistance schemes. To date, Congress has shown no disposition to follow that recommendation, and the Carter administration has already modified it.

D. Supplemental Educational Opportunity Grants (SEOG). Supplemental Grants began as the first large federal program of scholarships for needy undergraduates, enacted as part of the Higher Education Act of 1965. Unlike the three programs just described, SEOG funds are parcelled out by the colleges on the government's behalf and subject to its regulations. Although individual awards may not exceed $1500, and although the Office of Education must approve the "needs analysis" system the college employs to determine how much money to award to students at various income levels, it is up to the college to decide whom to assist and how to amalgamate a Supplemental Grant with other kinds of student aid. Hence it is the college, not the student, that applies to Washington for SEOG money. An intricate procedure governs the allocation of those funds among the nation's campuses, with the total appropriation first divided among the states, and with each institution's application then reviewed in light of the composite "need" of its students vis-a-vis the total available for applicant colleges within the particular state.

Several additional features of SEOG are noteworthy. First, because a Supplemental Grant can be awarded "on top of" a Basic Grant, thus raising the maximum federal stipend to $2,900, this program is particularly beloved by the higher-cost private colleges. Second, the White House has regularly attempted to eliminate this program, arguing that it is superfluous now that the Basic Grants program is operating. Third, in bestowing much-sought administrative flexibility on the colleges, SEOG makes it hard for a prospective freshman to know how much assistance he can expect from this program, since it is up to the college to decide, and such decisions are not normally made until applicants are selected and their various circumstances appraised in the context of total resources available to the institution for student aid.

E. College Work-Study Program (CWS).   Working one's way through college smacks of old-fashioned virtue. Having Washington pay for it, however, dates back only to 1964 when the Work-Study program came into being as part of the original anti-poverty legislation. Initially meant as much for job creation and economic stimulation as for student aid, the program has undergone several modifications and a transfer to the U.S. Office of Education. Presently it provides eighty percent of the wages paid to needy students for part-time work on campus or at nearby non-profit organizations. The employer supplies the remainder.

As with SEOG, Work-Study appropriations are first allotted by formula among the states and are then sought by the colleges and universities through application. As with SEOG, the schools have considerable discretion in parcelling out the funds among their needy students and are able to use a "needs analysis" system, such as that provided by the College Scholarship Service, that heeds a student's own financial situation as well as the cost of attending the particular institution.

Work-Study has won widespread popularity among the universities and in the corridors of Congress. It is the only one of the three "campus-based" programs to have been spared frequent attempts by the administration to do away with duplicative or superfluous student aid schemes. Neither a straightforward "handout" like the grant programs, nor something that must later be repaid by the students, Work-Study payments help students pay for college, and help colleges pay for useful work, without violating the puritan ethic.

F. National Direct Student Loans.   Known originally as "national defense loans," this program ranks as the forerunner of federal subsidies for needy undergraduates. Created as part of the National Defense Education Act of 1958, it provides federal "capital contributions" to colleges which they, in turn, can lend to their students at extremely low interest rates (3 percent). The college must itself supply 10 percent of the new capital each year, but it may also re-lend the principal and interest repaid by previous borrowers. Other provisions—such as deferral of interest until the borrower begins repaying his loan—make this a most attractive form of borrowing from the student's point of view.

G. Federally-Insured Loans.   The guaranteed loan program has several parts and works in a complicated way, but its underlying intention is straightforward. Eligible students obtain loans from banks, from their colleges, or from state agencies. Washington guarantees those loans against death, default, and other forms of non-repayment and, in addition, subsidizes the interest payments for students below a certain income level, thus allowing the lender to obtain a reasonable return on his money without burdening the needy student with usurious interest rates. In addition, Congress created the (privately capitalized) Student Loan Marketing Association as a "secondary market" for those loans so that lenders can recycle their capital.

Although the colleges participate in the administration of this program by certifying their students, only where the institution chooses to lend its own funds to its students does it really control access to this program.

H. State Student Incentive Grants (SSIG).   Created in 1972, the SSIG program attempts to encourage the states to provide scholarships to needy students by "matching" with federal funds the amounts the states appropriate for that purpose. Because it is quite small—$44 million for the entire nation in fiscal 1976—and because state scholarship programs have burgeoned in recent years, the federal payments do not come close to equalling the full amount in many jurisdictions, particularly since initial allotments are based on a population formula which is unrelated to the level of scholarship activity.

The states have considerable latitude in administering their programs, save that recipients must demonstrate "substantial financial need" and that individual stipends may not exceed $1,500. This latitude, however, has permitted the states to impose irksome limitations, such as confining their aid to residents who enroll at colleges located within the state's borders.

DOES IT MAKE SENSE?

Federal student aid is a booming business but an immensely disorderly one. The disorder ought not be lightly dismissed, for this category of government activity is important on several counts.

It is far and away the largest and the fastest-growing area of federal financial involvement with higher education. In that semiconscious, half-articulated way in which complex choices are often made in Washington, both Congress and the executive branch have decided to give priority to aid for students rather than assistance to colleges and universities. If additional funds are forthcoming for higher education, one can reasonably predict that most of them will be directed to helping students pay for college. The Republican administration was explicit about this, arguing that, as a matter of principle, "in most cases, aid should be provided to individuals rather than to institutions." But even the Congress, which has been more reluctant to abolish programs of assistance to institutions, has also acknowledged the primacy of student aid. In reporting out its 1976 amendments to the Higher Education Act, for example, the House Education and Labor Committee observed that "There is a consensus today that the proper Federal concern is for the student."[2]

For the vast majority of American colleges and universities, most of the federal money that makes its way into their coffers comes from undergraduate student aid programs. This is conspicuously *not* true for the hundred or so major universities, which receive far more in research and development funds, and it is also not true of a handful of private campuses that receive much of their income from philanthropy. But most private institutions get most of their revenues from student tuitions, and most public campuses also obtain the bulk of their non-state funds from student payments. Hence while the workings of the G.I. Bill, changes in the family contribution schedule of the Basic Grants Program, or the cost-sharing ratios of the Work-Study program are minor considerations for the nation's most eminent institutions of higher education, on nine campuses out of ten they are matters of some moment.

The escalating cost of education means rising tuition levels, especially in private colleges and universities where costs must normally be "passed through" to students. In a period when the economy is weak, when many families find their disposable income shrinking, and when excess capacity and slackening demand for higher education make it harder to fill the freshman class, increased tuition means that the health of the institution depends more on the ability of prospective students to locate sufficient financial aid to bring its prices within their financial grasp. Washington is by far the largest supplier of such aid. Although the nation has made great strides in equalizing access to higher education, a person's likelihood of attending college remains entangled with his socio-economic status. Many reasons may be adduced, not all of them financial, but it is clear that low-income people cannot afford to pay for college themselves, even when tuition is very low. Even a student living at home and commuting to a nearby community college must reckon with out-of-pocket costs which averaged $2,000 a year in 1975−76, and this figure ignores the income he may forego by electing to spend those hours in class rather than in gainful employment. According to the College Scholarship Service, a family ought not be expected to "contribute" that much to the college education of one of its children until its income reaches $19,000.[3]

Federal student aid, in short, is too important to be burdened with all the flaws and irrationalities that it now displays. One's sense of these will differ, of course, with one's perspective on the matter. The needy student plainly has different concerns than the taxpayer; the college president looks at the subject in still another way; and the state university executive has concerns that differ from those of the private college administrator. Nevertheless, three general points deserve attention.

1. The prospective student has great difficulty finding out how much federal student aid he can expect to receive. If he is eligible for G.I. benefits or Social Security student benefits, he can ascertain how much money they will supply. And if he is very clever, he can plug financial information about his own family, and the cost of attending a particular college, into a table that will show him how large a Basic Grant, if any, he can anticipate—provided the program is "fully funded." If he has a friendly banker willing to grant him a loan, he may even be able to determine whether a federal subsidy will reduce the interest he must one day pay on that loan. And if his state runs a model scholarship program, there is a chance he can obtain information about the size of his prospective grant from the state, some portion of which is probably supplied by the federal SSIG program. But he will have trouble doing all of those things, and even if he succeeds, he still will not know his "net price" of attending college, for not until he is admitted and has his financial aid application reviewed by the institution will he learn what assistance may come to him from the three "campus-based" programs. Hence at the

23

time it matters most—at the point where he is trying to decide whether to go to college at all, and, if so, which one to select—he has no way of knowing how much help Washington will supply or what his net cost will be.

2. The college has no way of knowing how much federal student aid money it can expect to receive, either. In a sense, this is the obverse of the student's problem, for if all the funds were channelled through the campus, the college would have greater certainty and the student less. As things stand, some matriculants arrive "carrying aid," while others must be assisted out of funds the institution administers, some of which it obtains from Washington. But even that process is unreliable, since the "campus-based" allotments require the college to apply for a portion of the state's share, an arrangement that serves some states better than others and that rewards the institutions adroit at federal grantsmanship. One could argue that, from the college's point of view, those students who qualify for veterans' or Social Security benefits, for a subsidized Insured Loan, for a Basic Grant, or for a state scholarship are the same as those with wealthy parents, in that all simply pay tuition out of the resources to which they have access, and that therefore the college should not fret about its inability to predict how much federal aid may arrive in the hands of its students. But that is a naïve view, since access to those sources of aid may well determine whether a student can apply—or be recruited—in the first place. Since it most assuredly affects how much aid he may require from the college's own resources, it also determines how much net income he will be able to provide for the institution.

3. Federal student aid programs treat the differing costs of various colleges, and the differing wealth of various students, in uneven and inconsistent ways. Neither the G.I. Bill nor the Social Security program pays any attention to the price of a college or to an individual's ability to meet that price himself. Well-to-do students receive exactly the same stipends as very poor ones; those attending a state college get the same amount as those choosing an expensive private university. The Basic Grants program pays some attention both to poverty and to costs of attendance, but the ceiling on individual stipends means that a student who has 40 percent of his costs paid at one college will—with the same grant—be able to cover just a quarter of his costs at another.

In the main, the three "campus-based" programs do the best job of reconciling the actual charges of a given college with the financial situation of a given student, but they have perverse effects outside the campus walls. A lower-middle-class student at one college may end up with a larger federal subsidy than a destitute classmate at another institution, depending on how successful their respective schools are in obtaining funds, how many others on campus qualify for aid, and which forms of assistance their respective scholarship officers choose to allot to which students.

As for guaranteed loans, the most obvious federal subsidy—the "special allowance" paid to lenders—is crudely related to income, in that student borrowers above a certain limit do not qualify for it at all, but the very poor and the not-so-poor are treated alike. Moreover, the largest *potential* subsidy—Washington's repaying the entire amount if the student borrower disappears, dies, or declares bankruptcy—is available to everyone who was able to obtain the loans in the first place, which process depends more on the habits of bankers than on the characteristics of students or colleges.

All federal transfer programs have their quirks, their inconsistencies, and their vexing procedures, and if one were to attempt to design a comprehensive student aid program that treated both college costs and individual means in a thoroughly reasonable fashion, one would find that it was very expensive and also quite likely to induce a number of dubious (if unintended) side effects. Nevertheless, the current array of federally financed student assistance schemes has more drawbacks than it needs and betrays all too well its origin in a half-dozen different acts addressed to as many different concerns.

Reforming federal student aid will not be easy, however. Each program has a body of supporters, jealous of its benefits and deeply suspicious of alterations that may curb some of those benefits and confer more of them on other constituencies. The veterans would oppose any move to introduce a "means test" into the G.I. Bill. The private colleges are wary of emphasizing the Basic Grants program and eroding the campus-based schemes. Their public sector counterparts object to heavy reliance on student loans because of the implication that students rather than society at large should pay the cost of their higher education. When, in 1975–76, Congress considered doing away with what many observers consider the least justified and most regressive aspect of the Basic Grants scheme—the "half-of-cost" limitation on individual stipends—the loud objections of a group of colleges that feared they might find it harder to

25

attract students sufficed to kill the intended reform. Even such an obvious and overdue correction as harmonizing the "state allocation formulas" of the three campus-based aid schemes meets with protest.

Just below the surface of these political disputes are fundamental disagreements about the rationale of federal aid to students. Making military service more attractive by subsidizing the college education of veterans suggests quite a different government objective than augmenting the income of poor persons who want to matriculate. Guaranteeing a loan reflects a conception of who should pay for higher education which is at odds with giving an outright grant to a student. Supplying enough money to get a student up to the door of a minimal-cost institution is not the same as providing enough resources to enable him to prospect among all the colleges which might admit him without regard to their charges. Guaranteeing every eligible student a certain sum of money, and then making sure he gets it, differs greatly from appropriating a particular total and then parcelling it out while it lasts. Stimulating the states to put more of their own resources into student aid connotes a different conception of federalism than putting Washington's funds directly into the hands of students, and that, in turn, is a different approach to government than supplying those same funds to the colleges for them to distribute as they see fit.

MONEY FOR INSTITUTIONS

The establishment and maintenance of colleges and universities has been a state and private responsibility since colonial days. In that respect, the United States differs from most other countries, where the well-being of institutions of higher education has been a direct concern of the central government. Although Washington has supplied some funds to institutions of higher education over the last century, it does not assume any responsibility for the institutions themselves; its outlays have been attached to other national purposes, and its beneficiaries have been constrained in what they could use the federal money for.

Some of these constraints are more rigorous than others, but the general point stands: the federal government did not set out to furnish unrestricted income to the nation's colleges and universities, nor to underwrite their ordinary activities. Instead, it has deployed resources to purchase particular services and to support designated activities. Colleges not wishing to provide those services or engage in those activities have always had the right to decline the funds, but if they accept, they accept the accompanying restrictions. In that sense, the financial relationship between the federal government and the nation's institutions of higher education is not that of patron and beneficiary so much as that of purchaser and vendor.

This statement needs several qualifications, for it is misleading to think of the ties between Washington and the campus as simply commercial. Shared and high-minded purposes are often involved. The university wants to train physicians, and the government wants more physicians to be trained. The result: a set of "capitation" payments to medical schools. A scientist yearns to study solar energy, and the government wants to encourage research in that field. The result: a federal grant to the scientist's host university to support his work. A college wants to experiment with a new sophomore-year humanities curriculum, and the government wants both to foster the study of humanities and also to encourage educational innovation. The result: a federal grant to that college.

Such harmony is not uncommon, and it may not matter to the university that concern for its welfare as an institution did not impel the programs which furnish money to it. Indeed, one of the reasons why Washington slipped into a pattern of "categorical" payments was the academy's fear that excessive federal control would follow if the government defined the institution's overall welfare as its primary interest. Limiting the purposes for which federal funds might be obtained was at once cautious and heedless, acknowledging the university's sovereignty, while enabling the government to pay for what it wanted without asserting any responsibility for the well-being of individual institutions or for higher education as a whole.

The government's organizational arrangements for disbursing money to the academy mirror this limited conception of the federal role in higher education. Dozens of Washington agencies make grants and award contracts to individual colleges and universities. In every instance, the purposes for which the funds are supplied are tied to the overriding mission of the agency. And nowhere, short of the president and the full Congress, can one identify anybody charged with supervision of the entire enterprise. No minister of education or university grants commission controls the spigots through which federal funds flow—or, as the case may be, drip—into the nation's colleges. No federal official reaches his desk in the morning sober with the knowledge that he is responsible for understanding, let alone doing anything about, the combined effect which federal funds might have on the health or quality of American universities.

There is something to be said for such fragmentation. For all the administrative confusion that it entails, it may well contribute to academic freedom. This view was expressed more than a decade and a half ago in a report to the Harvard faculty. It said

"By 1960 Harvard was participating in at least thirty-four categories of programs managed by two score Federal agencies, under the general oversight of a dozen Congressional committees. Since all the faculties were involved, though in widely varying degrees, Harvard's relationship with Washington was clearly managed on a highly decentralized basis.

While this decentralized pattern, with its heavy emphasis on particular fields and specific activities, has brought about a great many difficult problems, it has probably made it easier to maintain the essential academic freedom of the University. The Federal Government has clearly not interfered in the direction of Harvard's research projects. It has certainly sought to encourage, in fields colored by a national interest, research which our faculty members wished to undertake. The variety of sources of support helps make it possible for a distinguished scientist in a respected institution to obtain backing for his research on terms acceptable to him and his university. The image of a coercive government dictating what shall and shall not be done in university laboratories and libraries simply does not fit Harvard's experience with Washington. . . . From the point of view of the universities, it may be better to live with the difficulties of the present disorganized system than to increase the risk of political interference with university independence by putting all our eggs in one basket. . . ."[4]

In recent years, however, higher education spokesmen have shown greater enthusiasm for imposing more order on these chaotic administrative arrangements, and also for obtaining unrestricted federal "operating grants" to colleges and universities. In 1969, the American Council on Education declared that "the principal unfinished business of the Federal Government in the field of higher education is the necessity to provide support for general institutional purposes." Five years later, with a limited "institutional aid" program on the statute books but not funded, the Council repeated that "the entire system of higher education represents a national resource, the strength and quality of which should be a national concern. It seems clear that the Federal government should underwrite some portion of the cost of sustaining the system."[5] And when the perennial proposal for a Cabinet-level Department of Education won the support of the Democratic presidential candidate in 1976, many higher education leaders were pleased. Most, however, would hasten to add that general institutional support must be in addition to, not in place of, the welter of categorical programs already on the books, and that any raising of education's place in the federal hierarchy must not constrain the ability of other "mission-oriented" agencies to continue channelling such categorical funds to the campuses.

From their point of view, the existing congeries of federal programs has a number of drawbacks. There is a lack of congruence between Washington's interests and those of the university. Federal obligations to colleges and universities in Fiscal 1974 totalled approximately $4.5 billion.[6] The largest portion of these funds, amounting to $2 billion, paid for scientific research and development, and an additional $650 million supported other activities that fall under the heading of "academic science." The balance, about $1.7 billion, went for "non-science" activities, but the bulk of that category actually consists of student aid (the "campus-based" programs, where the funds go first to the university) and the training of medical manpower. (Tables II and III.)

At first glance, the federal "cafeteria" would appear to be serving up a nicely varied menu, but a bit more examination reveals that, for most colleges and universities, prolonged reliance on such a diet would result in severe institutional malnutrition. There is a great deal of money for research, for example, but little for teaching. One finds few signs of funds that can be used to underwrite the philosophy department, the school of public administration, the acquisitions budget of the library, or the college of basic studies, not to mention such vital but pedestrian functions as the heating plant, the placement office, and the department of buildings and grounds. Indeed, there is no sign of resources to pay for the university's cost of complying with such well-meant but potentially costly *federal* requirements as those of the Occupational Safety and Health Act, the Equal Pay Act, and the regulations of the Environmental Protection Agency.[7]

Of course, most federal payments include an administrative allowance or make some provision for "overhead," and it can certainly be argued that since "all money is green" any college with a skillful

Table II
Federal Obligations to Universities and Colleges, by Agency and Type of Activity, FY 1974
(Thousands of U.S. Dollars)

Agency	Total Obligations	Academic Science (Total)	Research and Development	R & D Plant	Facilities and Equipment for Instruction in Science and Engineering	Fellowships, Traineeships, Training Grants	General Support for Science	Other Science Activities	Non-Science Activities
Total	4,462,623	2,736,021	2,085,285	29,009	3,506	326,600	85,929	205,691	1,726,602
Department of Agriculture	260,696	260,696	96,703	0	0	0	0	163,993	0
Atomic Energy Commission	99,284	99,284	94,371	4,248	0	514	0	151	0
Department of Commerce	29,478	29,368	26,623	0	0	20	490	2,235	110
Department of Defense, Total	184,491	184,491	184,491	0	0	0	0	0	0
Army	43,060	43,060	43,060	0	0	0	0	0	0
Navy	80,285	80,285	80,285	0	0	0	0	0	0
Air Force	56,767	56,767	56,767	0	0	0	0	0	0
Other DOD	4,379	4,379	4,379	0	0	0	0	0	0
Office of Economic Opportunity	9,999	4,084	3,370	0	0	714	0	0	5,915
Environmental Protection Agency	30,919	30,919	24,121	0	0	6,798	0	0	0

Department of Health, Education and Welfare	3,233,788	1,515,553	1,129,171	14,524	371	301,541	64,209	5,737	1,718,235
National Institutes of Health	1,219,808	1,219,808	967,565	14,524	0	169,828	64,209	3,682	0
Health Resources Administration	662,420	20,892	16,219	0	0	4,536	0	137	641,528
Health Services Administration	69,056	3,015	3,015	0	0	0	0	0	66,041
Alcohol, Drug Abuse, and Mental Health Administration	213,290	192,030	80,591	0	0	110,521	0	918	21,260
Center for Disease Control	8,045	6,931	4,764	0	0	1,167	0	1,000	1,114
Food and Drug Administration	14,562	14,562	13,977	0	0	585	0	0	0
Office of Education	921,977	7,316	5,599	0	371	1,346	0	0	914,661
National Institute of Education	18,902	18,902	18,902	0	0	0	0	0	0
Social and Rehabilitation Service	42,570	29,952	16,394	0	0	13,558	0	0	12,618
Other HEW	63,158	2,145	2,145	0	0	0	0	0	61,013

Table II (Continued)

		Academic Science							
Agency	Total Obligations	Total Academic Science	Research and Development	R & D Plant	Facilities and Equipment for Instruction in Science and Engineering	Fellowships, Traineeships, Training Grants	General Support for Science	Other Science Activities	Non-Science Activities
Department of the Interior ...	23,761	23,761	22.201	0	8	0	1.552	0	0
National Aeronautics and Space Administration ...	98,904	98,904	91.957	59	0	1.227	0	5.661	0
National Science Foundation	449,566	449,566	376.096	10.178	3.127	14.444	17.807	27.914	0
Department of Transportation	12,814	12,814	11.472	0	0	1.342	0	0	0
Agency for International Development	18,863	18,863	18.416	0	0	0	447	0	0
Department of Housing and Urban Development	2,855	647	647	0	0	0	0	0	2.208
Department of Labor	7,205	7,071	5.647	0	0	0	1.424	0	134

SOURCE: National Science Foundation, *Federal Support to Universities, Colleges, and Selected Nonprofit Institutions, Fiscal Year 1974*. Detailed Statistical Tables, Appendix B, Table B–2, p. 3 (Washington, D.C., 1975).

NOTE: Table includes data from fourteen federal agencies responsible for more than 95 percent of all federal obligations to universities and colleges.

business manager can take advantage of federal funds earmarked for specific purposes to free non-federal funds for other purposes. This is a familiar technique and, within limits, a perfectly reasonable one. Nevertheless, the simple fact remains that, in keeping with its legislative origins, federal funds are intended in the first instance not to pay for what the college wants to do but, rather, for what the cognizant Washington agencies want it to do. Hence the yearning for "unrestricted" funds, too, if only to fill the many chinks left by the categorical programs.

The government's priorities change, sometimes rapidly and sometimes slowly, but almost never with any regard for the impact of those changes on the institutions receiving money from it. When a particular federal interest is growing, the availability of funds serves as a friendly bribe or "carrot" to lure universities into it. But when Washington's interest wanes, and the funds for it shrink or are diverted into another area of crescent enthusiasm, the universities frequently find themselves left with people and programs but without the resources to sustain them. The following table shows some of the ups and—especially in constant dollars—occasional downs in federal expenditures for basic research in colleges and universities between 1966 and 1974. (Table IV)

The large, diversified university can cope with these shifting emphases more easily than the small or specialized institution, but it is never easy to make such adjustments, particularly when a federal program or project phases out quickly, when unrestricted campus funds are scarce, and when tenured staff are involved. And when entire categories of federal activity dwindle, such as the now-notorious reduction of graduate student fellowships in the late 1960s and early 1970s, even the nimblest university is hard pressed to respond with anything but cutbacks in activities which are central to its institutional vocation.

For the past eight years, as enrollments increased with increases in student aid programs, as the cost of providing a college education soared, and as inflation exacted its toll, the money supplied directly by Washington to the nation's campuses has not kept pace. Hence the federal portion of their income has shrunk somewhat. (Table V)

A more worrisome trend can be discerned in the recent history of federal obligations for research and development on campus, and particularly in those funds intended for basic research where, in constant dollars, the total in 1974 had returned to the level of 1966. (Table VI)

Funds are distributed very unevenly among the nation's colleges and universities. This is not accidental, nor has it gone unremarked over the

Table III
Federal Obligations for Research and Development to Universities and Colleges, by Field of Science, FY 1974
(Thousands of U.S. Dollars)

Field of Science	Total
Total, All Fields	2,085,286
Physical Sciences, Total	261,997
Astronomy	31,823
Chemistry	83,157
Physics	131,625
Physical Sciences, NEC	15,392
Mathematics	51,931
Environmental Sciences, Total	174,769
Atmospheric Science	46,158
Geological Science	37,748
Oceanography	67,098
Environmental Sciences, NEC ..	23,765
Engineering, Total	174,803
Aeronautical	11,901
Astronautical	1,196
Chemical	10,089
Civil	23,327
Electrical	34,151
Mechanical	15,476
Metallurgy and Materials	39,129
Engineering, NEC	39,534
Life Sciences, Total	1,128,236
Biological	516,214
Clinical Medical	376,747
Other Medical	212,879
Life Sciences, NEC	22,396
Psychology, Total	56,265
Biological Aspects	33,487
Social Aspects	21,323
Psychological Science, NEC ...	1,158

Social Sciences, Total	114,679
Anthropology	3,973
Economics	19,704
History	975
Linguistics	2,334
Political Science	3,600
Sociology	18,186
Social Sciences, NEC	65,907
Other Sciences, NEC	122,606

SOURCE: National Science Foundation, *Federal Support to Universities, Colleges, and Selected Nonprofit Institutions, Fiscal Year 1974*, Detailed Statistical Tables, Appendix B, Table B–13, p. 23 (Washington, D.C., 1975).
NOTE: NEC means "Not Elsewhere Classified."

years, and in many cases there are plausible reasons for it. A college without a medical school, for example, could scarcely expect to reap much of the sizable federal harvest in bio-medical research and health manpower training. A university that lacks a college of agriculture is simply out of the picture so far as most of the programs of the Department of Agriculture are concerned. A school that stresses the performing arts would not expect to receive much money from the National Aeronautics and Space Administration. More fundamentally, the lion's share of the federal awards of grants and contracts to colleges and universities comes in the realm of scientific research, and most—though not all—of those expenditures follow procedures that emphasize the ability of a particular scholar or institution to undertake a given project and carry it out with skill. The federal agency is under some pressure to scatter its research money across the country, but far greater pressure pushes it to use strictly intellectual standards and variants of the "peer review" process to award its funds to the most capable scientists.

Hence for most colleges and universities, money from Washington means money for student aid, perhaps a loan with which to construct a building and maybe some small grants to individual professors. There are approximately three thousand institutions of higher education in the

Table IV
Estimated Federal Basic Research Expenditures in
Universities and Colleges, by Selected Field of Science,
1966, 1970, 1974
Current and Constant (1967) Dollars
(Dollars in Millions)

	1966	1970	1974
Engineering			
current	$151	$185	$175
constant	156	161	121
Chemistry			
current	60	69	75
constant	62	60	52
Environmental Science			
current	47	76	112
constant	49	66	77
Clinical Medicine			
current	279	352	433
constant	288	306	299
Psychology			
current	30	41	56
constant	31	36	39

SOURCE: National Science Board, *Science Indicators 1974* (Washington, D.C.: Government Printing Office, 1975), Table 3–9, p. 196.

United States but, year after year, one hundred of them obtain two thirds of all federal funds allocated directly to colleges and universities. In research, this concentration is even more pronounced; here, the leading one hundred institutions regularly receive 85 percent of the total, and only one school in five receives anything at all.

For the few, these funds matter enormously. In Fiscal 1974, the least of the leading one hundred recipients garnered $11 million, and twenty-

Table V
Federal Funds as a Percentage of the Total Current
Fund Income of Colleges and Universities
(By Control of Institution, Selected Years, 1939–1974)

	1939–40	1949–50	1959–60	1969–70	1973–74
Private Institutions	0.7	8.6	19.4	20.7	18.6
Public Institutions	10.3	9.6	16.6	15.8	14.6

SOURCE: Susan C. Nelson, "Trends and Issues in the Financing of Private Higher Education," paper prepared for a Brookings conference on "Public Policy and Private Higher Education," Revised draft, February 1977, Table 2–1.

two universities received more than $40 million apiece. Among the twenty-two private campuses that the Carnegie Commission classifies as "Research Universities I," federal funds supplied 34 percent of their "educational and general" revenues in 1973–74. At Harvard—which ranked fourth among institutional recipients of federal obligations—Washington supplied $63 million that year, or 27 percent of the university's overall income, and the federal reimbursement of indirect costs alone (i.e., overhead payments) was equivalent to the entire budget of a medium-sized college.[8]

There is a problem here, but it has two sides. On the one hand, the major universities have grown very dependent on federal funds. On the other hand, most of the nation's higher education institutions get very little money from Washington, and most of what they do get actually comes as student aid, even though the peculiarities of the programs may mean that in the first instance it is channelled to the campus. This income is welcome to most institutions, but since it supplies less than 8 percent of their "E & G" revenues it is simply not very consequential. Whereas one could fairly say of the major research universities that the sudden disappearance of federal funds would leave them nearly unrecognizable, there are thousands of campuses where the federal "institutional" payments just do not make much difference. For a stable, prosperous college, that independence from Washington is surely to be celebrated; for a strug-

Table VI
Federal Obligations and Expenditures for
Research and Development, and for Basic Research,
in Colleges and Universities, 1964–74
(Millions of U.S. Dollars)

	1964	1966	1968	1970	1972	1974
Federal obligations to colleges and universities for research and development						
current dollars	$ 976	$1252	$1398	$1447	$1853	$2085
constant (1967)	1046	1292	1351	1270	1492	1496
Estimated federal basic research expenditures in universities and colleges						
current dollars	767	1009	1251	1296	1419	1514
constant (1967)	829	1041	1203	1127	1142	1046

SOURCE: National Science Foundation, *Federal Support to Universities, Colleges and Selected Nonprofit Institutions, Fiscal Year 1974*, p. 3, and National Science Board, *Science Indicators 1974*, (Washington D.C.: Government Printing Office, 1975), Table 3–9, p. 196.

gling, financially marginal school, however, such freedom is a mixed blessing.

Exceptional situations abound. No simple characterization of the effect of federal "institutional" support could do justice to its great variety. Rarely, for example, does the entire university derive equal financial benefit from Washington. Some parts of the institution are markedly "richer" than others—and, of course, that much more dependent on the government agencies which support them. Where there is a medical school, usually it is the leading recipient of federal funds. At Harvard, the "medical area" (schools of medicine, public health, and dentistry) received 61 percent of its income from federal sources in

1973–74 and in doing so accounted for more than half of the entire university's federal revenues; the law school, by contrast, obtained just 5 percent of its receipts from Washington, the business school 2 percent, the school of design 10 percent, and the divinity school none at all.

Medical education and bio-medical research remain fine examples of activities where the federal interest and the university's interest come together and where categorical programs may serve both interests. Despite the constant debate about the terms of those programs—how much money, how many conditions—it is clear that if the $1.25 billion that Washington paid to the medical schools in 1974–75 had instead been channelled into some ''general assistance'' scheme for which all colleges and universities qualified, markedly less would have gone into medical training and research, and financial distress of major proportions would have enveloped the medical schools and their universities.[9]

One obstacle facing anyone seeking ''general aid'' to colleges and universities is the hostility of the current beneficiaries of categorical programs to any scheme that might reduce their revenues for the benefit of other institutions. Moreover, federal officials tend to believe that the money they spend for categorical purposes was intended for those purposes, not for the general support of institutions that help to carry out those (and many other) purposes. Hence any move for institutional aid would require additional resources in a period when ballooning student aid schemes lay claim to additional funds and when the recipients of categorical programs also want to have increased appropriations for their own projects.

Additional problems abound. How, for example, would funds for general support be allotted? An identical lump sum paid to every college and university would clearly be ridiculous, when Ohio State University enrolls 50,000 students and nearby Columbus College of Art and Design has fewer than 800. But a ''per student'' (or capitation) payment ignores the enormous range of cost differences in American higher education. A university that is heavily involved in graduate training, for example, spends—and needs—much more ''per student'' than a community college. And what about financial strength? Some schools are prosperous, others near bankruptcy. Some are sustained by their states, others by wealthy benefactors, while others rely chiefly on their students for income. What ''incentive and reward'' effects would a federal subsidy yield? Would federal funds replace other revenues or augment them? Would they make a significant difference for campuses faced with acute fiscal problems? Perhaps more important. is that the right test of a federal program, implying as it does that the rationale for federal support is the maintenance of failing institutions?[10]

Countless formulae have appeared over the years, and in 1972 Congress actually wrote one of them into law. It was a complicated affair in which colleges were entitled to "cost of instruction" allowances based primarily on the number of federally aided students they enrolled. Despite the ardent pleas of the higher education associations in Washington, however, no funds have ever been appropriated for this program, and by 1976 Congress had all but forgotten it. The most recent higher education amendments stress two other approaches to institutional aid: increased "administrative allowances" tacked onto the major student assistance programs, and a financial "trigger" that obliges money to be appropriated for these categorical "institutional" schemes when funds for student aid exceed a certain level. To date neither Congress nor the executive branch has been ready to designate "general support" of colleges and universities as an appropriate purpose for the national government. Neither the strengthening of weak institutions, nor the burnishing of strong ones has elicited much enthusiasm on the banks of the Potomac. The responsibilities of general support are easily left where they have always been, in state and private hands.

TAX BENEFITS

The least recognized form of federal support for higher education is embedded in the tax code, not in the education laws. In 1976, the federal treasury received $1.9 billion *less* revenue than it could otherwise have expected as a result of taxpayers availing themselves of provisions associated with higher education.

A lively controversy surrounds the entire subject of "tax expenditures." Many tax reformers consider some or all of these provisions "loopholes" whose "cost" to the government should be tabulated and whose wisdom should undergo searching scrutiny. But others object even to listing tax expenditures, arguing that the action implies that the entire gross national product somehow "belongs" to the federal government, which graciously consents to leave some funds in private hands by making exceptions to what would otherwise be a 100 percent tax on everything.

Be that as it may, the Congressional Budget Act of 1974 required that tax expenditures be enumerated, and this is now a regular feature of the president's annual budget and of the budget calculations of the Congress.

Scholarships, fellowships, and kindred benefits to students are exempt from taxation. This applies to veterans' benefits, as well as conventional student aid from public and private sources. These tax exclusions reduced federal revenues in 1976 by $500 million. This revenue loss may be thought of as an indirect form of student aid, since if those taxes had been paid, a corresponding addition to direct student aid outlays would have been necessary in order to attain the same level of "postsecondary purchasing power."[11]

It may also be noted that these are relatively progressive features of the tax laws. About 48 percent of the (non-veterans') student aid tax expenditure accrues to persons earning less than $7,000, and another 37 percent to those with adjusted gross income of $7,000 to $15,000; 92 percent of the tax expenditure associated with the exclusion of veterans' benefits goes to those earning less than $15,000 a year.[12]

Parents providing more than half the support of a child may continue to claim the $750 dependent's exemption for that child so long as he is a full-time student, even if his own income exceeds $750 and thus would normally have disqualified him for that parental exemption. This special treatment of student dependents cost the treasury $720 million in 1976. The provision dates to 1954, when the gross income test was eliminated for student dependents. It serves to increase the disposable income of families with tax liability who have children who are students with earnings of their own. Clearly, its "value" rises as the family's tax bracket rises; at the median marginal tax rate of 20 percent, a $750 exemption is "worth" $150, while for families at the highest marginal rate (70 percent) the same exemption is worth $525. Thus it is not surprising that 44 percent of the benefit from this tax expenditure accrues to those earning more than $15,000. Its defenders argue, however, that it offers needed and desirable relief to parents who continue to support their offspring in college. It may thus discourage students (and their parents) who would otherwise seek "emancipation" so that they could qualify for the additional student aid they might be eligible for if family earnings vanished from their "need" calculations.

Individuals and corporations making charitable contributions to colleges and universities may, within certain limits, deduct those contributions from their taxable income. In 1976, such deductions cost the treasury about $700 million. (Included in this figure is a small amount for elementary and secondary schools.) The charitable deduction differs from the other higher education tax benefits in three respects. First, the expenditure entitled to favorable tax treatment in this instance is one that yields resources directly to the college, rather than to its students or their parents. Second, the total sum affected by the tax law is much bigger than that connected with higher education; six out of every seven dollars lost to the treasury as a result of the charitable deduction result from contributions to other than educational institutions. Third, this provision arouses heated controversy in which liberals devoted to higher education find themselves on opposite sides of the policy fence, permanently divided by their attitude toward the charitable deduction.

The effect of private philanthropy on institutional well-being is not negligible. Although the proportion of the nation's higher education budget supplied by voluntary support has shrunk somewhat in recent years, such gifts remain in excess of $2 billion per annum.[13] They are particularly important to private colleges and universities, which receive three-quarters of this money (though they enroll just one-quarter of the students) and which, on average, obtain 10 percent of their revenues from this source. In addition, the income from endowment, which may reasonably be seen as the accumulation of past gifts, yields another 5 percent of the revenues of the private institutions.

Even within the private sector, however, philanthropy has a most uneven impact. Some institutions receive many millions, while others get practically nothing. A handful obtain three-quarters of their "E & G" revenues from current gifts and endowment income, and hundreds of them obtain more than one-third of their revenues from those sources.[14] At places such as Claremont, Chicago, and Princeton, voluntary support in 1974–75 came to more than $3,000 per student; were it to disappear, those campuses would have to impose a drastic increase in their tuitions or obtain a vast increase in other revenues in order to maintain their accustomed standard of institutional living. On the other hand, philanthropy yielded less than $100 per student in 1974–75 to schools such as Northeastern, Duquesne, and Villanova, and for numerous other colleges and universities, income from this source was not large enough even to report.

Some institutions would fare better if Washington eliminated the tax expenditure associated with voluntary support of higher education and then allocated revenues resulting thereby to all colleges and universities according to a simple formula. On the other hand, many institutions— including the most distinguished—would fare far worse under such an arrangement.

The federal government has no voice in deciding which colleges and universities (and other eleemosynary organizations) benefit from voluntary support. If it did, such support would no longer be "voluntary" in any reasonable sense of the term. Voluntary support, as we know it, benefits those institutions that by dint of hard work or good fortune have succeeded in attracting donors and benefactors.

Tax reformers generally object to the charitable deduction because the taxpayers who derive the greatest benefit from it tend to be those with high income, whose high marginal rates, propensity to itemize their deductions, and ability to make large gifts maximize the value to them of the charitable deduction. Nowhere is this clearer than in the case of colleges and universities, which obtain more than 70 percent of their (individual) gift revenues—including 88 percent of their capital gift income—from the very small number of donors giving more than $5,000 apiece. Thus it is not surprising that three-quarters of the "benefit" from (individual) charitable deductions for higher education accrues to taxpayers earning more than $50,000 a year.

An important question about the charitable deduction concerns the extent to which it "induces" gifts. Obviously the deduction costs the treasury only about 30 percent of the amount that colleges and universities receive in voluntary support. But would the gifts have been as numerous and as large if they had not been deductible? Practically everyone who has looked at the subject agrees that the eradication of the charitable deduction, unless accompanied by new programs of governmental assistance, would result in a decline in college and university income which would slightly exceed the additional revenues to the federal treasury. In 1973–74, for example, one analyst estimates that the absence of the (individual) charitable deduction would have cut the revenues of higher education's private sector alone by $250 million, while adding $230 million in federal tax revenues.[15]

In addition to the three enumerated above, a number of other federal tax benefits, some obvious, some well-hidden, assist colleges and universities. The institutions themselves, for example, share the general exemption from corporate taxation which the Internal Revenue Code grants to non-profit organizations. Thus a college fortunate enough to realize a surplus does not pay income taxes on it. The federal deduction for (non-business) state and local taxes also yields a sizable subsidy for colleges and universities supported by state and local governments, as does the tax exemption of interest on state and local bonds, many of which were sold to finance the construction of higher education facilities.

The most widely discussed of other tax benefits for higher education, however, are those which have never been enacted, such as a credit or deduction for college tuition. Their supporters contend that student aid programs do little for middle-income families trying to meet the rising cost of college, and that the tax system offers a way to lighten that burden with minimal red tape. The Senate has several times approved a "tuition tax credit," but to date that idea has not found favor with the House of Representatives. It is apt to keep coming up, for it has obvious political appeal. College and university spokesmen are generally able to contain their enthusiasm for it, however. They point out that most of the people who would benefit from it already attend college. Unless it were very generous, indeed, hence extremely costly to the treasury, it is not apt to widen college access or choice very much, but rather to reduce the pain of expenditures which college students, their parents, and extant sources of financial aid are already making. In addition, any provision that makes tuition less burdensome for the ordinary college student is viewed by some educators as an incentive to the states to curb their institutional subsidies and replace them with higher tuition rates.

CONCLUSION

"The federal government has no inclusive and consistent public policy as to what it should or should not do in the field of education. Whatever particular policies it seems to be pursuing are often inconsistent with each other, sometimes in conflict. They suggest a haphazard development, wherein policies of far-reaching effect have been set up as mere incidents of some special attempt to induce an immediate and particular efficiency."

National Advisory Committee on Education, 1931[16]

Nearly half a century after President Hoover's advisory committee bemoaned the lack of clarity and consistency in national policies affecting education, the map of federal financial involvements with the nation's colleges and universities has grown no easier to read; indeed, it is harder to find one's way on it than early observers could ever have dreamed.

The explosion of discrete programs, each aimed at "an immediate and particular efficiency," has continued. Neither in Washington nor on the campus can one locate a soul who could name, let alone explain, all of them. Every cranny of the federal establishment houses programs or other provisions by which government funds (or funds that, because of the provision, never reach the government) gush or trickle onto the nation's colleges and their students. Practically every institution is directly affected, and many students are too, although for many of them the effect remains indirect.

In the early 1960s, thoughtful observers discerned on the horizon "an enlargement of the Federal interest to coincide more nearly with the national interest" in higher education. They expected Washington to begin aiding colleges and universities *qua* educational institutions, and anticipated a reorganization of the federal government that would simplify and thereby encourage efforts to comprehend the entire subject.[17]

For the most part, they were wrong. Higher education policy in Washington has remained piecemeal, and the administration of federal higher education programs has stayed so decentralized as to daunt anyone in the Congress or the executive branch who might have liked to grasp its totality. The tax benefits endured, and in the realm of institutional support the government added a number of categorical programs, enlarged some and shrank others, but always in accord with purposes to which higher education was ancillary, and through agencies that viewed colleges as instruments suited to helping the agencies carry out their own purposes. The tasks which the universities might set for themselves evoked scant interest in Washington, save where they overlapped with a passing federal enthusiasm.

The national government has greatly increased its outlays for higher education, but the bulk of this growth has come in student aid, an activity which most people favor but one that qualifies as a limited form of income redistribution at least as well as support for higher education.

When one adds up all the programs and examines the range of academic activities that they help pay for, one could argue that, in fact, the "federal interest" in higher education has come to coincide with a larger portion of the "national interest." If that is so, perhaps there is no need to inveigh against the seemingly inadvertent way in which the pieces of the mosaic fit into place. Indeed, one might have greater cause for alarm if some comprehensive government master plan ordained all these developments. The inefficiencies, odd gaps, and occasional inconsistencies in the pattern of federal support may be necessary concomitants of a flexible and responsive set of financial arrangements where the recipients are as diverse and as jealous of their sovereignty as the nation's colleges and universities.

But there are at least equal drawbacks in these arrangements. Heightened sensitivity to federal regulation of higher education reflects as much as anything else the frustration of educators who sense that if they have been "bought," the price was too low, that the money they receive from Washington does not justify the enormous complexity of dealing with the federal government, and that the government is acting more like a creditor than a patron. Many colleges and universities, faced with a decade or more of what is variously described as "steady state" or severe retrenchment, find on the banks of the Potomac more problems than solutions, more irritation than succor.

Thus one encounters such utterances as Kingman Brewster's celebrated quip that Washington has adopted a "now that I have bought the button, I have a right to design the coat" approach to higher education.[18]

Withal, the situation shows few signs of changing to suit the academy, and one is therefore drawn to the view that the academy will have to live with it, pushing for modest alterations and fighting unwelcome developments, but not effecting any thoroughgoing change in the ways the government treats it. Some colleges will make good use of federal funds. Others will find this more difficult. Perhaps the most important accommodation is to accept the fact that unrestricted support has little chance, and that any increase in federal funds for higher education will likely take the form of more aid for undergraduate students, primarily through programs that channel the money directly to the individual rather than through his college or university. The challenge to the institution is to shape the terms of that aid so that the students it wishes to enroll find the federal programs serviceable, and to obtain sufficient funds to keep the programs true to their promise.

Categorical programs will continue, too, but their size and shape will follow from the "missions" of the sponsoring agencies and the priority those missions receive in the overall federal budget. If Washington were to revive its earlier emphasis on scientific research and development, for example, the major universities would doubtless benefit, but no amount of campus clamor about vanishing funds for graduate fellowships (or whatever) will result in more federal dollars for that purpose unless elected officials can identify it with other, larger purposes. But higher education need not adopt a passive stance. Its leaders can strive to enlarge the categories of academic activity which the government deems part of its mission—such as the relatively recent addition of arts and humanities—and can endeavor to demonstrate the value of particular federal strategies that serve their institutions well. They can also keep a wary eye on such mundane but important facets of federal relations as overhead payments, can push for the longest possible ''advance warning'' of shifts in government spending priorities, and can rally their trustees and alumni to press for larger appropriations.

With respect to tax benefits, the most the academy can expect is to retain those its students and donors now enjoy. The only additional measure that stands much chance of enactment is a tuition tax credit, and it is not a very good idea compared with other uses to which the same resources might be put.

One must reckon also with the strong possibility that federal outlays for higher education may not increase much in the next several years, if only because the shrinkage of veterans benefits will create some slack within the government-wide totals. The academy will have to scramble even to persuade the president and Congress that the funds recovered from the G.I. Bill should remain within the orbit of higher education.

An additional possibility, deserving of both hope and caution, is that of forging better links between federal policies and those of the states. Most national higher education programs ignore state boundaries and deal directly with individual campuses or students; only a few attempt to coordinate with the activities of the state governments. For many institutions, particularly the research universities, this seeming gap actually has some value, but for other schools it may produce more confusion than creativity.

No blinding flash of political and intellectual lightning will melt the present array of federal postsecondary activities into a single, elegant set of policies. No new Lorenzo will suddenly stride forth from the U.S. Office of Education—and if one did, the Office of Management and Budget and a horde of congressmen would quickly bury him under a mountain of *Federal Registers*. Higher education policy will remain a complex and incremental affair, adding new programs, re-calibrating old ones, transfusing some with resources and bleeding others, demanding much from its beneficiaries and thereby altering their own priorities, complicating their institutional lives, and hastening coronaries among their leaders. Improvements may be made on the margin, but the academy itself has no consensus as to what constitutes an improvement; hence every change will be seen by some as a dubious one.

The higher education community has little trouble agreeing that federal policy displays defects, but when the time comes to specify them and to propose agreeable remedies this unanimity regularly breaks down. Every faction is jealous of its benefits, wary of sudden change, and fearful that a carefully added total might turn out to be less than the sum of its parts. Over the years, this conservatism and its expression in federal policy have not served the academy badly, and they have served the government rather well. Since this pedestrian "buyer-seller" relationship seems destined to continue, one is well advised to search out its strengths and—always on the margin—try to offset its weaknesses. One would be wrong to call it patronage, but one can try to behave as if it were.

NOTES

1. James A. Perkins, "Coordinating Federal, State, and Institutional Decisions," in *Education and the State,* ed. John F. Hughes (Washington, D.C.: American Council on Education, 1975), p. 189.

2. U.S. Office of Management and Budget, *Seventy Issues: Fiscal Year 1977* (Washington, D.C.: Government Printing Office, January 21, 1976), p. 98; U.S. House Committee on Education and Labor, *Higher Education Amendments of 1976,* Report to accompany H.R. 12851, Report No. 94–1086, U.S. House of Representatives, 94th Congress, 2nd Session, p. 4.

3. The cost figures come from College Scholarship Service, *Student Expenses at Postsecondary Institutions, 1975–76* (New York: College Entrance Examination Board, 1975), Table 6, p. viii. For "family contribution" estimates, see College Scholarship Service, *CSS Need Analysis: Theory and Computation Procedures* (New York: College Entrance Examination Board, 1975), Table F. The figure cited here represents the gross income of a family with two children, one of them in college, that would sustain a "family contribution" of $2,000. This figure includes estimates of the cost of providing room and board in the home, as well as tuition, transportation, books, and miscellany.

4. Daniel S. Cheever, "Harvard and the Federal Government (A Report Delivered to the Faculties and Governing Boards, September, 1961)," *The Graduate Journal,* 5 (1962, Supplement), 121–135.

5. American Council on Education, *Federal Programs for Higher Education: Needed Next Steps* (Washington, D.C.: American Council on Education, 1969), p. 17; American Council on Education, *Federal Programs in Postsecondary Education: An Agenda for 1975* (Washington, D.C.: American Council on Education, 1974), p. 9.

6. National Science Foundation, *Federal Support to Universities, Colleges, and Selected Non-Profit Institutions, Fiscal Year 1974,* Surveys of Science Resources Series, NSF 76–305 (Washington, D.C.: Government Printing Office, 1976), p. 3. The activities represented in this figure are not wholly comparable to those included in the $4 billion for 1976 shown in Table I of the text, but much more information is presently available on the FY 1974 expenditures, hence they are used here.

7. Carol Van Alstyne and Sharon L. Coldren, *The Costs of Implementing Federally Mandated Social Programs at Colleges and Universities,* Policy Analysis Service Special Report (Washington, D.C.: American Council on Education, 1976).

8. Harvard University, *Financial Report to the Board of Overseers of Harvard College for the Fiscal Year 1973–1974* (Cambridge, Mass., 1974).

9. Carnegie Council on Policy Studies in Higher Education, *Progress and Problems in Medical and Dental Education* (San Francisco: Jossey-Bass Publishers, 1976).

10. For a good discussion of institutional aid, see Carnegie Commission on Higher Education, *Institutional Aid* (New York: McGraw-Hill, 1972).

11. Social Security student benefits (and all other Social Security benefits) are also free from income taxation, but are not included in this figure.

12. U.S. Senate Committee on the Budget, *Tax Expenditures*, Committee Print (Washington, D.C.: Government Printing Office, March 17, 1976).

13. The Council for Financial Aid to Education estimates that voluntary support for colleges and universities totalled $2.24 billion in 1973–74, $2.16 billion in the following year. See *Voluntary Support of Education* (New York: Council for Financial Aid to Education, 1974 and 1975).

14. Patricia Smith and Cathy Henderson, *A Study of the Private Sector of Higher Education; Part One: A Financial Taxonomy* (Washington, D.C.: Policy Analysis Service, American Council on Education, February 10, 1976).

15. Susan C. Nelson, "Trends and Issues in the Financing of Private Higher Education," paper prepared for a Brookings conference on "Public Policy and Private Higher Education." Revised draft, February, 1977.

16. Report of the National Advisory Committee on Education, *Federal Relations to Education*, Part I, "Committee Findings and Recommendations." (Washington, D.C., 1931), p. 8.

17. Homer D. Babbidge, Jr., and Robert M. Rosenzweig, *The Federal Interest in Higher Education* (New York: McGraw-Hill, 1962), p. 186.

18. Kingman Brewster, "Coercive Power of the Federal Purse," *Science*, 188, no. 4184 (April 11, 1975), 105.

Harvard's School of Education and the Federal Government: Institutional Effects of Interaction in the 1960s

Arthur G. Powell
Harvard University

(1)

Federal assistance to universities not only produces or fails to produce the programs or products officially intended. It interacts subtly with the unique histories of institutions, their existing cultures, and future ambitions. Although it is useful to consider the effects of government programs completely on their own terms—how wise were their intentions and how valuable their results—it is also helpful to examine the broader impact of government funding on the institutions themselves. Do federal funds encourage continuity or discontinuity, stability or disruption? To what extent do government funds cause change of any kind? How do they support or subvert institutional purposes?

This discussion explores some of these questions through the example of the Harvard Graduate School of Education. If federal involvement has institutional effects, the experience of this institution should be revealing. Between the mid-fifties and 1968, the federal role in the annual budget of the Graduate School of Education increased from 5 percent to

51

62 percent. Most of that increase occurred in the five years after 1963. After 1968 a substantial decline in support took place. By 1975 the government provided only 20 percent of the School's funds. During the years of federal activity a continuing discussion ensued about how a school of education like Harvard's could best be supported financially and what its central mission should be. Our main concern is the connection between these institutional dilemmas and federal support.

The next section establishes the context of fiscal dependence on outside sources which preceded federal subvention and accompanied it. The third section describes the continuing tension between Harvard's desire for general funding of ongoing activities and the government's primary interest in additive special projects. The fourth section assesses the extent to which Harvard became financially dependent on government monies. The fifth section explores how federal funds accelerated an internal crisis concerning the proper mission of a graduate school of education.

(2)

Harvard University's "every tub on its own bottom" fiscal decentralization required that its School of Education be responsible for generating its own income and balancing its budget more like an independent institution than a department within one university. Substantial support from external sources characterized the Graduate School of Education's finances for decades prior to any federal involvement. Moreover, the shifting nature of that support had profound impact on the purpose of the School.

Early in the century the study of education at Harvard had been propelled forward not by internal university backing but by the contributions of businessmen. They believed that public schooling could adjust American youth to the requirements of an industrial order and that university courses in professional education could be decisive instruments to achieve that objective. In the twenties and thirties, the acquisition of an endowment allowed the School to withdraw from direct school reform and to attempt to upgrade the quality of training given to prospective professionals. When, at the end of the Second World War, endowment no longer could carry that burden and no other sources of income seemed available, the School adopted a primarily research mission by which it hoped to parlay minimal resources into maximum influence.

During the 1950s the School began to achieve national recognition as a creative and growing enterprise. The financial base for this sudden progress was provided by private foundations, which discovered public education as a major interest in the aftermath of the baby boom and cold war. Before the fifties endowment and tuition income had covered nearly 100 percent of basic or "core" expenses for faculty salaries, financial aid, and administrative support. But by 1953 the foundations provided approximately 40 percent of core expenses and 55 percent of total expenses (which included funded research and miscellaneous special projects). In 1960 the Ford Fund for the Advancement of Education alone provided 29 percent of all core income.

Although the directions in which foundation dollars pushed the School were quite different from those its senior administrators intended to follow at the beginning of the 1950s, they were consistent with Harvard's educational biases and provoked no sense of discontinuity or of undue outside pressure. Harvard, in fact, became increasingly instrumental in affecting foundation priorities, especially those of the Ford Fund, and in generating monies that could be applied flexibly to meet internally defined needs. By the end of the fifties the School's reputation was based on expanded practitioner programs in teacher education and school administration, funded respectively by the Fund for the Advancement of Education and the Kellogg Foundation; and on the advancement of scholarship in social science and humanistic disciplines related to education, funded largely by the Carnegie Corporation and the Rockefeller Foundation.

As this mission took shape, the principal administrative concern shifted from program development to program stabilization. How, assuming that foundation support was only temporary, could basic, core expenses be financed permanently? Efforts to increase endowment and tuition income were the most obvious and most pursued strategies but, increasingly, federal assistance in this task also seemed feasible.

Until 1956, the scale and influence of federal support to the School had been limited and usually indirect. During the Second World War, various federal contracts had helped stimulate interest in research and development. After the war, anxiety over the end of G.I. Bill benefits, which had provided unexpected core revenue, provoked a search for new sources of students. This in turn led Harvard to find common cause with emerging foundation interests in the national shortage of educational personnel. Throughout the fifties, in addition, a few faculty received research support from agencies such as the National Institute of Mental Health. But in 1955 only 5 percent of total income derived from government sources. Only after congressional funding in 1956 of the Cooperative Research Act and the decision, at the same time, of the National Science Foundation to fund in-service training of teachers of school mathematics and science did federal concern for education *per se* begin to affect the School. Following the Sputnik scare a year later and passage of the National Defense Education Act, Harvard realized that substantial federal assistance was likely. Largely through NSF in-service programs and Cooperative Research Program grants, federal assistance increased to approximately 25 percent of total income in each of the years between 1958 and 1963.

Since federal support on this scale was wholly new to the School's experience, much faculty discussion centered on its probable institutional impact. One issue was federal control over academic decisions, as exemplified by cold-war requirements such as loyalty oaths, disclaimer affidavits, and security clearances. But these requirements were not regarded as serious or long-term threats; they were tied to specific programs which could be rejected if too obnoxious, and were opposed by many thoughtful public officials who saw them as short-lived. The greatest potential danger, instead, was thought to be the centrifugal pull of enticing federal programs unrelated to the School's principal programmatic mission. Unless the School disciplined itself in the scramble for federal dollars, Dean Francis Keppel warned in 1959, it might "lose its central purpose and become a holding company for the solution of *ad hoc* problems defined by outside forces."

Here too Keppel was optimistic. The dilemma was thoroughly familiar to an institution whose history was so closely linked with outside funding. The tug-of-war between the specific and usually new projects of funding agencies and the more general institutional assistance sought by university administrators was a well-known condition of the grantsmanship game. Ford Foundation officials, for example, were well aware of Harvard's fundamental interest in institutional support, no matter how cleverly that interest was disguised by specific proposals. They kept a vigilant watch (with imperfect success) over the consistency between preliminary budgets and actual expenditures. Keppel hoped for the development of personal relationships with federal officials to promote close affinity between Cambridge and Washington priorities. Moreover, he hoped that the variety of potential funding agencies within the federal establishment would allow for diversity of viewpoints and even competition, so that institutions would have the same range of options which prevailed in the foundation world. Especially after the 1960 presidential

Table I
HGSE Income Availed of

	U.S. Government	(%)	Total
1962–63	$ 769,595	(23)	$3,334,059
1963–64	1,042,560	(30)	3,463,992
1964–65	1,868,842	(44)	4,236,075
1965–66	2,951,792	(52)	5,629,456
1966–67	4,520,743	(62)	7,332,021
1967–68	4,685,682	(57)	8,188,711
1968–69	3,302,487	(43)	7,719,352
1969–70	2,674,196	(37)	7,283,824
1974–75	1,228,495	(20)	6,166,685

elections, Keppel used his considerable professional prestige and contacts within the new administration to advocate more general, multi-year support to advance and stabilize institutions like his own. The chances for success seemed promising, not only because the federal education bureaucracy as it related to institutional grants was relatively unformed and malleable, but because Keppel himself became the United States Commissioner of Education in 1962.

(3)

Following enactment of the Great Society legislation after 1964, federal assistance to the Graduate School of Education rose dramatically beyond the expectations of the late 1950s. (See Table I.) By 1967, 62 percent of all income derived from federal sources. The School's total annual income had first exceeded one million dollars in 1958. Five years later the government alone provided an equivalent sum. By 1968 the School's income exceeded $8 million, and the federal contribution approached $4 million.

The most striking aspect of this vast change between 1963 and 1968 was the general unavailability of federal funds for program support or institution-building. Government assistance was not designed to stabilize the programmatic mission which had developed in the fifties, but instead to create a small number of large research and development projects. All were expected to produce visible educational products outside the main currents of the School's regular activities. The four largest projects—in 1966–67 they alone accounted for 76 percent of all government support to the School—created a comprehensive secondary school for the Western Region of Nigeria ($2,389,654 from the Agency for International Development); a high school physics course ($4,348,927 from the Office of Education); a computer-based vocational counseling system ($1,829,663 from the Office of Education); and a research and development center for inquiry into individual and cultural differences in education ($4,077,246 from the Office of Education).

Federal concern for tangible research and development products was in marked contrast to previous foundation interests, and tended to disperse financial power over grant expenditures from the School's central administration to faculty project directors. The tendency away from institution-building was thus doubly reinforced by both the government's preoccupation with visible products and the inevitable tendency of faculty project managers to husband resources under their control for narrowly focused project ends. Only in the case of the Center for Research and Development on Educational Differences (and also in the Nigerian project, where the project leader was the School's associate dean) did the central administration retain the kind of control it had routinely held over most foundation grants of the fifties. The R and D Center became the main example of the School's efforts to use federal project money for more general institutional support.

In this effort the School was encouraged by Commissioner Keppel's explicit intention to focus Cooperative Program Resources on long-term inquiry in general problem areas and thus make relatively unrestricted funds available to strengthen basic instructional programs. Harvard had been chosen in 1964 as one of the first federal R and D centers in education. In part, the R and D center idea had been modelled on Harvard's previous experience with Ford funds, and Harvard was led to believe that it would be able to continue under Center auspices the same kinds of activities begun with Ford backing. These activities had had two broad purposes: to stimulate school improvement through projects jointly undertaken by the School and cooperating local school systems (such as team teaching), and to provide long-term support for certain core Harvard activities in training teachers and administrators. Authority over the Ford grant had been centered unmistakably in the Dean's office, where the largely unrestricted funds were strategically deployed to cover core expenses such as staff salaries and financial aid.

The original U.S. Office of Education guidelines for R and D centers did not envision program support in this general sense. But the School believed Keppel would soon succeed in altering the guidelines and that, for the moment, a proposal could be submitted "broad enough to encompass the interests and needs of the . . . Graduate School of Education, and narrow enough to permit an effective concentration of research and development energies over an extended period of time." The chosen theme, individual and cultural differences, was in fact a broad rubric under which monies could be appropriated to a variety of faculty whose work and salaries were thought most promising of support. Enthusiastic about research, but conscious of the growing dangers of fragmentation and the "holding company" model, Dean Theodore R. Sizer attempted to connect the R and D Center to existing core programs of the School. Of course part of his motive was financial: he wanted to replace dwindling foundation support for core activities with federal money, and saw the R and D Center as the most appropriate point of leverage. But he also wanted the Center to be the "glue to hold the whole faculty together," to integrate research and development with the activities (and budgets) of the training programs, to counter the growing centrifugal tendencies.

Over thirty projects operated simultaneously in the Center's peak years. But as time went on, the gap between Harvard and federal intentions widened rather than narrowed. Keppel did not succeed in making the R and D centers a vehicle for federal strengthening of the basic operations of a few major schools of education. Moreover, the Office of Education administrators were increasingly committed to the ideal of focused social science research.

In the summer of 1966, a scathing federal site evaluation remarked that "Although research and development centers are supposed to have a clearly defined purpose, the Harvard center does not." The evaluators found no "clear configuration" among projects and suspected that the label educational differences was an "umbrella for funding projects rather than . . . a point of departure for an integrated frame of reference.' It was difficult to tell "where the activities and personnel of the Center stops and the School of Education's program begins. . . . There is little feeling that the Center has a unity of purpose, of facilities, of personnel, or of a program separate from that of the Graduate School of Education.'' Harvard readily agreed with this description, but drew different conclusions. It felt that leading Office of Education officials embraced a linear or ''pipeline'' model of educational change, which assumed that social science could contribute to education by an orderly process of research, development, demonstration, and dissemination. Harvard opposed this model of highly targeted research, both on substantive grounds and because the model implied a narrow and separate role for federal support rather than the more flexible sponsorship of institutional growth Harvard preferred.

Although Harvard subsequently attempted to meet federal criticism by focusing its efforts more carefully, the difference in viewpoint remained fundamental. In 1967, by mutual agreement, the Center was phased out. The School accurately predicted that other sources within and outside the government would refund most of the major projects. There was no need for a humiliating concession to the research production schedules Washington required. For its part the Office of Education had no desire for an ideological battle over the proper meaning of program support and was pleased to pay the price of helping to refund the larger projects under non-Center auspices in return for the elimination of a visible alternative to highly targeted research and development.

Harvard's failure to convert federal research and development funding into more general institutional support was disappointing but precipitated no financial disaster. The mid-sixties' years of federal ''soft money'' expansion in research and development were also years of expansion of the older core program mission inherited from the end of the fifties. Between 1963 and 1967 the number of permanent faculty, paid almost entirely from non-federal sources, rose from sixteen to twenty-six. The number of full-time equivalent individuals with teaching appointments paid for by what the School considered core resources (reasonably stable, non-government funds) rose from about thirty-five to fifty-three.

Part of this expansion was financed by income from new endowments raised principally by the president of the University; between 1964 and 1966 endowment income alone increased by $328,000. Tuition income also increased, though less dramatically. Moreover, predictions of sudden foundation withdrawal from program support proved unduly pessimistic. Ford, for example, made an additional, largely unrestricted grant that enabled program support to continue until 1967 as well as other more restricted grants that the School in part turned to its own requirements for core backing.

Finally, the institution benefited somewhat from an unexpected new source of unrestricted income, the recovery of funds for indirect expenses incurred on research and development projects, or overhead. In 1968 alone the School received $729,000 in overhead income from the government. Senior officials of the School believed at the time that a portion of overhead income would remain to absorb core expenses even after incremental indirect costs of federal projects had been covered. The amount of funds "left over" for core application varied according to the project. Internal estimates suggested that only 25 percent of overhead collected from the Nigerian project was needed to pay for the incremental indirect costs associated with it. The comparable estimate for the physics curriculum was 50 percent. It is not clear how accurate these estimates were, nor is it easy to recover data to answer the question authoritatively. Some senior officials claimed that, if overhead "profits" were made on some projects, they in part went to cover overhead costs in other projects that were not fully reimbursed. Yet if the overhead "profits" for the two projects above are correct—as estimated by the School's own administration at the time—some $761,000 of overhead income from those projects alone was available to fund the general expenses of the School.

Even though the purpose of federal grants in the mid-sixties was not to provide institutional support, and despite Harvard's lack of success in modifying that policy, overhead income from the several research and development projects became one of several sources of unrestricted income which permitted the core instructional program to expand. Before 1962, internal financial analyses rarely mentioned overhead as an important source of unrestricted income. Similar analyses after 1967 always viewed overhead as a principal component of core revenue.

(4)

Although the federal R and D programs were designed to add activities to the School rather than subsidize ongoing operations, by 1966 Harvard felt dependent on government funds for partial support of its basic activities. The dean's financial advisors told him that "It would be nice to be able to report that withdrawal of government support would be matched immediately by equal reduction in expenses. This isn't so." Part of this sense of dependence derived from the practical necessity to incur staff contractual obligations that extended beyond the period guaranteed by appropriated federal funds. The government funded multi-year projects on an annual basis, but Harvard frequently had to make longer commitments to attract professional personnel. Long-range budget planning was far more difficult for federal projects than for foundation projects; the difficulty was compounded by changing overhead rates and the unpredictability of when committed funds would actually be received.

The sense of dependence stemmed, in the second place, from the realization that certain individuals employed on government funds had gradually assumed roles in the School's general affairs, in addition to their project activities, that could not be easily abandoned even if federal funds disappeared. In effect, the pool of professional researchers and administrators attracted to the School by the expansion of soft-money activities became an internal personnel pool for the assessment and recruitment of potential regular faculty. If in the middle sixties fifty-three "full-time equivalent" teaching faculty were supported by core resources, a total of ninety-five individuals actually held teaching appointments (an increase of forty over 1960). Many individuals, that is, held teaching appointments and participated in some aspects of regular instructional programs whose salaries were paid from government funds and not from core resources. The size and diversity of the curriculum thus indirectly grew as a result of federal grants for research and development.

It is easy, however, to exaggerate and misunderstand these kinds of dependency on government money. In general, soft-money research faculty who also participated in instruction did so not at the School's instigation nor as a covert device to replace core faculty support with government dollars. The young researchers themselves pushed for teaching appointments and the chance to offer courses because their own long-range career ambitions were usually to find regular university teaching positions. They desired, for their own advancement, the experience and credentials that could be provided only by direct involvement in the School's academic programs. Thus, their role in instruction was mainly dictated by their own needs rather than by the School's interest in "free" instruction.

In addition to the factors of discrepancies between assured income and contractual commitments, and the role of soft-money faculty in the School's regular programs, the sense of institutional dependence on government funds was heightened by the presence of overhead income which could help meet the rising costs of administrative functions and services. Federal assistance had transformed the sheer scale of the School's operations from a budget of less than a million dollars in 1957 to one of more than eight million a decade later. The School misjudged the ways this escalation of short-term support would indirectly affect the components of the core budget. Financial planning in the early and middle sixties was based on the 1950s assumption that faculty salaries and financial aid would continue to be the predominant core expense categories. In 1954, for example, 54 percent of core expenses supported faculty salaries, and 19 percent funded financial aid. When the institution forecast its immediate financial future, even as late as 1963, it assumed that sixty cents of every new core dollar raised in the following four years would be available to underwrite faculty salaries alone. Administrative and maintenance expenses would remain constant despite institutional growth, subject only to a 4–5 percent annual inflation factor.

Yet by the middle sixties these crucial assumptions began to break down as the shift in the scale of operations, along with the rising rate of inflation, provoked not only a rapid rise in administrative and service costs but a rise in the *fraction* of available core dollars they consumed. Part of this new expense burden was first assumed directly by federal research and development project budgets, then indirectly in overhead recovery, and eventually by other core resources. The School's first full-time fiscal officer, for example, was initially employed to monitor the budget of the R and D Center as a line-item direct federal cost. The function proved to be indispensable even after the demise of the Center, and the salary was justified as reasonable overhead support to all the School's fiscal affairs. More generally, building maintenance expenses jumped from 6 percent of core expenditures in the mid-sixties to 14 percent a decade later. Library costs, pushed upward by the operating expenses of a new building funded in large part by a federal facilities grant, rose in the same period from 3 percent of core expenses ($59,000) to 10 percent ($362,000). Central administrative services rose from 27 percent of core in 1964 to 35 percent in 1975. Institutional expansion, regardless of the funding source, created demands for more central services and facilities which could not easily be reduced even if income declined. A high level of overhead recovery was helpful not only to fund these new expenses, but to preserve the availability of other core income for faculty expansion.

By the end of the 1960s it was apparent that the School's core expenses, especially those for faculty salaries, were overextended and that some retrenchment was necessary. The precipitating event was the fortuitous completion in 1968 of many of the large research and development projects and the corresponding decline of overhead income by $313,000 in 1968–69. It was easy to conclude that this decline in federal overhead had "caused" the fiscal problems which ensued, and it was true that the School—and the University administration—had misjudged the stability of federal support for research and development. As late as 1967 the School had found it "sensible and prudent" to assume that no decrease in the level of R and D involvement was likely.

Yet overhead was but one source of unrestricted income, and its reduction was but one factor in the late 1960s fiscal instability. After 1966 no further major increases in endowment occurred, as all fund-raising energies were devoted to completing the new library. Tuition income actually decreased in 1967, the first such setback in nearly two decades, as a greater program emphasis on doctoral and research training caused a reduction in the size of large practitioner-oriented Master's programs. Foundation involvement in core support dropped to a trivial level. And, along with all this, inflation continued to grow, especially in service areas least susceptible to immediate control. Declining federal assistance was thus only one factor that led inexorably to both a reduction in the percentage of core income available for faculty salaries (24 percent in 1975, compared with 38 percent in 1964 and 54 percent in 1954) and in the actual number of core full-time equivalent faculty positions (thirty-six in 1975, compared with fifty-three in 1967).

Ironically, the retrenchment at the end of the sixties was accompanied by new federal policies which promised general institutional support of precisely the kind that the School had coveted at the beginning of the decade. These new policies passed through two phases. The first supported financial aid for graduate students in education on a far broader front than before and dramatically increased the financial aid available to students enrolled in basic instructional programs. Beginning largely in 1966, the older NSF money was supplemented by three-year doctoral fellowships for research training from Title IV of the Elementary and Secondary Education Act, three-year fellowships to promote college teaching from Title IV of the National Defense Education Act, and one-year fellowships for prospective and experienced teachers under Title V of the Higher Education Act. In 1967–68 the School awarded 153 federal fellowships worth nearly $808,000. It could lament that a few of its basic programs, notably educational administration, were ineligible for federal assistance and that the fixed nature of federal stipends reduced the number of students who might participate and eliminated the capacity to match fellowship awards to actual need.

But the most serious complaint was that these fellowship programs were discontinued almost as soon as they were established. The national sense of a shortage of education personnel, both in quality and in quantity, which had informed passage of the legislation, abruptly disappeared at the end of the sixties. By 1972 all the major fellowship programs were making no new awards. The programs did not last long enough to affect institutional planning. At first, some relief was given to core allocations for student aid, but soon core contributions increased and increased more sharply when the fellowship programs ended. Core income from tuition and endowment provided $135,000 in fellowship assistance during 1966; nine years later it had grown to $439,000. For the first time in two decades, neither government nor foundations provided significant monies for student aid. In the face of a desperate need for new sources of core income to hold retrenchment to a minimum, the School seized upon tuition income as the one source of unrestricted funds most open to immediate increase. The substantial increase in tuition income which occurred in the early 1970s was achieved mainly through increases in tuition fees rather than through increases in the size of the student body. In 1963 tuition contributed 40 percent of core income; in 1975 it contributed 60 percent. But one price of this greater reliance on tuition increases was a corresponding increase in financial aid, an increase which after 1972 was borne mainly by the School's own core resources.

The second phase of more general federal assistance explicitly supported program development. The Education Professions Development Act of 1967 sought to fund not only student support but other program costs including staff salaries. Moreover, funds were available to assist the older major program areas of administration and teacher education, the latter through the Training the Teachers of Teachers project (TTT) of the Bureau of Education Professions Development. In 1971, in addition, NIMH provided program support to the School's training program in clinical psychology. Thus all three of the practitioner areas which the School had viewed as basic in 1960 had received or were about to receive program support by the end of the decade.

Yet this assistance also was short-lived. Funds for teacher education ended in 1973 after four years of operation. (Previously Ford funds had assisted this function for fifteen years.) Support for administration ended a year later, and aid to clinical psychology is currently ending. Made much more cautious by the decline in federal R and D assistance, the School never relied on EPDA program support to provide long-term institutional support. And especially after the 1968 elections, no one believed that program support was likely to last. It was viewed not as a means for further expansion or to salvage the expansion of the sixties, but as a means to buy time. Federal program support, while it lasted, was used to finance the transition to a smaller core faculty. In only this indirect and unanticipated sense did the late and brief federal interest in program support contribute to institutional financial stability.

In purely fiscal terms, then, the effects of federal subvention on the stability of the School's basic or core program were real but limited. In the years of greatest expansion and greatest optimism about a continuing high level of federal support, the most significant federal contribution to unrestricted income, overhead, was indirect and but one among several sources of core income. When more direct forms of general institutional support finally emerged from Washington, financial optimism had already waned. A far more wary mood about the duration of federal largesse prevailed; the newer federal dollars were used far more cautiously and for purposes of consolidation and retrenchment. Certainly the vast inflow of research and development money had helped fan the flames of expansionism; but federal dollars were only one factor in overexpansion. Despite the marked reduction of federal support after 1968 the institution adapted its expenses to fit its income remarkably quickly and with trivially small deficit budgets.

(5)

The most significant connections between federal subvention and the retrenchment of the late 1960s are revealed in the substantive directions the retrenchment took. The most serious consequence of federal involvement was not on financial stability but on institutional purpose and mission. At the end of the decade, pressures within the School shifted from expanding and stabilizing the program mission inherited from the 1950s to adding a new mission. Federal research dollars were an important catalyst in furthering the growth of this additional goal. At first, when income from many sources was expanding and financial optimism prevailed, it appeared that both old and new missions might be accommodated within the core budget. But when retrenchment became necessary and choices had to be made, the power of the newer ideas was felt.

Through their catalytic—and unintentional—effects on internal ideology, federal funds made their most lasting institutional impact.

Some of these effects were obvious from the outset and caused no sense of conflict of purpose. Even if the School had wished to insulate its ongoing training operations from the federal projects for research and development, which it tried at all points not to do, the fact that expenses of a few of those projects in any given year surpassed the entire core budget would have made some spill-over effect likely. The clearest initial effect was to enhance the importance of research and development as both a faculty activity and a training priority. Although these functions had been hardly absent in the fifties, and indeed had been viewed by President James B. Conant as the institution's *raison d'etre* at the beginning of that decade, foundation priorities had encouraged practitioner training and inquiry in disciplines related to education rather than applied research designed to produce educational products or solve educational problems. Applied research was immeasurably strengthened by federal support.

Federal dollars transformed the roles of several established senior faculty, in professional fields such as social studies education, science education, and guidance, from a primary emphasis on the instruction of prospective practitioners to a primary emphasis on research, development, or the management of those activities. The ease with which these role changes were accomplished, along with the unwillingness of faculty to revert back to former roles when projects were completed, revealed the heady lure of research and development over the more mundane and less prestigious task of training educators. A common outcome of a research and development project in such areas was the stimulation of organized doctoral programs which emphasized R and D rather than practitioner training. The apprenticeship possibilities for advanced students on projects, with the precious attraction of financial aid in the form of research assistantships, altered student career hopes as much as those of the faculty who taught them. None of this was intended by the government, nor was it a unique effect of federal funds alone. Foundation funding patterns in the sixties also became more project-oriented and more concerned with discrete results. (In fact, it was unusual for the government to fund new ideas from their inception. More typically, its role was to support on a large scale ideas which had first been developed through another funding source. Thus the physics curriculum began with Carnegie support, and the international activities which led to the Nigerian project started through Ford and Carnegie grants.)

Yet the fifties practitioner mission was not merely balanced by research and development. It was more directly challenged in other unplanned ways. The variety of federal projects, and especially the variety of efforts supported by the Research and Development Center, became conduits for the penetration of unfamiliar ideas into the institution as a whole. As the sixties progressed it became harder to accommodate these ideas to the older mission. Here again the role of government was not intentional. Indeed the new ideas were often opposed by administrators in the Office of Education. Nor was the incorporation of controversial ideas associated with government money alone. The foundations were often more sympathetic and supported their development after Washington backed away. Only in matters of scale was federal money unique.

During the 1966 evaluation of the R and D Center discussed earlier, federal officials and their consultants were not only critical of the absence of an administrative structure and research focus distinct from the activities of the rest of the School. They were also concerned about the substance of the work supported by the Center. Of the many projects, some employed research designs consistent with modern social science methodology. But many other projects were not "research" in the sense of dispassionate, controlled inquiry. They embraced more passion, more activism, and more reformism. Their substantive themes were urban education and the limits of formal schooling.

An internal study of the Center discovered that the "most extended and heated issue" under debate was the Center's capacity to reform urban schools. A variety of Center projects, some of which had a research focus, explored urban issues. The result was the re-establishment of ties (broken since early in the century) between the School of Education and the local urban communities of Boston and Cambridge. Administrative liaisons with these cities were appointed; curriculum projects in Roxbury were begun; a Harvard-Boston summer training program was undertaken; and studies started on Negro teenagers and on the effects of desegregation. Although most of these activities were conducted by white administrators and researchers, R and D Center funds brought the first blacks to the School's professional staff.

At the same time, other Center projects (and some of those mentioned above as well) emphasized a second theme: that education occurred in many places besides schools and perhaps could best be improved if schooling itself was not the primary focus of reform efforts. This second theme became explicit when the hostile federal evaluation forced the Center to devise a more precise mission than educational differences. The most comprehensive focus seemed to be on "*expanded educational opportunities* (or environments) . . . not restricted to schools and schooling." The Preschool project, for example, stressed family rather than school settings and focused on an age group that did not attend school at all. Other projects analyzed adolescent subcultures and the cultural roots of mental abilities, adolescent identity formation, focusing on non-school factors, and the unintentional effects of the public schools' social system on pupil learning. One of the largest projects, a staff seminar on secondary education reform (called the "Shadow Faculty" because it had a program but as yet no power to implement it), emphasized the restoration of links between school and other community agencies.

Yet the Center's leadership knew that the expanded education theme would not appeal to the Office of Education, which emphasized schooling, any more than urban activism would appeal to Washington administrators committed to social science research methods. More significantly, the leadership realized that the new themes conflicted at crucial points with Harvard's own institutional mission. The simultaneous emergence of a moral commitment to urban educational reform and of growing doubts about the efficacy of schooling as a principal means to achieve that reform created a center of frustration and criticism of the School's traditional mission. If the educational value of schooling was limited, so was the program mission the School had been attempting to expand and stabilize financially. If the problem of secondary education was the restoration of community and not academic learning, why stabilize a teacher education department organized according to the major academic subjects taught in schools? If what happened to children outside school was at least as important as what happened in school, why should Harvard practitioner programs exclusively train school-based workers, like guidance counselors and principals? If the central educational problems were urban, why were the School's recruitment and placement efforts geared to a primarily suburban clientele? If academic inquiry in discrete disciplines had had little effect on solving social problems, why had the School developed doctoral programs in just those disciplines, rather than interdisciplinary studies more explicitly committed to problem solving?

As a result of this criticism, the withdrawal of the federal dollars that had enabled these ideas to enter the School was accompanied by an active search for new dollars to keep them going and deepen their influence. In

67

the short run, new foundation grants, particularly from Ford, continued the urban theme within a new Office for Metropolitan Educational Collaboration. In addition, the Center had decided prior to its demise to undertake an extended study of the limits of schooling, to be led by Christopher Jencks. The idea, given an enormous national boost by James Coleman's federally sponsored study of *Equality of Educational Opportunity*, continued to develop at the School through Carnegie sponsorship of reanalysis of Coleman's data and Jencks's subsequent volume on *Inequality*.

But the new themes flourished not only because new sources of soft money supported them. Increasingly, they and the individuals who expressed them penetrated the core budget and competed for increasingly scarce core resources with the older missions of practitioner training and discipline-based scholarship. OMEC was transformed into an administrative unit concerned with field activities, headed by a new associate dean. A member of its staff occupied another associate deanship. A key R and D Center associate became director of the teacher education program. Others joined the regular faculty, and three professorships of urban policy were created.

In effect, the Shadow Faculty and other sympathetic individuals became a Shadow School of Education. Funded at first entirely from the outside, and mainly by federal dollars, the new themes became a potent countervailing force to the old mission by the end of the sixties. Although the battle of 1967 over continuation of the R and D Center seemed to be mainly with Washington, the more compelling dispute was internal.

The government had not attempted to promote this ideological instability. But the existence of large sums of research and development money along with (for two years) flexible rules about its use enabled Harvard's administration to encourage a variety of new ideas. The same process frequently occurred in even the most product-oriented R and D projects outside the Center. The curriculum and counseling projects already mentioned created not only a climate of faculty acceptance to possible changes in the teacher education and guidance areas, but opened up opportunities for the dean's office to institute changes furthering the new spirit of urban and nonschool reform. It was relatively easy, for example, to develop a broadened notion of counseling which emphasized the social sources of psychological instability and to persuade the guidance program to abandon its traditional concern for individual, school-based remediation. Federal monies for R and D in that area both deflected faculty commitments and created vacancies which individuals holding the new beliefs could fill.

If government money expanded the School's ability to broaden its mission, it did not mandate that that result would occur. The outcome was not foreordained. Both federal funds and Harvard administrative will were essential. Nor, again, were government funds the only sources involved.

Just as the government did not intend to provoke an internal Harvard debate about how its own resources should best be used, it also did not intend to establish when the debate would climax. But the reduction of overhead income in 1969 made Harvard see that retrenchment, and therefore choices, were essential. Guidance had already disappeared into the new program in clinical psychology and public practice. Now the old teacher education department was eliminated as well, and in its place a new program called Learning Environments was given core support. Learning Environments was the direct heir of the Shadow Faculty.

Federal program support, which had begun in 1968, made this reorganization more orderly and less painful than might otherwise have been the case. The government's intention in giving program support for teacher education through TTT (Training the Teachers of Teachers) was indeed institutional development. But the government's objective was to improve the education of teachers and teacher educators, not to subsidize the elimination of such training. The gap between what the government wanted and what in fact happened was not provoked, this time, by policy disagreements between federal grant officers and Harvard officials. Unlike the experience of the R and D Center, a genuine collegial respect prevailed between Harvard and Washington administrators of TTT. The disagreement instead was internal, between the School's administration and the TTT faculty. Because the government never stipulated that a coherent training program be created with its funding, and because the principal Harvard faculty involved lacked tenure, the School's administration was able to control TTT expenditures in much the same way as it had controlled R and D dollars earlier. The TTT faculty group desired incremental change in teacher education at Harvard. They consisted largely of men not involved in the R and D Center, whose careers had suffered from the disruption of the old guidance program and the waning of support for academic teacher education. The School's administration, in contrast, wanted to funnel more resources to the remaining Shadow Faculty group, now ready to implement its proposals through establishing a new alternative school in Cambridge. In addition, TTT funds seemed a heaven-sent chance to provide resources to the underfinanced but well-organized group of black students and faculty whose demands for resources were a natural outcome of the moral concern for urban improvement.

Thus, the long hoped-for program support for teacher education led to the funding of two ventures—the Cambridge alternative school and a black school in Roxbury—that had not been mentioned in the original prospectus at all and which were beyond the control and interest of the key faculty who had procured the grant. Their share of the program became far smaller than they had expected. By 1970, the Shadow Faculty group had not only established its alternative school but had designed the new training program called Learning Environments. The positions of the TTT junior faculty were eliminated. The last links with the older mission of teacher education were cut. The function of program support in its final years was to support faculty who would leave the School once the federal grant ended. Except for Learning Environments, TTT did not fund program development but provided a financial cushion to make program dissolution more orderly.

Surprisingly, the reaction from Washington was not disapproval that original intentions were not carried out. In part this was due to ignorance of Harvard internal politics and trust in the School's administration. Indeed the Harvard administration had been privately consulted on which EPDA projects it most wanted funded and had been allowed to exert a crucial veto over faculty proposals. The original TTT proposal had been extremely vague; federal subvention was principally a vote of confidence in the School and its ability to use the funds wisely. The federal administrators expected Harvard's focus, as well as their own, to become more specific as time went on.

This is exactly what took place. As Harvard endorsed Learning Environments and its program of greater community involvement, and also the efforts of black students to improve a school in Roxbury through greater parental control, these same ideas became popular in Washington. If the original TTT prospectus proposal at Harvard was rather white, suburban, and school-based, what Washington and the Harvard administration soon wanted was urban, black, and community-based. An early federal site evaluation praised the urban and community control themes before they had been implemented at all and demanded further changes in the original proposal. Harvard had reached essentially the same position and accommodated itself without protest to the new federal demands.

Federal "policy" had come full circle. Ideas which had been opposed by one agency in 1966 were now mandated by another agency four years later.

The path of program-support dollars to the field of school administration was less tortured. The crisis in mission at the School did not destroy the area of school administration as it did destroy guidance and teaching. Indeed the demise of the latter two strengthened administration. When program support came to the latter area, there was greater agreement between the School's central administration and its faculty leaders in the field of school administration. As with TTT, generally close personal realtionships prevailed between Harvard and the federal grant officers. Federal funds assisted the already-planned redirection of Harvard efforts toward urban problems, enlarged and broadened the student body, and allowed new subjects such as organizational behavior to enter the curriculum. Long the area of the School most dependent on external support for faculty and students, the administration area was a prime beneficiary of cuts elsewhere. By the mid-seventies when federal program support had ended, most of its faculty were finally supported by internal core sources.

(6)

At the beginning of the 1960s the Graduate School of Education hoped that the expected large-scale federal involvement in its affairs would not precipitate a centrifugal expansion in peripheral directions desired by Washington but would instead undergird essential institutional functions. The School had a clear idea what its core program was; it needed stable dollars to pay for it and imagined the government to be one promising source. Subsequently, the feared centrifugal explosion occurred. The core mission was fractured, but the government's responsibilities for this were less direct than had been foreseen.

The financial and intellectual instabilities of the late 1960s were more the result of actions taken freely by Harvard than of actions taken by federal officials. These instabilities were not inevitable outcomes of increased government subvention. Rather, government monies amplified tendencies already present at the School. Harvard overestimated its ability to maintain a stable consensus for its program mission, and underestimated the capacity of large amounts of new money to expose the fragility of that consensus.

The School used R and D Center funds to develop exciting ideas which had previously been outside its sense of central mission. Once present, these ideas demanded a larger place and helped undercut both school-based practitioner training and research in the traditional disciplines. Even when certain developments seemed beyond anyone's intention, such as the role changes of key senior faculty, the initiative for how to exploit these changes remained at Harvard and offered many options. Again and again federal money created administrative opportunities to choose continuity or change. And again and again Harvard opted for change. The balance of power lay mainly with the School; the government was weaker than outsiders supposed. The government hoped to establish a targeted R and D enterprise and failed. It hoped to ensure financial aid for research training for certain careers, like sociology; it largely failed. When program support eventually came, the School successfully transformed this to its own purposes as well.

The differences between older sorts of external suppport and government funding was not in their capacities to alter institutional mission, but in the elusive indirectness of the government's influence. Unlike businessmen reformers at the beginning of the century, or foundations during the fifties, the federal government rarely tried to change the Graduate School of Education or mold it to its purposes. It primarily attempted to purchase a variety of products. But by providing the means for new ideas to enter the institution, by offering possibilities for change for administrators to exploit, by reshaping the scale of institutional operations to hasten both the dominance of R and D and the growth of larger administrative services, federal influence was substantial. Yet it seems less specific and more "structural" than, for instance, foundation involvement with the reform of teacher education. It was usually intended to affect the periphery of operations rather than to advance specific reforms in central mission. Still, the assistance had a volatile effect at the Graduate School of Education, more volatile than the more direct foundation influence of a decade earlier. The decisive factor in volatility was the internal institutional climate of the School itself. By the mid-sixties, serious criticism of the school-based, profession-based, and discipline-based reform mission of the fifties had arisen. Federal funds accentuated that internal conflict; they did not create it.

72

The Interaction of State and Federal Policy

James A. (Dolph) Norton
Chancellor, Ohio Board of Regents

I would like to commend the planning committee for this Conference on recruiting Dr. Finn and Professor Powell to prepare the papers which opened this meeting. Each report deserves wide circulation. Dr. Finn has presented a succinct overview of one of the most involved minefields of public policy. Professor Powell's report seems to me to be a most balanced evaluation of the emotion-laden interplay between federal grants and institutional development. I have learned a great deal, confirmed some of my own perceptions, and been reassured that a full discussion did need some of the perspective that comes with my background.

My invitation from Professor Todorovich reported that " . . . all the experts we consulted (advised) that our program would be one-sided if it did not include someone who brought to our session the perspective engendered by familiarity with state patronage of higher education." While the role of either state or federal governments as patrons, contractors, or suppliers of higher education services is important enough for a full conference, the fact that state government does provide about 55 percent of the tax dollars expended means that many policy issues are raised and perhaps illumined by state experience even though the emphasis is on federal policy.

You recognize, I am sure, that no state's experience accurately portrays that of the other forty-nine. You know as well that within any state the dynamics of law and practice give rise to different and changing situations and perceptions. I am more comfortable with those caveats even though we in Ohio have just gone through an extensive and broadly participatory process developing the 1976 version of the Master Plan for Higher Education, and I have just been through a series of eleven meetings around the state talking with most of the members of the legislature.

In Ohio each state-assisted university, college, community college, technical college, or university branch receives an annual subsidy appropriated *to it by name* by the General Assembly. The amount of each subsidy is determined by multiplying the anticipated number of full-time equivalent students in each of sixteen categories of courses by the amount of subsidy appropriate to that category. The appropriate amount of state subsidy is based on the average actual expenditures by all the state colleges and universities for courses in each category minus the fees which the legislature expects the student to pay. In appropriating for upcoming years the legislature advances the expenditures by a certain percentage to cover anticipated inflation. After students are actually enrolled there is a mechanism for adjusting the appropriation downward, and, if money is available, upward. Since 1968 the appropriations have kept up with inflation and increases in the number of students except last year when the unanticipated enrollment was so large.

When the university or college receives its subsidy, it puts it with student fees and other income and operates the institution.

There are a few other appropriations. Student aid goes to public and independent school students; a small appropriation encourages developmental education; funds are provided beyond the per student subsidy to help develop our four newest medical schools; and so on; but about 78 percent of the appropriations for higher education go in the student based general subsidy.

The state audits the books, and there are some restrictions—a few rational and some difficult to fathom—but generally practice follows the policy urged and defended by the Board of Regents: autonomy, as much as possible, in university activities.

As I understand Dr. Finn's interpretation of the term "patron," the state of Ohio could be called a "patron" of the public universities and colleges. It undergirds, coerces on some points, demands cooperation on others, oversees in minor ways, and appreciates the quality work they do.

Actually, Ohio is concerned with a full range of the services called post-secondary education. In addition to its coordinating and planning

74

functions for public institutions, the Board of Regents authorizes new programs for the independent sector and administers a student aid program that assists both public and independent college undergraduates. A Board of School and College Registration on which I sit oversees the proprietary sector, and the State Board of Education oversees the post-secondary vocational school programs. In some ways Ohio is more systematic than many states, but to an outsider most state systems do not look much like a system.

Across the country the picture seemed so disorderly that the national government used its ability to seduce with dollars to entice almost all the states to establish or designate a truly comprehensive planning agency. The authority was in Section 1202 of the Higher Education Act amendments of 1972, and the state agency responses are called 1202 Commissions. We were lucky in Ohio. The 1202 duties closely approximated the statutory obligations of the Board of Regents; the Governor designated our agency; we received some additional funding and elevated to a somewhat higher priority some items on our work program—a study of two-year campuses and articulation, a policy statement on independent colleges, an inquiry into the role of proprietary schools, and so on.

A brief summary such as this gives a picture of organization to some very fuzzy relationships. But it also gives some background for identifying some problems and some conclusions.

One problem is the relationship of federal programs and state agencies. For the public sector, basic support does come from state government. It is precisely this support which makes it possible for the federal government to come along with a few dollars and get tremendous responses to its needs or wishes.

Think of the expansion of medical schools bought with two-thousand-dollar capitation grants while the states were trying to manage with three or four times that input. The privilege of setting research priorities came with a few dollars when the basic physical plant and intellectual infrastructure were bought by the state.

Now I am as opportunistic as anyone, and our state grabs dollars that fund the incremental activities that spice higher education. But it stirs resentment having to fight the arrogance of a new idea some Congressional staff person had at the last minute or of a priority change that can be made by the federal government with near impunity because the states cannot back out of basic support. No one likes new battles when they are already hard pressed, but a fact of life for state agencies is that they and the universities must be engaged in the processes of the federal government.

This has some benefits. Second in importance to few things—moderately adequate funding and a good academic tradition—is some mechanism for helping a very conservative system change. Trying to redirect even a small part of academic institutions can be very frustrating. The United States has witnessed some rather extreme change techniques in the past decade, and a productive system need not go to extremes. In spite of the low priority the leaders in a particular state might put on some of the goals fostered by the federal government, it is good to have a change agent at work.

This is the value of the foundations as well. Some persons have decried their failure to continue basic support. They are too small, of course, to undergird all the efforts of higher education and should be valued for the potential they offer to keep the system flexible, even if their priorities may not exactly match one's own.

This is an appropriate point to note that states probably should be the basic patron for higher education. Their politics are complex enough, but the thought of introducing federal politics to basic funding is frightening. No college would ever collapse, even with a total loss of mission or gross mismanagement. There is little enough potential for discontinuing a school now; almost none in the state-assisted sector. But the lesser fiscal capacity of states may give us some freedom from saving every school.

As I look at academia and governments, particularly at the remarkable wedding of agriculture, higher education, and government, I know that universities and their leaders play the political game as successfully as anyone. State coordinating boards—even those prompted as 1202 Commissions—are a new part of the picture; institutions find their life more complicated. But they can be allies as well as intruders and they are there, another of the players in a game with no limit on the number of participants.

What Is All the Shouting About?

Kenneth S. Tollett
Howard University

Since I have difficulty talking and thinking while at the same time sitting, I'm going to stand. (This should by no means imply I have difficulty chewing gum while walking.) That difficulty may be because I feel somewhat in an adversary position. My thinking and talking abilities were nurtured in law school and executed on the whole in court rooms. When I first began my career as a lawyer, in trying cases, I always stood, and I was very uncomfortable trying a case at the counsel's table.

I should make a disclaimer at the outset. I'm not so blessed as Sidney Hook with the perspective of not having a partisan ideological commitment. I do have a commitment. Indeed, I should say the reason I express this commitment is to let you know what it is in advance. Two years ago in an article in *Daedalus*[1] on education and community, I tried to develop the importance of intellectual integrity. I think that in order to engage in a useful dialogue on any issue, it is extremely important to put commitments, biases, and what-have-you on the table. I don't think any of us are devoid of commitments and biases. The question is how to deal with them, how to bring them to the surface and take them properly into account, and how to make the kind of discounts that need to be made as a result of being aware of a person's ideological commitment.

I welcome the opportunity to come here to comment on Government as a Patron of Higher Education. What I propose to do in the few minutes allowed me, and I wasn't told specifically how many minutes I had, which is very dangerous for an academician and lawyer. I shouldn't have said that, I could have gone on as Professor Powell did. Please don't take that wrong because I should say, I'm going to talk not only about Government as Patron of Higher Education but allude also to some of the other papers that I read in preparation for this conference. I'm going to do it because I'm not going to be able to stay here for the entire Conference since I'm on the Visiting Committee to the Graduate School of Arts and Sciences at Harvard which is meeting this afternoon and tomorrow, and I have to go there to participate in their deliberations. I'm going to organize my remarks around what the Institute for the Study of Educational Policy is doing. I'm going to do that because the Institute for the Study of Educational Policy is predominantly black, and like most other black institutions in our society, it is probably unknown to you or is to a certain extent invisible. The Institute for the Study of Educational Policy has three program objectives, and I believe I can make my comments on the proper role of law by saying a few words about each one of those program objectives and how they relate to the papers that have already been presented and will be presented here.

The first program objective is to issue annually a comprehensive report on the status and situation of blacks in higher education. I should say at the outset all of these program objectives have as their ultimate goal devising strategies and means for providing educational equity for blacks and other disadvantaged groups. And I should say at the outset that I do have a commitment toward educational equity for blacks and other underprivileged and oppressed groups. Now, we already issued a report, *Equal Educational Opportunity for Blacks in U.S. Higher Education: An Assessment,*[2] which to a large extent reviews federal legislation and discusses its impact on equal access to higher education, distribution of blacks in higher education, and the retention of blacks in higher education. The report also deals with the economic return to blacks in higher education. It enables me to make a first point that I would like to make regarding the relationship between the state and the university.

Our status report indicates that the role of the federal government in higher education has been very constructive on the whole. Blacks have made significant progress in obtaining access to higher education particularly as a result of the Higher Education Act of 1965 and also the Higher Education Act of 1972. We see the role of government as being on the whole favorable, and initially I should say that we are very much disturbed by those who seem to be extremely concerned about what the federal government is doing in higher education. People who say it's over-reaching, that it is ensnarling universities in red tape, trouble us somewhat because we are not sure whether they are preoccupied with the red tape, and so forth, or are in some way not pleased with the support and advancement the federal government has brought to blacks in higher education. Indeed, Chester Finn's reference to the federal government's emphasis on money to support students, we think, is very good. The biggest obstacle to blacks obtaining access to higher educational institutions is financial. Therefore the focus of federal money upon students, on needier students, we think, is a salutary thing and we've proposed that not only should this focus of the federal government continue but also should be expanded.

Now the second program objective of the Institute for the Study of Educational Policy is to monitor and evaluate the impact of law, social science, and other research on the status and situation of blacks in higher education. Those who talk against the expanding role of the state and federal government in higher education, it seems to me, are harking back to what I suppose political philosophers have called the "night watchman's" theory of government. A "night watchman" theorist would say the role of government should be minimal. Perhaps, in an ideal society or state, that would be good, but, I think, it is inevitable that the role of government will expand in most complex industrialized societies. Of course, you know better than I, at least certainly as well as I, that the expansion has been to a large extent a response to the expansion of the power of capital and other institutions in our society. The Interstate Commerce Commission grew up out of the great power of the railroads. Every other regulatory commission that has developed in our country developed in response to concentrations of power in the private sector or to some other problem that had developed there. This response had been essential and thus, it seems to me, one is taking a rather conservative, retrogressive view of things if he thinks we can return to a "night watchman" concept of government. It is neither possible nor positive.

Indeed, we have been looking at the role of social science research, and we will be publishing next year a book called *The Changing Mood: The Eroding Commitment?* in which Dr. Faustine Jones, a Senior Fellow on our staff, tries to document that there has developed in our society a neoconservatism which would like to limit the role of government, which claims that social intervention can not effect significant social change, and that there is no correlation between educational inputs and educational output. Therefore, this neoconservatism would contend it doesn't matter whether you put additional funds into the higher education of the disadvantaged or the oppressed. We're very much concerned about this movement and again would say that it is retrogressive, that is, misconceives the role of government. Indeed I'd like to say that my own view of this development of neoconservatism, this new climate of opinion, can be analogized to earlier states' rights rhetoric. That is to say, in the abstract, talk about a "night watchman" government, a minimal intervention of government in society generally and in higher educational institutions in particular, is very similar to the talk, since the establishment of this government, that freedom in the states, freedom in our society could best be preserved by retaining a maximum amount of power in the states to deal with the various problems in those states. And I should add immediately that it is my view that just as historically the position of state's rights disguised hostility toward blacks, many of the proponents of government non-interventions are anti-black. Indeed, I think I could prove to you if I had time here, that the advocacy of this position almost from its inception, certainly after the adoption of the Constitution, was designed at that time to preserve the institution of slavery and after the Civil War was designed to preserve a segregated society and Jim Crowism. And I put it to you that those today who talk about a minimal theory of government, to me anyhow, are disguising a hostility toward blacks.

Moreover, I should add that it is amazing to me that the greatest attack on affirmative action in our society has come from the university community. It is coming stronger than it came from private industry or even the labor unions. And, I repeat, from my viewpoint this attack disguises a hostility toward the advancement of the interests of blacks. I resist the attacks the same way I resisted the claims of states' rights. It should be said here in passing that since Dr. Finn made an allusion to the Tenth Amendment, I do not think the Tenth Amendment reserves education to the states necessarily. It is a states' rightist position to say that the Tenth Amendment reserves to the state entirely the function of education.

The University Centers for Rational Alternatives has certainly suggested that we should rationally discuss these matters and that to be fair about it one should give some reasons why he feels that the hostility to the federal government intervention disguises hostility towards blacks. I'll give a few.

Certainly I don't think that the centrifugal impact of federal largess that Mr. Powell alluded to has caused any great disruption at Harvard School of Education. Indeed, it seems to me that the bottom line of his review of federal money at Harvard is that it did not have any untoward effects. It did not have any significant negative impact on Harvard.

Dr. Finn's remarks also certainly did not suggest that the role of the federal government had harmed the intellectual enterprise in any way. Now if that's so, why are we so agitated about the government intervention and regulation?

Well, perhaps, I should here allude to Mr. McGill's paper. It is not fair to discuss his paper before it is presented, but it indicates the tremendous burgeoning of federal regulations in society at large and in universities in particular. These regulations have always been there. One schooled in the law knows that advanced and complex societies produce more and more laws as they advance. This is inevitable. It will continue.

Certainly, we want to make the rules and regulations that we live under more rational, we want them to be fair, we want to provide notice and hearings and the like. But there is no way to live in a complex society without having an expansion of laws and regulations. If one is aware of that, then why is there this tremendous outcry and outrage over them? Well I have to submit to you that the tremendous outcry and expression of outrage over government regulations have come mostly in the last three or four years of affirmative action, as it has gained some momentum and is going to have some impact on higher educational institutions—bringing in blacks, women, and other groups that have been excluded from these institutions.

Yet some would respond that universities are governed by merit. Well the short answer to that is, where was meritocracy for the prior three hundred years of our history as far as blacks and even women were concerned? There wasn't that much preoccupation with it in the past, so that there is something disingenuous and dishonest about talk today that merit governs the university and that affirmative action programs, special minority admission programs, and other such programs violate the intrinsic values of higher educational institutions.

I put it to you that when one looks at law and the relationship of law and higher education, one can make a strong case for a requirement that insofar as the federal government has anything to do with higher educational institutions, it must be committed to (and it has in fact adopted this position) universal access. You would think our government would be for

81

social equality, diversity, pluralism, and equity in higher education. And I think you might say the absence of coherence, to a certain extent, in educational federal policy has nurtured diversity and pluralism in our higher educational system. If one tried to rationalize it more, set up a bureau of education with a central role like the role of educational bureaus in Europe, we would lose a lot of the value and bases of success in our system.

Indeed, a recent report of the American Association of Higher Education by Burton R. Clark and T. I. K. Youn[3] very forcefully makes a point that higher education has advanced in America very well because of its pluralism and diversity and because of the lack of central control; and that European countries which are trying to move toward equality, universal access, and the like are beginning to model or at least are trying in some way to bring into their systems some of the aspects of the higher educational system of the United States. In other words, what is being complained of by some, the lack of coherence, a single policy, you might say, centralized direction, actually is probably the reason why we have maintained diversity and pluralism in our higher educational system, which provides a broad cross-section of institutions in which a broad cross-section of individuals may attend. We have community colleges, liberal arts colleges, comprehensive universities, research universities, and private and public institutions. We have sectarian colleges, all women colleges, all men colleges, and predominantly black colleges. This smorgasbord of higher educational institutions does not provide a pre-arranged coherent meal, but one certainly has a good opportunity to have a good diet, if he or she chooses well.

Reference to the variety of our schools brings to mind two very important cases about which I would like to say a few words. The first one is the *Adams-Richardson-Weinberger-Matthews* case which is concerned with the desegregation of education in kindergarten through post-secondary institutions. At one state of the litigation the friends of predominantly black colleges thought the court was going to insist that schools could not be identifiably black. We do not think that is either good law or good public policy. These schools have been and continue to be an invaluable public asset. They have educated a significant number of successful black leaders and professionals. They should not be eliminated or merged into larger white universities in the name of integration or getting rid of duplication. If this happened, important needs and aspirations of blacks would be frustrated. The 1964 Civil Rights Act and the Equal Protection Clause of the Fourteenth Amendment were enacted and adopted primarily to help or benefit blacks, not hurt or frustrate them.

Another case worries me even more because the Equal Protection Clause, which is the major source of the mandate to integrate, is being used as a vehicle to embarrass and threaten integration. The case is *Bakke* v. *University of California Board of Regents.*[5] The *Bakke* case worries us very much. Those who are knowledgeable in the matter know that if the California Supreme Court decision is upheld in the United States Supreme Court, minority admissions programs in graduate and professional schools would be practically destroyed. If one is opposed to these programs, he is also opposed to the expansion of the participation and the maintenance of the entry of blacks into medical, law, and other professional schools. A private report of an outstanding law school stated that if they did not have a special minority admission program, they might have one black law student. The prestigious distinguished school was not Harvard, by the way, since you know I am associated with Harvard; it's not the University of Chicago, since some of you may know I once served on the Visiting Committee to their Law School.

What I want to put to those of you here who take the neo-conservative position, intentionally or not, is that the effect of it unquestionably is that there will be a restriction on the entry of blacks into professional schools.

In closing, I'd like to say something about the constitutionality of special minority admissions and affirmative action programs because to me those are what this conference is really all about. This is a conference that is ostensibly concerned with the proper role of government, but I really think the bottom line is how can you continue to do battle with the federal government's effort to push affirmative action. The discussion in McGill's paper about the labyrinth in regulations and so forth is very good. In a sense he is disguising (I don't say he's doing this intentionally) for this Conference its hostility toward affirmative action, special minority admissions programs, and other efforts to advance the interests of blacks.

The Thirteenth, Fourteenth, and Fifteenth Amendments were adopted in reaction to slavery and to efforts to reimpose it in a different or modified form. The Thirteenth Amendment abolished slavery. The Fourteenth Amendment made blacks citizens of the United States. The

Fifteenth Amendment guaranteed the right to vote. Therefore it is a misreading of the Constitution from my viewpoint to say the Constitution is color blind.

The Constitution as far as the Thirteenth, Fourteenth, and Fifteenth Amendments are concerned is pro-black. Indeed, Justice Miller in the *Slaughter-House Cases*,[6] which was the first case that passed on the Equal Protection Clause, said that he doubted that there would ever be an occasion in the history of this country that the Equal Protection Clause would be used except for the vindication of the rights of the recently freed slaves. This was a contemporaneous interpretation of the Fourteenth Amendment's Equal Protection Clause. Of course, as you know this is not the way that the interpretation of that clause developed.

Corporations are treated as persons and, therefore, got tremendous benefit from the Equal Protection Clause. In a study reported in 1960[7] it was found that over 75 percent of the cases involving the Equal Protection Clause actually involved corporate or other economic interests rather than minority groups or blacks, although clearly the provision was there for that purpose.

Now if one engages in a structural analysis of the Constitution, that is, if one looks at these three provisions together, looks at the mischief they were trying to correct, and looks at the way they went about trying to correct that mischief, one will see that their overriding objective was to provide equity and justice for blacks. Therefore it is not a violation of the Equal Protection Clause for the state to have a special minority admissions program in order to get rid of the vestiges of slavery. Indeed the *Jones-Alfred* case,[8] which applied the 1866 Civil Rights Act, stated that Congress was empowered to prohibit discrimination in the sale of houses because discrimination in the sale of houses was a vestige of slavery. I put it to you that the disadvantages that blacks suffer in our society today in obtaining positions in higher education, in employment, and in admission to higher educational institutions are vestiges of slavery. Thus, the federal government and even the states, by virtue of the Thirteenth, Fourteenth, and Fifteenth Amendments, are empowered to institute programs to eradicate those vestiges and take color into account.

Let me close with a statement of what I consider education to be. Education is an intellectual process that creates and transmits knowledge, structures cognitive powers, enriches and enhances sensibility, and develops a capacity in individuals and groups to understand their relationship to others and their relationship to nature. Even if one did not want to take the Constitutional view I have of the Thirteenth, Fourteenth, and Fifteenth Amendments, the intellectual enterprise can not be pursued properly unless one has a broad cross-section of intellectual perspectives. Therefore, it is critically important for universities, if they are going to advance knowledge, if they are going to nurture learning, to have the perspectives of the rich, the poor, black, white, male, and female in significant numbers. Ultimately the pursuit of truth can not be done well without this broad cross-section, and therefore I put it to you that ultimately the justification of special efforts to bring blacks, women, and others into higher educational institutions for full participation is not just social justice, is not just a matter of providing equity for others, but it is for sustaining the requirements necessary to pursue knowledge in an effective and desirable way.

NOTES

1. K. S. Tollett, "Community and Higher Education," *Daedalus* 104 (Winter, 1975):278.

2. Institute for the Study of Educational Policy, *Equal Educational Opportunity for Blacks in U.S. Higher Education: An Assessment* (Washington, D. C.: Howard University Press, 1976).

3. B. R. Clark and T. I. K. Youn, *Academic Power in the United States,* ERIC/Higher Education Research Report No. 3, 1976 (Washington, D. C.: The American Association for Higher Education, 1976).

4. *Adams* v. *Matthews,* 536 F. 2d 417 (1976).

5. *Bakke* v. *The Regents of the University of California,* 553 P. 2d 1152 (1976), *certiorari granted* 45 U.S.L.W. 3555 (U.S. February 22, 1977) (No. 76–811).

6. *Slaughter-House Cases,* 83 U.S. (16 Wall.) 36 (1873).

7. K. S. Tollett, "Blacks, Higher Education and Integration," *Notre Dame Lawyer* 48 (October, 1972):189 at 200, fn. 45.

8. *Jones* v. *Alfred H. Mayer Co.* 392 U.S. 409 (1968).

Patronage and the Academy

Robert F. Sasseen
San Jose State University

This panel's topic is the Role of the Federal Government as Patron of Higher Education, and a commentator is assigned the task of discussing the papers prepared on that topic. Before discharging that responsibility I cannot resist the temptation to reply briefly to Mr. Tollett's remarks.

Mr. Tollett has asserted more than once that the motive of this conference and of the academy's concerns about the role of government in higher education is, at bottom, simply "hostility to affirmative action, special minority programs and other efforts to advance the interests of blacks." The arguments advanced in opposition to governmental intrusion into academic affairs are dismissed as unprogressive at best and, at worst, as disingenuous expressions of racial prejudice. Such assertions are often greeted by a pathetic display of public confessions lamenting past sins, proclaiming true conversion and protesting the authenticity of the commitment to justice, equality, and the cause of the disadvantaged everywhere.

However, I am told that only God can read the human heart and that confession is good for the soul if between thee and me. This much should be said. If arguments against a public policy are to be dismissed out of hand as mere protestations of prejudice or interest, then the principle of equal treatment suggests a similar dismissal of the arguments in support of that policy. But this approach makes an anguished cry for justice no more worthy of serious attention than a naked demand of self-interest. It makes public discourse impossible. It transforms public deliberation into public relations and makes public debate an instrument in the struggle of interests for partisan advantage. Fortunately civility demands a different approach, and the public interest requires it. Deliberation is essential for the discovery of what is just in any case, and genuine deliberation takes seriously serious arguments about the public good. This conference aims to foster public deliberation about the role of government in higher education and, in fidelity to that purpose, let us turn now to the papers prepared for this panel.

The two papers complement one another and may serve as a useful introduction to the conference. But they force one to question its necessity. Both papers conclude with a rather sanguine view of federal involvement in the academy, and the problems described appear on balance to be rather minor, if irksome.

Mr. Finn's paper introduces us to the nature and extent of federal involvement in higher education. In his account, the federal government serves as rich uncle for needy or otherwise deserving students; as jealous contractor for particular services; and as indulgent, if not careless, tax collector. His survey gives us a clear appreciation of the vast complexity of federal involvement and suggests some of the difficulties arising from its uncoordinated and sometimes conflicting largesse. The paper amply demonstrates his thesis that, if government has served as benefactor, its beneficence does not make it a patron since the aim of its aid has not been to promote the ends of higher education.

This fact may suggest problems of a fundamental kind, but Mr. Finn's approach is more cautious and pragmatic. He concludes that federal involvement in higher education has not served the academy badly and has served the government rather well. Its blessings appear to outweigh its evils and, in any event, there is not much that can be done to remedy the defects noted. One can expect, at most, marginal adjustments which may lessen friction between the academy and the federal government, but which will not change the basic nature of a generally beneficial relationship.

Mr. Finn's picture of the forest is complemented by Mr. Powell's intriguing account of a branch on a stalwart tree within that forest. Mr. Powell's paper describes the transformation of Harvard's School of Education in the sixties in response to its receipt of considerable federal patronage. That patronage was accompanied by unsuspected and perhaps excessive, but not altogether unintended, changes in the nature of the

School of Education at Harvard. If the conclusion of Mr. Finn's survey was cautiously sanguine, Mr. Powell's is downright optimistic. Federal patronage unleashed "new energies" which moved the School in new directions, to the substantial benefit of both the School and the country. His analysis of the School's experience has persuaded him that the University need not become, as many fear, a "holding company" for a variety of federal projects unrelated to, or even subversive of, its central purpose. His analysis suggests an alternative model of the relation of government and the academy. According to that model, the University should receive limited federal funds for discretionary program development, centrally administered by the University for the benefit of all.

The sanguine conclusions of both papers contrast sharply with the picture others have drawn of the sorry state of the current relation between the academy and the federal government. The Report of the Secretary's Work Group for the Consolidation and Simplification of Federal Reporting Requirements—(a title, perhaps, which may indicate part of the problem)—notes, for example, that a mutually supportive attitude between government and the University has degenerated into an adversary relationship. "Those who write administrative regulations have over the years assumed a defensive posture and, when in doubt about legislative intent, include every conceivable topic, definition, area of applicability, reporting and record keeping requirement, time limit, and penalty." The situation seems desperate and "strong executive action is needed to reverse this arrogation of power by the bureaucracy!" The Work Group has recommended various reforms which would be helpful if adopted. But the prosaic character of the reforms suggests that the problems in the current relation may be exaggerated by those who cry that the academy has sold its birthright for the noxious porridge of federal support. In fairness to Mr. Tollett, it should be noted that perhaps his remarks may have been prompted by the optimistic appearance of these papers and their failure to note anything fundamentally wrong in the current relation between the academy and the federal government.

Before disbanding the conference in the comforting belief that the relationship is basically a healthy one, however, it is necessary to confront the questions suggested by Mr. Finn's paper. Can that relation be genuinely beneficial if it is true that government is not, in any proper meaning of the term, a patron of higher education? Indeed, a more careful reading of Mr. Powell's paper suggests that there is both reason to doubt its optimistic conclusion and evidence enough to suggest the existence of a fundamental problem both in the academy and in its relation to the federal government.

According to Mr. Powell's account, Harvard's School of Education had emerged from World War II as a small, unprestigious school concentrating on the education of doctoral students and research in the social sciences. With the help of considerable support from private foundations, the School remade itself and, by the mid-fifties, had apparently settled upon a new mission. That mission was to maintain a large, primarily master's level program designed to prepare practitioners for the mainline school careers of teaching, guidance-counseling, and administration. The School then turned to the federal government for aid in the confident expectation of avoiding the mistakes of the past, in the optimistic hope of stabilizing its core budget by reducing its dependence on outside funding. At the same time, the School was prudently wary of government involvement in its affairs. The School feared, not an overt threat to the academic freedom of teachers and students, but the more subtle dilution of purpose through government support of centrifugal elements tangential to its central mission. However, it was believed that this error could be avoided by careful selection among the variety of sources of funding in the federal government. Thus the School sought federal funds in the effort to expand its faculty and programs and to resolve the fiscal instability previously caused by excessive dependence on foundation support. It believed it could do so without compromising its established mission of school-oriented education

But what happened? If I understand Mr. Powell's account correctly, the School realized none of its dreams and most of its fears. Federal dollars had become a larger part of the School's core budget than ever foundation dollars had been. When the federal bubble finally burst, a precarious fiscal stability in its core budget was ultimately achieved, but only by dramatic program retrenchment, painful faculty cuts, and increased tuition. More significantly, its central mission of school-oriented education had been "fractured" almost beyond recognition. The much feared dilution of purpose and centrifugal explosion in peripheral directions were both stimulated and accelerated by the nature and extent of the federal support. School-oriented teacher education, if it did not disappear entirely, had become greatly subordinated to a new thing called "learning environments." School guidance-counseling had become lost in a new program of public psychology, and school administration had been redirected toward reformist community involvement. This is quite a change. If it were to be judged by the intentions at the beginning, it must be judged well-nigh a total disaster.

Mr. Powell, however, knows that he judges the change from a different perspective. His sanguine conclusion no doubt springs from his approval of the new directions established by the "new energies" unleashed with the help of the federal patronage. The new directions are characterized in his description of the R & D Center established with the federal funds. The "emphasis" of the Center permeated the School and decisively colored its mission. According to Mr. Powell's account, that emphasis consisted in the abandonment of research in the usual sense of dispassionate, controlled inquiry; the celebration of experiential learning and the restoration of community in place of academic learning; and the substitution of expanded educational opportunity for school-oriented teacher education. This new emphasis, of course, is not unique to Harvard, and many have come to question its propriety. Certainly we should. For the change approved by Mr. Powell appears to consist in a further politicalization of the academy, in its subordination to the aims of the current regime. Even if we approve those aims, we must question that subordination and its implications for the freedom of the academy which, I take it, has its ultimate foundation in the transcendent mission of the quest for truth.

But if Mr. Powell's sanguine conclusion is thus questionable from the viewpoint of the academy's highest purpose, it is no less questionable from the government's point of view. Indeed if I were a conscientious public administrator, I would be tempted to infer from Mr. Powell's account, not the desirability of the model he suggests as an alternative to the "holding company" model, but the necessity of rejecting it lest I betray the public trust in the disbursement of funds. The R & D Center and the TTT project were two of the main programs established with federal funds, and neither one achieved the purpose for which the aid was granted. If we were to judge the experience in terms of the intention of the federal administrators in granting the aid, it must be judged no less a failure than if judged by the intention of the School administrators in seeking the aid. The government failed to get what it sought and the School got the very thing it had hoped to avoid. Thus from many points of view—from that of the government and the School in the beginning and from that of the academy's highest and perennial purpose—the experience with federal patronage in this instance appears to have been less than satisfactory. It is difficult to discern in that experience, or at least in Mr.

Powell's account of it, a firm foundation for his sanguine conclusion regarding the relationship between the academy and the federal government.

Mr. Powell implies that the chief cause of "fracturing" the School's original mission and of diverting the federal funds from their intended purpose was the School's administration and that part of the faculty which it created and favored. He observes that "the balance of power lay clearly with the School," that "the government was weaker than the outsiders supposed." Federal patronage created administrative opportunity to choose continuity or change. The School's administration repeatedly opted for change. It would appear that the drastic change in the character of the School, if occasioned by federal patronage, was caused by ambitious and enterprising administrators who may not have seen clearly where they were going but ardently desired to go somewhere. This suggests a problem within the groves of academe and, if patronage was the apple, raises the question of who played Eve and who, the serpent. If it is proper to consider the question, it is necessary to recall that the apple of private foundation support had also occasioned extensive changes in the School during the period after World War II. It would appear, at least from this instance, that the academy is not immune to the temptation to taste the fruit of the tree of power and influence.

Mr. Finn's paper suggests that what may have once been a temptation has now become a necessity. The dependence of many universities on federal patronage is so extensive that it is difficult to imagine their survival without its continuance. But, as Mr. Finn suggests, federal patronage affects even those institutions which receive no direct aid. He notes, for example, that tuition-dependent colleges may be tempted, or compelled by economic necessity, to change their admissions policies in order to increase the proportion of their students eligible for federal financial assistance. Since student aid is largely predicated on need rather than ability, such a change could have a profound effect on the character of the college.

The conclusion warranted by both papers is that federal patronage cannot help but affect the character of the institutions which receive it. The papers suggest that such patronage cannot help but weaken the academy's sense of its essential purpose and, given the nature and extent of the patronage, must inevitably make it less capable than ever of fidelity to that purpose. This may well be a necessary effect, and not merely the result of the imprudence of administrators, at least to the extent that the purpose of the patronage is inconsistent with the aim of the university. If that aim is the quest for truth and the education of genuine students for the mature life of free men and women, thoughtful citizens may find just cause for alarm in the present relation of the university and the federal government. The alarm would be justified if it is true that the United States is best served by an academy which remains faithful to its essential purpose.

The problems in that relation, however, are not limited to the role of the Federal Government as Patron of Higher Education. The considerable nose of patronage was soon followed by the massive camel of regulation, and it is the nature of federal regulation which has occasioned the most controversy. Since that regulation is the subject of later panels, it may be sufficient now to distinguish two types of regulation. The first is tied directly to the patronage and consists in the necessary rules and procedures for ensuring adequate accountability in the expenditure of public funds. No one questions the legitimacy of this type of regulation, though many have suggested that the rules and procedures should be improved to better recognize the particular character of the academy and thereby to lessen their harmful effects.

Patronage, however, is merely the vehicle—or excuse—for the second type of regulation which is otherwise wholly unrelated to the purpose or nature of the patronage. Such regulations are general in nature and have nothing to do with the administration of a particular grant or form of federal aid. They are designed instead to subordinate the academy to particular public ends. It may not be an exaggeration to note that the power of the government as contractor to issue such regulations is to the university what the commerce clause was to business in the thirties. Partisans of the particular ends favor such regulations and can see in the opposition to them only a contrary partisanship. But the issue is surely more complex and justifies serious concern. The issue is a fundamental one which requires for its proper resolution an understanding both of the nature of a democratic republic and the proper freedom of the academy.

We were told in the introduction to this conference that our task was to examine the problems in the current relation of government and the academy, and to discover bold new solutions. It is necessary to understand a problem in order to know whether a proposed solution, however bold, is a good one or not. We must thank the authors of the two papers for the help they have given us in understanding the current problem in its depth as well as its exent.

The Frankenstein Fallacy

Martin Kramer
Director for Higher Education Planning, HEW

Let me comment first on the picture of overwhelming complexity in federal programs described by Mr. Finn. In his oral remarks, which may have been the only ones some of you heard, he makes this a ridiculous picture. I think Dean Sasseen and I, both reacting to his written paper, felt that he drew a picture more sinister than ridiculous. I think I see in his characterizations something that I would call the Frankenstein fallacy. If you recall the movie *Frankenstein,* there were two things wrong with the monster. First, he was very ugly because he was put together out of parts from many different cadavers. But there was a second thing wrong with him, and that was something wrong with his mind. The fallacy I'm pointing out here is to identify these two sources of horror—to think that what is menacing or malevolent about federal action is the fact that it is put together from so many component programs. I'm inclined to agree with the Harvard Report that Mr. Finn quotes, which sees the diversity and fragmentation of federal aid as a great support and strength. And indeed, a diversity of support as between federal government, philanthropies, state government and student tuition is also a source of strength.

Complexity is not always the enemy of freedom and safety. In a decent society it is safe for citizens to go to bed on election night even if they don't understand how a voting machine works and even if they don't understand how the electoral college operates. You can deposit your money in a regulated bank without understanding or worrying about the complex audit rules the bank examiner follows.

There are federal program complexities which are also not threatening, and as examples, let me cite most of the federal student aid rules. However bizarre and however irrational they may be on particular points, they are not generally threatening to academic freedom. Nor are the rather detailed rules for the accountability of student aid funds. These require certain kinds of evidence that a student is officially enrolled and the like, of which we will be seeing a great deal more as federal efforts increase to prevent fraud and abuse in the student aid programs.

I think it would be very unwise to regard such dimensions of complexity as threatening to academic freedom. One way to think about the matter is to note that one has only so much capacity for watchfulness and that capacity ought not be frittered away on things that are not genuinely threatening. There may be things that we should fear, but we should not be indiscriminately fearful on grounds of complexity alone.

Given these reactions to Mr. Finn's paper, you can imagine how congenial I found Mr. Powell's paper. I read him as saying that the evil of government patronage may not be so much that it bullies as that it confuses. It seems somehow to release aspects of competitiveness among academics from precisely those restraints which, within an established academic discipline, make competition so extraordinarily productive and benign. In particular, it produces what I think of as the institute syndrome, a malady characterized by Young Turks finding it possible to set themselves up as a separate establishment independent of their disciplinary peers. Research overhead, as Mr. Powell points out, can make this kind of entrepreneurship highly attractive to the parent institution if the overhead rate is over-generous, as it tended to be in the late sixties. I sometimes wonder if the vulnerable institutions we call universities would not be better off if they could bargain away some portion of their overhead rates for an insurance policy to limit their risk of declining federal project support, to, say, a maximum reduction of 10 percent a year.

My reaction to Mr. Powell's paper, then, would be that he is perhaps too modest in his conclusions. It is perhaps not a set of particular circumstances at the Harvard School of Education or the nature of education as an academic discipline that made the School vulnerable to the events he describes, but something far more general that we should all worry about.

THE COSTS OF EDUCATION

Introductory Remarks

Richard A. Lester
Princeton University

Because of some observations made in this morning's session, perhaps I should indicate in this introductory statement that I was, from 1968 to 1973, dean of the Faculty at Princeton University, and the first four of those years I was chairman of the Equal Employment Opportunity Committee at Princeton. In that position I was primarily responsible for the drafting of the first comprehensive affirmative action plan for Princeton, which was submitted to the Office for Civil Rights of HEW in March 1972. That plan was one of the first, if not the first, of the university affirmative action plans to be approved by HEW after Revised Order No. 4 was issued in December 1971.

Furthermore, my book, *Antibias Regulation of Universities,* published in mid-1974, set forth in detail a program of affirmative action for the federal government to apply to university and college faculty. I ha,e long been an advocate of effective and intelligent affirmative action to improve the employment opportunities for women and minorities. From 1961 to November 1963 I was vice chairman of the President's Commission on the Status of Women and, thus, share some responsibility for the Equal Pay Act of 1962 and a number of other actions that are partly the result of that Commission's work.

Before I introduce the members of the panel for this afternoon's session, perhaps I should say a few words about our subject by way of background.

As the discussion this morning indicated, the costs of government regulation of employment for nondiscrimination and affirmative action purposes are of various kinds and of varying degrees of difficulty to isolate and measure.

First, there are the additional monetary costs which are fairly clear and definite. They are the budgetary costs that universities incur for the salaries of additional personnel and computer and other direct expenses for the preparation and administration of affirmative action plans. For some major universities those money costs have amounted to hundreds of thousands of dollars. A significant amount of such costs, in the case of faculty, may have been misdirected and wasteful, partly because of the unsound methodology required for goal determination and the knowledge deficiencies of the OCR enforcement staff.

Second, there are what might be called the displacement costs, which represent the time and energy that regular personnel (the president, deans, faculty, and other employees) divert from their normal work to meet the federal regulatory requirements which may force waste and inefficiency.

Third, and perhaps still more difficult to assess fully, are the effects that the regulations and the enforcement pressures have on the institution's teaching and research programs—the effectiveness of the faculty—over the long pull. A simple example in this category of costs is the following provision in Revised Order No. 4 for the past five years: "Neither minority nor female employees should be required to possess higher qualifications than those of the lowest qualified incumbent." Imagine the ultimate real cost of strict enforcement of that provision on a distinguished university.

The requirement that any practice or means used in the selection of faculty must be statistically validated in each part is really asking for the impossible in the case of highly individualistic professional work and workers. The strict enforcement of such a requirement would, in many cases, force the abandonment of professional judgments in the selection of faculty, with the attendant costs to the long-term effectiveness of a university's educational and research programs.

Pointing out such costs is not to deny, slight, or overlook the great costs of race and sex discrimination to individuals, to institutions, and to the nation and society generally. But on the same grounds, reverse discrimination also has great immediate and ultimate costs to individuals, institutions, and society.

Thus the question of the costs of a federal regulatory program is much broader, longer, and more complicated than might be supposed by a person who has not had extensive experience in a major university, subject to the various aspects of federal regulation of faculty employment under executive orders and anti-discrimination legislation.

The Costs of
Government Regulation

Donald Hornig
Former President, Brown University

INTRODUCTION

Higher education in the United States has traditionally been supported by
states and local communities, if public, or through tuition and private
philanthropy, and most of the regulation, such as it was, took place
through state and local governments. Such regulation I shall not discuss,
in part because of the variety and diversity of situations, but also because
the principal concerns at present relate to the federal government. Of
course, to some extent what can be said of the impact of regulation by the
federal government applies as well to regulation by other governmental
bodies. In any case it should be clear at the outset that this paper is based
on the experience of the president of a private university who has
experienced the restraints accompanying reliance on federal funds, but
who has also experienced the restraints accompanying foundation grants
or private philanthropy and the even greater restraints imposed by short-
ages of funds. There is very little in the way of hard data or analysis on
which to base the judgments presented here. The author has consulted
other university administrators and discussed his experiences with them
but has not attempted a survey.

   The last thirty-five years have seen a most remarkable evolution in
the relations of the federal government to universities. Prior to World

War II the federal government simply wasn't involved. During World War II they formed a successful partnership for the conduct of war-related research and the specialized training of personnel at many levels and in a wide variety of areas. Subsequently that initital experience has broadened and deepened. The university scientific community, backed by the wartime experience, successfully persuaded the government and the public that scientific research in universities was a national asset and federal expenditures on basic research in universities, principally in the physical sciences and in the health related sciences, expanded steadily until they levelled off in the late 1960s at around $2.5 billion per year. In this same period the federal government increasingly saw the universities as a national resource which could be instrumental in meeting a variety of national goals such as:

1. to educate an increasing fraction of the rapidly rising population of young men and women
2. to overcome barriers of race, sex, and economic conditions which had been shamefully neglected
3. to develop the knowledge needed to address a wide variety of national problems
4. to provide sources of advice and analysis to all parts of the government.

To these ends a bewildering array of federal programs were set up to provide scholarship, fellowship, and loan funds, to finance the construction of facilities, and to fund research on countless problems. It was not long before a significant part of the financial support of all institutions of higher education came, directly or indirectly, from the federal government. However it followed inevitably that if colleges and universities were indeed a precious national asset, if they provided the research on which our future security, health, and well being depended, if their degrees were the keys to professions and many jobs, if they were a driving force for social improvement, the government could not simply provide funds with no strings. It would inevitably attempt to guide all these activities in what the many semi-independent agencies of government conceived to be the national interest. I presume that the consequences of this guidance is what gives rise to the topic of my paper.

Before discussing costs it should be said at the outset that most observers anywhere in the world would agree that we have developed a very diffuse higher educational system which is probably the best in the world. It produces outstanding scholarship and it teaches an enormous variety of students from widely varying backgrounds, with aspirations in many directions. Beginning with the Morrill Act in 1865 the land grant colleges introduced a new conception of public service which has added a unique dimension to American higher education. It seems to me that the pluralism in institutions, in curricula, in governance, and in sources of support has been a major source of strength in American higher education because of the flexibility and vitality it has engendered. I mention this now, not to begin an analysis of the American higher education complex (Note: it is surely not a *system*), but to say two things. First, federal funds have certainly been an important contributor to the health of the enterprise. What is more, whether one considers it desirable or not, the chaotic way in which funds have moved from many federal agencies to the schools and colleges through thousands of programs has been consistent with the tradition of pluralism. Second, it is because we have done so well that we must recognize the fragility of the enterprise and be sure that even if the benefits of federal participation have greatly outweighed the costs, we do not introduce elements which may eventually damage some aspects of the fabric irreparably and irreversibly. I believe this is the origin of the present concern over regulation.

REGULATION AND AUTONOMY

In one respect almost any regulations exact a price. From the beginning American schools have experienced a high degree of autonomy. This has taken the form of autonomous boards for private universities and colleges, boards of regents to isolate state schools from excessive involvement in the political and governmental process, in the existence of separate higher educational systems, no two alike, in each of our fifty states, and so on. It is manifested in the internal separation of powers which places curricular control and the selection of faculty in the hands of faculties rather than the administration. This autonomy has allowed each school to find its own niche, to meet the needs of its clientele and to do the things it can do best in its own way. Any attempt to impose common regulations on this melange detracts from the autonomy which institutions of higher education treasure. Some of the deep resentment at all regulation undoubtedly derives from the sense of loss of freedom and autonomy, whatever the result.

Beyond that one must look at the nature of the regulations and the nature, as well as magnitude, of the costs. In many areas regulations are plainly needed and the arguments for institutional autonomy are not persuasive. For example, regulations related to the proper expenditure of public funds, reporting procedures, and accountability for funds are surely appropriate. However, regulations which require pointless and arbitrary modifications in accounting procedures or which require that the same financial data be reported in a variety of formats, for example, introduce needless costs. Similarly, regulations concerning equal employment opportunity and affirmative action are surely appropriate. It might be argued that since these involve fundamental human rights, educational institutions could be counted on to lead the way whether or not federal law or regulations were involved, but the record of past discrimination is so blatant in *all* of our institutions that the need for corrective action surely outweighs the claims of institutional autonomy. But again, if the regulations do not address the root problem but generate pointless paper work instead of action, there is an unnecessary cost which undermines both the institution and the social goals. A class of regulation which raises the most fundamental problems are those relating to the educational process itself, such as the Buckley amendment with respect to student records and recent efforts to shape medical school curricula through legislation.

DIRECT COSTS

The costs of regulation, too, take many forms. First, there is the simple, out of pocket cost of the staff additions and so on, needed to comply. This is, in general, the cost of the increasing bureaucratization of our institutions in response to the requirements for increased and different record keeping, further correspondence, and varieties of formal procedures to replace older informal ones. However, increasing bureaucratization is forced on us by many factors, by the necessity to understand our operations and to make them more effective, for example, so that it is not usually obvious how much of the recently added cost should be ascribed to federal regulations and programs.

A start has been made though by Carol Van Alstyne and Sharon L. Coldren in a report entitled "The Costs of Implementing Federally Mandated Social Programs at Colleges and Universities." In that report they studied six schools including a large state university, a large public community college, two private universities with teaching hospitals, a private comprehensive college, and a private liberal arts college. The federal programs studied were:

- Equal employment opportunity: Title VII of the Civil Rights Act of 1964, as amended by the Equal Employment Opportunity Act of 1972
- Equal pay: Equal Pay Act of 1963
- Affirmative action: Executive Order 11246, issued in 1965, as amended by Executive Order 11375 to include discrimination on basis of sex, 1967
- Age discrimination: Employment Act of 1967, as amended
- Wage and hour standards: Fair Labor Standards Act (FSLA), as amended
- Unemployment compensation: Social Security Act of 1935; Employment Security Amendments, 1970
- Social security tax increases: Social Security Act of 1935; Employment Security Amendments, 1970
- Health maintenance organizations (HMOs): Health Maintenance Organization Act of 1973
- Retirement benefits: Employment Retirement Income Security Act (ERISA) of 1974 (Note: public institutions excluded)
- Wage and salary controls: Economic Stabilization Act of 1970 (Note: public institutions excluded; nonprofit institutions exempted January 25, 1974
- Occupational safety and health: Occupational Safety and Health Act (OSHA) of 1970
- Environmental protection: Regulations implemented under several laws by the Environmental Protection Agency

For the purposes of this Conference, programs such as Social Security do not seem relevant since they supplement, and in part replace, programs such as TIAA or state pension plans which are adopted voluntarily by the institutions. The direct costs by institution are shown in Table 1.5b from Van Alstyne and Coldren. The average institution spent just under one percent of its total budget on these programs. The highest, which includes a hospital whose costs were not separated, was 2.25 percent.

Stated as a fraction of total budget, these costs do not seem over-

Table 1.5b
Trends in Costs of Implementing Federally Mandated Social Programs, 1965–1975
By Institution, Excluding Social Security Taxes

Institution	I	II	III	IV	V	VI
Control and Type	Public State University	Public Local Community College	Private University, with Hospital	Private University, with Hospital	Private Comprehensive College	Private Liberal Arts College
Highest Degree Offered	Doctorate	Associate	Doctorate	Doctorate	Master's	Master's
FTE Enrollment, 1974–75	33,000	23,000	8,000	10,000	3,000	2,000
Expenditures, 1974–75	$213,000,000	$44,500,000	$160,000,000	$86,000,000	$12,500,000	$10,500,000
1965–66	438,470			110,736	2,158	4,540
1966–67	348,809			193,370	32,958	320
1967–68	176,467			313,004	62,958	345
1968–69	346,265	1,263		332,922	93,558	375
1969–70	683,645	80,186		1,091,829	92,958	58,239
1970–71	856,429	103,663	617,400	393,022	92,958	52,421
1971–72	880,932	115,710	623,750	758,711	93,928	42,407
1972–73	819,815	135,570	349,590	771,208	99,070	34,303
1973–74	1,156,583	141,954	962,940	1,006,506	146,590	39,464
1974–75	1,302,545	180,764	865,840	1,939,573	166,277	87,871

SOURCE: American Council on Education, Policy Analysis Service, Data compiled by the Special Costs Study Task Force, Spring, 1975.

whelming and one must ask immediately why they are so keenly felt on almost all campuses, both by members of the faculty and of the administration. I believe there are several reasons. First, most institutions operate at the limit of their resources and have had to eliminate programs and faculty members in recent years. Hence these expenditures are properly measured against programs or people which would not have been eliminated (or might be added) in their absence. Viewed in this perspective, the cost of these programs consumes perhaps a fifth of the library acquisition budget or a sixth of the scholarship budget. No matter how legitimate the costs are, they are quite properly seen as a real diversion of funds from educational purposes.

A second reason for the great concern is the rapid rate of growth of these costs as illustrated in Exhibit 1.2 from Van Alstyne and Coldren. Some, such as EEO and OSHA, have come into being in the last five years. The totality appears to be doubling in roughly five years, although there is reason to hope that as staffs, reporting and data collection systems and so forth are in place and the capital expenditures required by OSHA have been completed, they may come to equilibrium and the rate of cost increase fall off. There seems to be little confidence, however, that this will actually take place.

One of the great frustrations attending these expenditures is that so much of the effort seems misplaced. For example, in connection with affirmative action enormous efforts have gone and are going into data collection, reporting, analysis, and projection, none of which help to employ people. The greatest obstacle to minority employment is the very tiny pool from which candidates must be drawn; yet, fellowship funds are not available for graduate study by minority students. In the case of women the analysis carried out for EEO purposes has helped to document that there is an adequate pool of talented women which continues to be underutilized, even in the sciences. But again, a better use of funds might be to at least experiment with assisting women through the very difficult early professional years when they must simultaneously establish a family and carry out the academic research and teaching on which a tenure decision will usually be made while they are in their early thirties. In many cases the regulations have seemed more appropriate to commerce or industry than to the teaching and research situation of a university or college. In sum, if regulations do not intrude on the central educational process, the greatest concern is not with the *existence* of the regulations but with their *character*.

Exhibit 1.2
Trends in Costs of Implementing Federally
Mandated Social Programs, 1965–1975
Combined Costs at Six Institutions by Program

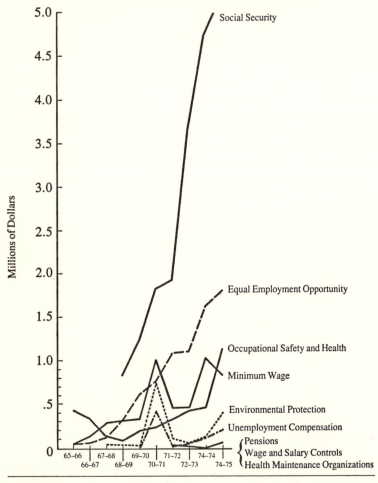

SOURCE: American Council on Education, Policy Analysis Service. Data Compiled by the Special Costs Study Task Force, Spring 1975.

INDIRECT COSTS

Possibly more important than the direct costs are the indirect costs of regulation. A major one is the unreimbursed diversion of faculty time from teaching and research to committee service and a wide variety of more or less administrative duties. This has particularly been the case in connection with affirmative action procedures in which faculty members screen and draft replies to large numbers of applicants. In his annual report for 1974–75, President Bok at Harvard estimated that 80,000 hours of faculty time were consumed to comply with federal regulations. Another indirect cost is the diversion of administrators' time and attention from the educational process to legal and bureaucratic problems and to explaining the differences between a university and a business to federal officials who do not understand the problems which federal regulations have created.

Very few institutions, including Brown, have attempted to determine the total costs. However, in his 1974–75 annual report, President Bok states "At Harvard, the total cost of administering five government programs—equal employment opportunity laws, the Buckley amendment, occupational health and safety rules, environmental protection, and pension reform—has been running from $4.6 to $8.3 million per year." With a total budget of about $250 million this implies that the indirect costs may be two to three times the direct costs. If that is typical it presents very serious problems for financially beleaguered institutions.

There is another indirect cost which must always be weighed. This is the effect of regulations on the character of the institution and its ability to carry out its central purposes. For example, university administrations and their budgets have grown relative to the rest of the institution as more elaborate budget and fiscal systems, personnel classification systems, better record keeping and information systems and so on are installed. The governance of universities is consequently becoming more centralized and this changes the relation among faculty, students, and administration. It is not clear how much of this new managerial approach can be ascribed to government regulation. There is good reason to believe that internal forces are also pushing institutions in this direction; the number of deans tends to grow at least as fast as the number of budget officers. Nonetheless, the requirements of the federal government for data, both personnel and financial, as well as the budgetary requirements of state and municipal governments, have certainly catalyzed this trend.

Another such indirect effect is the psychological cost of insincere or meaningless efforts. This is particularly true of affirmative action where efforts may be concentrated on the formalities, on assembling appropriate pools, and screening by formal criteria and writing impressive reports instead of hiring men and women. This sometimes results in a charades playing posture which both hurts affirmative action and the institutions.

CONCLUSION

In my view all of the programs considered constitute legitimate costs to be charged to the higher educational enterprise. On the other hand, there is no question that they constitute a genuine diversion of funds from other educational activities. Furthermore, they impose indirect costs in the form of strains on university functions and unreimbursed faculty time.

The question is: what can be done? It would, of course, be nice if education and charitable organizations could be reimbursed for at least their out of pocket expenditures. However, with the decentralization of our system and the lack of any agency responsible for the overall health of higher education, this seems unlikely.

In that event what is clearly needed are regulations which: (1) infringe on the autonomy of institutions and their ability to deal with each problem according to their special requirements and capabilities to the minimum extent compatible with the fundamental purpose and (2) do not raise costs needlessly. Regulations need to be reasonably unambiguous and left intact long enough so that institutions can plan intelligently. Surely some means can be found so that parallel authority does not exist in several agencies, all of whom require slightly different sets of information covering the same subjects and who sometimes generate conflicting requirements.

In short, the principal step is to draft intelligent regulations which are appropriate to educational institutions.

The second step is to insure that federal officials who enforce the regulations understand the special nature of educational institutions and the differences between them and business organizations.

The responsibility for doing this rests, in the first instance, with the Congress and the executive agencies but the institutions of higher education also bear a heavy responsibility. Their responsibility is to make clear, while laws and regulations are being drafted, what their impact will be and how desirable goals can be achieved at least cost to the institutions. It is to work with the agencies and their personnel to the end that regulations can be intelligently administered and educational problems understood. Various associations and a number of individual institutions have worked hard to do this. However, the fact that the problems are still with us indicates that a renewed effort is in order.

generates much of the interaction between the government and the university community.

Based on perceptions gained from our study, we found, even beyond government funding, that significant government impact on higher education stemmed from the implementation of federal policies with respect to social justice, manpower development, science, defense, and taxation, all entirely outside of the educational sphere and most providing no direct funding whatsoever. We found that these had far greater financial impact on higher education than did any explicit federal policies or programs specifically designated for the support of higher education. In general these impacts of government flowed from policies in areas of national interest completely outside of education; many of these impacts were unintended and some were scarcely recognized. If there is no explicit recognition of a national interest in higher education, then higher education has no weight in balancing policy trade offs with national interests which have been well articulated in other areas. For instance, education benefits for veterans were replaced with in-service educational opportunities for the volunteer army, thus ending the largest single program of financial support for students on the basis of analysis of the needs of the military, with scant or no explicit attention to the impact of that decision on higher education finance.

For our Task Force cost study we included those federal programs which impinged upon higher education institutions because they were employers or research contractors, not because they were educational enterprises. We looked at these costs to determine who bears them.

There has been an evolution of policy with respect to how to deal with these federally imposed costs. We started out, as we've heard earlier in the day, with arguments that the federal programs ought not to apply to higher education, either because colleges and universities had better performance records and "deserved" protection from federal enforcement agencies, or because the federal programs constituted too great a threat to academic autonomy or educational quality. I think I detected some of that type argument in Professor Lester's earlier works and in some of the introductory remarks which he made today. But I doubt that higher education can defend its performance as superior to the performance of other sectors and on that basis justify deflection of federal policies. And with respect to the alleged threats to educational quality, women and minorities historically saw race and sex used to intervene as negative weights before merit was even taken into consideration in employment decisions.

I believe we have moved into a second phase with respect to our attitudes towards these federal programs and the costs associated with them. Now, in general, we accept the contention that the regulations *do* apply to higher education, but if they apply, then there are costs of implementing them which must be met. Those who have written the laws and who administer them are beginning to recognize that there are indeed costs involved in implementing these regulations, but then they argue that the higher education institutions must bear those costs just as does any other enterprise. That attitude was reflected, I think, in some of the statements made by Mr. Chambers. I would argue, however, that we have to move into a third phase in developing our policy stance with respect to who bears these costs. A more defendable position is that the laws apply to higher education institutions but that there are the costs, and the nonprofit educational enterprises are less able to recover those costs than are profit-oriented firms.

I'd like to put forward an assertion that nonprofit higher education institutions are indeed different from most profit-oriented firms because, in general, they must bear a relatively larger share of those costs as they are less able to shift them forward or backward. To begin with, in the profit sector the costs of regulation are generally reflected in a higher price for the products, which is paid by all those who purchase it and which is therefore spread rather broadly across the consumers. In higher education, however, we don't have a single source of income, the price paid by consumers. Rather, higher education institutions have a complex financial structure with a large number of sources of income, including the tuition paid by students and their families, state and federal support, as well as private philanthropy, including both endowment income and current contributions. If costs increase but the increases are not spread across all the sources of income, then the institutions, out of necessity, may have to raise tuition, because tuition is the one source of revenue over which they have more immediate control. In consequence, a larger than proportionate share of these cost increases may be shifted to the students—with adverse effects on the ability of the students and their families to pay for those costs, and on educational opportunities.

On the other hand, it is likely that the institution may have great difficulty timing increases in tuition with increases in cost, simply because tuition charges are published in bulletins as much as a year earlier. The charges listed take on the effect of commitments made to the students. Mid-year changes in tuition levels would also necessitate recalculation of need-based student financial aid. The complexity of all this means simply that the institutions cannot, on a month-to-month basis, change prices as can, for instance, a steel manufacturer.

Further, institutions cannot cut costs readily, quite apart from tenure obligations, in large part because of annual contracts with faculty and staff, and program commitments to students for the academic year.

And colleges and universities have decentralized administrations; compliance with federal requirements such as affirmative action, has to be implemented in perhaps as many as 200 departments. Consequently, compliance may be more costly to implement in a college or university than it is in an industrial firm with a central hiring office.

There is another consideration for colleges and universities in meeting the costs of federal regulations. It flows from and is the obverse of the benefit that higher education, as nonprofit, institutions derive from their tax exempt status. The other side of the tax benefit is that when costs are imposed, the institution bears the burden of the full amount of those added costs. In contrast, if costs are raised for an industrial firm and their profits are reduced as a consequence, then the federal taxes are also reduced. There is a difference in the impact on the budgets because the federal government bears a portion of the added costs of the firm which must be borne fully by the nonprofit educational enterprise.

Another consideration is that profit-oriented enterprises and nonprofit educational institutions may be treated differently with respect to their ability to recover indirect costs or overhead which may increase because of government action or requirements. Educational institutions may be forced into what we call marginal cost pricing, whereas industry may be permitted to use average cost pricing in negotiating cost recovery rates. For example, research may be considered by the government to be an added activity of an educational institution and as a central activity of an industrial contractor. An illustration of the practical effect of that distinction would be, for instance, that the transition costs in shifting from one program to another, where researchers might be carried on administrative overhead without chargeable projects for extended periods, would be includable in the indirect costs of the industrial firms but not of the educational institution. Still another difference in the cost impact of government activity on educational institutions as compared with industrial firms is that the costs of plant and equipment are reflected in depreciation which is recoverable to a private firm, but which is not necessarily fully reflected in the cost accounting that a college or university has in contracts with the federal government.

For these reasons, I think that it is likely that the nonprofit educational institutions may be far less able to recover the costs of federal regulation than are industrial firms.

We have heard assertions that these costs are inflationary. I'm not sure that they are in all cases. To a very large extent, the costs of not regulating, of not making the improvements in our social system, are borne predominantly by those who are now disadvantaged. Consequently, regulations in the domain of social justice are likely to shift costs rather than add costs. Many of the "costs" of regulations which institutions bear, from a larger social perspective, are really costs which have been shifted to institutions that were borne by women and blacks and other minorities.

Also, to a very large extent the costs of regulation which we calculate are offset by benefits which are not measured and included in national income accounts. It is entirely possible that if we had a larger conception of what the net social products of all of these governmental activities were, the costs may indeed not be inflationary at all.

We have little hope, however, that the costs of regulation are likely to be reduced or the increases slowed down in the near future. After we completed our Task Force study, we found, in just one intervening year, that we had not included programs which are just coming on line now, particularly programs responding to the needs of the handicapped, which are anticipated to be relatively costly.

I want to say just a word about the costs of regulation relative to the costs of other federal actions as they impact on higher education. In our study, we looked at twelve federally mandated social programs. Eleven of them involved regulation. The twelfth did not involve federal regulation but was a program of taxation; that was social security. When we are looking at costs to colleges and universities of government activity, there is a question as to whether we should include the costs of social security, partly because there are those who argue they are really borne by the faculty in the form of lower wages. But the complete shifting of the burden of employment taxes to the employees takes place, if at all, only in the long run. And year-to-year increases in the social security tax outlays by institutions have been so large (as much as 25 percent), it is likely that in the short run they are not shifted—which results in substantial current cost impacts.

But we have spent the last two or three years in higher education totally preoccupied with the costs to institutions of regulation and ignored the sharply increasing costs of taxation to the "so-called" tax-exempt colleges and universities. Based on our Task Force study, when we calculated the dollar impact on the budgets of the institutions, the eleven regulatory programs on which we are focusing these two days of discussion accounted for half of the added costs and the other half was accounted for by one tax program, the increases in the social security tax base and tax rate. Social security has not, in the past, been regarded as a public policy issue in the higher education community because it replaces what would otherwise be required by way of private pension plans or state retirement programs. But social security is not simply a pension plan; it is a tax transfer system, shifting resources from those currently employed to those not currently employed. And the impact of this employment-based tax transfer system is particularly severe on higher education, because it is much more labor intensive than most industries. To generate $100,000 in revenue may take five times as many people in an educational enterprise as in a profit-oriented firm. While we have spent two or three years totally preoccupied with the costs to the institutions of federal intervention in terms of regulation, we have ignored general tax issues or defined them as not issues for consideration by higher education. In addition to attention to the costs of regulation, we ought to look at issues of general taxation as large areas of interest concerning the relationships between the federal government and the higher education institutions.

While institutions are exempt from income taxes, and generally from property and sales taxes, they are not exempt from employment taxes. I was staggered to find that the share of total federal revenues which comes from taxes on employment has risen to 30 percent. To the extent that we shift toward taxes on employment and away from taxes on income, the relative benefits of our tax exempt status are eroded. That is something we ought to pay some attention to.

I also think that there is an issue broadly affecting the relationships between government and the university, arising from the differential tax treatment of human capital and physical capital. That should be the subject of a far larger discussion on another occasion.

Let me close simply with several observations on coping with these costs of governmental activity or reducing them. There was discussion today in several of the papers of the possibility of reimbursing institutions for these costs. There is a practical difficulty, however, because the costs arise from so many and widely ranging governmental activities. Consequently reimbursing for specific costs, accounting for them program by program, is extraordinarily complex. On the other hand, nobody is adding up the individual cost components to derive a measure of the total impact of these governmentally driven costs on higher education.

In analyzing these costs we should move beyond mere identification of the costs of federal programs to analysis of their cost effectiveness. We've got some encouragement that this is actually going to take place on at least a small scale with the Paperwork Commission now looking, not only at the number of forms and the burden of filling them out, but also at the usefulness of the data collected.

If we shift to cost effectiveness as the basis of our policy analyses, we must, however, define the goals of those policies. Here I think it is terribly important that we separate those goals which are truly educational goals from those which are social goals. There are very good reasons for making that distinction from a budgetary standpoint when we look at higher education among federal and state spending priorities. For instance, if the vast sums allocated to student aid are characterized as spending for educational goals, they are taken from education budgets. But if they are characterized as income maintenance programs and spending for broader social goals, arguments can be made that the funds for that purpose should be added to the budgeted amounts available for education. So I think we should move to cost effectiveness and we should be very clear about the goals of the programs and distinguish between educational and social goals. I also believe that when we examine the cost effectiveness of social programs, we will find that the achievement of goals, particularly in the affirmative action area, is not necessarily related to costs. It may actually cost more to resist compliance with federal requirements than to carry out the programs. We will find that performance often results from differences in management style and in commitment, rather than in cost.

We heard a great deal today about moving away from external regulation, to internal or self-regulation, moving away from meeting process requirements to performance. It seems to me, however, that up to this point practically nothing has been said as to what the standards of performance are or ought to be. I think it is incumbent upon the institutions to be very specific about what performance standards they will meet, and how soon, in claiming that they will do a better job with voluntary compliance, removing external pressures.

A closing remark. When regulatory reform is discussed, a great deal is said about the necessity for de-regulation, moving away from federally

An Institutional View of the Costs of Government Regulation

Charles M. Chambers
George Washington University

In exploring how the government acts as regulator of the academy, one should take a moment to consider an example of those actually regulated. Because of the numerous, separate categories of regulatory activity at the local, state, and national levels, it is unlikely that any one institution could adequately reflect the entire phenomenon and the costs it produces. We do not suggest that the following review of current sentiments which have been expressed at the George Washington University is comprehensive. We do feel it would be of interest to this conference for two reasons. First, it offers a benchmark from which other conference deliberations can be measured. Second, there is perhaps a more acute awareness of these issues here than on other campuses. After much thought we published a "Declaration of Independence, *circa* 1976" in the April 19 issue of *The Chronicle*. This awareness has recently been enhanced by the work of a large interdivisional committee which conducted a survey and self-study of government regulation at the University. While this may not lend all that much credibility to our discussion, it does suggest that a plurality of viewpoints across our University have been considered. We do note that the opinions expressed here are the sole responsibility of the author and do not necessarily reflect official university policy. Let us begin by presenting a few brief facts about the University and our approach to costs and regulation.

The George Washington University is private, nonsectarian and was chartered by Congress in 1821 ostensively to fulfill President Washington's oft-stated hope "for the erection of a university at the seat of the Federal Government." It has an enrollment of some 22,000 students in twelve academic schools and divisions. Its programs are comprehensive, but have general emphasis in the areas of government, law, public affairs, and international affairs. It granted 4,400 degrees last year, has library holdings of 700,000 volumes and a portfolio endowment of $14 million. The President is the chief executive officer, the Provost is the second ranking administrative officer, and the various vice presidents serve as chief officers in their respective areas. The current budget is over $124 million and the University expects a $5 million surplus in the current operating year. Grants and sponsored programs are at a level of some $26 million per year.

Next, in considering the economic impact of regulation, we approach the element of cost quite broadly. We include not only direct costs which can be found in the various budget accounts, but also the indirect costs into which various overhead items are pooled. We also consider types of imputed costs. Two major ones are dislocation costs associated with lost opportunities and risk costs associated with institutional planning in an uncertain environment. We ignore specific dollar amounts in all of these costs for the following reasons. First, such amounts would invariably be out of context with other University expenditures and therefore would be relatively meaningless. Second, because we do not yet have accurate quantitative methods for assessing all relevant economic costs, precisely stated dollar amounts can be misleading. Third, we have found that some of the costs which appear to be caused by regulation must be adjusted or discounted to account for other nongovernmental effects.

Third, we note that regulatory costs arise from a large number of separate agencies at many different levels. To simplify our discussion, we take an administrative law approach. In this approach an agency operates as both a legislator and an adjudicator. Within broad bounds it can both make its own law and then enforce it. As a guide to understanding how the different costs arise, let us recall the several stages at which an agency interacts with a university. Initially the agency promulgates regulations through its rule-making authority. Second, it conducts judicial type hearings and makes findings of fact. Third, it is able to enforce compliance and impose penalties either through its own discretion or through a court of appropriate jurisdiction.

Although the administrative process is not based on the traditional adversary relationship, parties such as universities involved in agency examinations become seriously concerned about the quality of such procedural protections as due process, freedom of information, exhaustion of appeals, etc. Also, this is a relatively new phenomenon in the affairs of state and it is not yet clear how traditional checks and balances serve to temper misplaced zeal. Of particular concern is what authority is actually delegated by enabling legislation to the agency, and what abuse of discretion is possible by appointed officials. Many of these factors enter the cost analysis whether it be a simple matter before a board of zoning appeals or a full-scale contract compliance review by the Department of Labor.

With this introduction, let us now turn to actual types of costs borne by this University. First, we recognize that government creates certain minimum costs which we cannot criticize. They are properly imposed by government as being necessary to the sound functioning of society in general. We accept them as costs of doing business in both our corporate and educational pursuits. Because of the constitutional guarantees of equal protection and the prohibition against prior restraints, we expect these costs to be borne equitably by all American enterprises. They serve the common good and are part of our shared duty to obey the law.

A second source of costs are associated with programs sponsored by government contracts and grants. Because we receive benefits from these programs, we expect a certain amount of concomitant costs. A part of these costs is administrative in nature and serves to assure the govenment that our stewardship of funds from the public treasury is trustworthy. Another part is the opportunity costs of attracting attention, submitting proposals, and maintaining reserve staff. These costs have been and continue to be reasonable business expenses. On the other hand, there is a growing practice by the government to use its contracting prerogatives to require a unilateral acceptance of numerous standard provisions by the University. These provisions demand certain behavior on our part in general operational areas outside of the actual scope of the contract or grant. Examples are:

Small Business Representation
Minority Business Subcontracting
Small Business Subcontracting

Labor Surplus Area
Affiliate Business Association Data
Profit/Not-for-Profit/Non-Profit Status
Contingent Fee
Employment of Handicapped
Civil Rights
Nonsegregated Facilities
Affirmative Action Program
Accuracy of Subcontractor's Certifications
Buy American
Human Subjects
Conflict of Interest
Wage Determination Methods
Assurance of Insurance
Care of Laboratory Animals
Cost Accounting Standards
Employment of Former Agency Personnel
Clean Air and Water Compliance
Independent Price Determination

If our acceptance of a contract or grant from a categorical program is an exercise of free choice in an arm's length negotiation, then it is perfectly proper for the government, as the other contracting party, to dictate provisions of its own choosing. Our concern here is that transactions between a university and the government are rarely even-handed. Many of you know how awkward it is for a university to ask for additional compensation to meet the costs of complying with the many standard provisions. We feel that the general problem here is that governmental sponsorship of programs at universities goes far beyond the mere procurement of products and services to meet its own needs, and represents a direct contribution to the academy as a deserving social institution. Thus the government should be more willing to accept these associated costs. Finally, we note that this discussion begs the question of whether obtaining compliance by force of contract provision is in the best interest of either the government or the academy, even if all costs are paid. We will return to this issue in more detail later.

Let us now turn to a large category of costs that have come about because of recent awareness of such needs as equal opportunity for minorities, women, and the handicapped; protection of student rights;

safe operation of hazardous laboratories, etc. Many spokesmen have bewailed the high cost of complying with government regulations in these areas. However, before acting too quickly to mete out blame, we should look more closely at the larger social forces acting here. We know that in the last decade or two there has been a tremendous amount of social evolution in this country. We believe that much of this evolution has been inevitable and that whether or not the administrative agencies were active we would today have the additional costs of fulfilling our new social obligations. During this time we have observed that the government has acted in a number of regulatory ways ranging from a most astute and effective spearhead for social progress to little more than a political opportunist capitalizing on the public conscience. While we are embarassed to acknowledge that we have not been as progressive in practice as we preach in the classroom, we nevertheless cannot give full credit to the government for this awareness and thus cannot blame all of our costs on the government. In the final analysis the government is the prime protector and defender of the rights of the individual citizen, and we recognize that the piper must be paid. In all honesty, we must discount a number of the costs which appear to be caused by regulatory compliance requirements. In general, the remaining costs are reasonable given the bureaucratic machinery necessary to assure ourselves and the agencies that we respect compliance. Later, we will give our own examples of how the costs can escalate when the regulatory process is poorly administered.

At this point, we would like to note that in an assessment of the impact of costs, the quality of compliance is only a relative factor. Because elements of human intent and good will are involved, it is not possible to guarantee perfect compliance regardless of how much is expended. In a large institution the problem becomes one of span of control in the implementation of policy. A system of communication, data collection, and audit is established to give adequate notice to subordinates of their duties and responsibilities and of the supervision and oversight that will verify their compliance. What is frequently lacking in the equation is an understanding by the regulatory agencies themselves of the inherent limitations in organizational systems whenever a comprehensive, accurate, and immediate response is required from a large operation. Many of these agencies seem blissfully unaware of generally accepted accounting procedures and the levels of confidence which any audit or verification scheme can be expected to achieve in terms of the effort expended.

Finally, there is another small category of costs associated with equal opportunity which we in higher education cannot honestly charge to the federal government. As many of you will recall, Lyndon Johnson exempted higher education from his compliance orders in the mid-sixties. While this was certainly considered a boon at the time, it did mean that when full affirmative action became inescapable for publicly supported institutions, we had to react quickly and incurred what might be called "catch-up" costs. Instead of amortizing the expense of the learning curve over a more reasonable period of time, universities developed hasty, expensive, and probably inefficient compliance plans. One particularly poignant example in this category occurred with the Berkeley model episode in 1975, which we will describe later.

When all of the above effects are considered, we have found that in the ordinary course of events, government regulation *per se* has not proved to be terribly expensive for us. Lest this be interpreted as an endorsement of regulation, we hasten to add that our story does not stop here. We have undergone a number of unfortunate experiences which raise much deeper and more serious problems about the ultimate cost of regulation in higher education. This second tier of costs is characterized by more subtle effects and like an infection, these costs can spread throughout the academy and reach fatal proportions before serious symptoms appear. Let us consider some of these.

As a relatively new member of the family of governmental methods, the administrative process has shown an exasperating proclivity for caprice. Such niceties as relevance and materiality in matters of discourse which we inherited from the English common law are conveniently omitted. Because an agency is ostensibly finding facts in a matter at hand, rather than judging the guilt of a defendant, investigations can easily escalate into grand jury type dragnets, e.g., "tell us everything, and we will decide what bears on your involvement in the matter at hand."

For example, in an investigation of discrimination in our admissions and academic services to first-year law students, a local compliance agency asked for "the records of all students who have attended law school during the previous three years." This required over three thousand records covering a span of some six years. In order to protect the students' confidentiality, our law school had to make a great effort to keep the records anonymous by hand editing every record. On several occasions in the future the same data was requested by different investigators who apparently were unaware that their agency had already received the data.

A much more serious example arose in 1975 when the U.S. Office of Civil Rights found that it did not have sufficient time to complete the compliance reviews of affirmative action plans for universities prior to award of federal contracts. Using its agency discretion, the Office required in effect that our University along with many others submit a plan based on the Berkeley model. To do this, we would have had to prepare masses of irrelevant data and analysis at a cost of thousands of dollars, and in the process we would have declared —against our self-interest— that we were noncompliant. As many of you know, only a dramatic public protest resulted in a drastic modification of the required plan to a much more reasonable scale. We appreciate that controversial agencies with insecure departmental postures are anxious to use all of their prerogatives to show how effective and dynamic they can be. At times, we become so frustrated and weary at what can only be termed harassment, however benign, that we even lose sight of our due process protections and appeal rights, and just long to see some light at the end of the tunnel.

In the research administration area, we have found some anomalous requirements from sponsoring agencies. Some have actually asked principal investigators directly to submit financial reports of their activities which should "not be used for reconciliation with other fiscal reports" coming from our University's treasurer's office. It is hard to know what possible use the agency could make of such spurious reports. It does raise serious problems of conflict of interest and breach of employer-employee relationships as between the researcher, the university, and the sponsoring agency.

In summarizing these examples, we find ourselves somewhat nettled by the "bad boy" mentality which is all too prevalent here. The philosophy seems to be that if a university has the opportunity to do wrong things, it will do so unless constrained in advance. This is a concept which most of Western Civilization left behind with Saint Augustine. We feel that the approach of self-regulation is worthy of consideration and would do much to curtail excessive costs. Eventually, when compliance begins to affect academic autonomy, the academy had no choice but to step in *as a whole* and insist that, one, it is better able to make the value judgments, and, two, it is the only proper one to do so.

Another serious type of cost which we find is that the pressure to conform to an acceptable agenda of social priorities inevitably leads to acquiescence in other areas. At issue here is both the plurality of higher education and the survival of the liberal arts tradition. Both are priceless, and the loss of either one cannot be measured in purely economic terms. Our concern here goes much beyond the often retread undergraduate curriculum. It extends to the inventive, scholarly, propagative, and authoritative functions of the academy, all of which are susceptible to grave harm. With government agencies currently emphasizing career education, we find ourselves being shepherded step-by-step into one great national model for higher education. While the problems in this area are of course much broader than the topic of this review, we do see regulation, in its many forms, as having a major negative influence on the self-determination and autonomy of higher education.

Related to this concern is the area of accreditation, both general and professional. It is difficult for any regulator to look out over his domain and not feel that accreditation is a necessary and proper item for his attention, if he is to fulfill his agency's mandate. We do appreciate that the government, as trustee of the public treasury and guardian of the individual consumer, does have a vested interest in assuring that tax revenues are used in a creditable fashion. Yet, it is frightening to imagine what more aggressive regulation by government agencies in this area would cost us.

In a further area, we believe that the government has not made an adequate effort to understand and respect the realities of financing higher education. While not strictly regulation, this lack of respect can and does produce additional costs for us. For example, in sponsored programs our indirect costs for pooled items are reimbursed on the basis of a negotiated overhead rate. The cost accounting standards used to categorize direct, indirect, allowable, and unallowable costs come from a rule making procedure. Rule changes recently proposed would result in universities underwriting even more of their overhead in conducting government programs. A second example involves student financial aid. We all know that tuition grants cover only a portion of the total cost of education for each student. In accepting student financial aid through government programs, we are forced to meet the additional costs from other private sources.

In concluding, we would like to consider two final areas which seem to us to be potentially extremely perilous. One might even say we have saved the best for last! As mentioned earlier, we have not yet found the legitmate costs of compliance to be an excessive burden. We are left with a disquieting sense that if present trends continue, we face nothing but a future of escalating costs of regulation. The first area involves universities being expected to seek out, identify, and report instances of student noncompliance with the terms of their individual arrangements with sponsoring agencies. The two most offending agencies are the Veteran's Administration and the Immigration and Naturalization Service. Both require certain levels of class attendance and other school behavior of students receiving their benefits. Aside from the serious ethical problems and the conflict of interest involved in our serving as both a bloodhound and a watchdog for these agencies, we feel that it is totally improper for any such agency to attempt to delegate any part of its investigative and/or enforcement authority to someone (us) who is a nonincumbent third party to the arrangements. The cost of policing all of the many and varied arrangements which our students may have with government agencies, such as guaranteed loans, would be astronomical, and would greatly compromise our academic sensibilities. The great danger here is that an agency which feels it is too understaffed to properly administer and supervise its own programs, can too easily believe that universities, who after all are getting all the money eventually anyway, should play a larger role in keeping everything under control.

Second, we find ourselves spending more money than we would like for what might be called "risk abatement." Costs are associated with uncertainty in planning, and the more uncertainty, the greater the costs. Of course, we all expect a certain amount of uncertainty. Through luck and what might pass for rational business judgment, we hope the good and bad will average out, and we can accept our fate, pay our bills, and move onward. In recent years we have had our own laments about the short-term priorities and fluctuating patterns of federally sponsored programs. This doesn't concern us terribly. Yet when the uncertainty becomes irrational and its effects sporadic, we don't know where to turn. We are thoroughly bewildered by the haste with which new regulations are forced into the Federal Register before even the most elementary consultive and deliberative scrutiny can occur. We sense that there is something much more invidious than just expediency involved here. Recall that it was only over the most surprisingly bitter opposition by the agencies themselves that Lyndon Johnson ordered the thirty-day pre-effective notice period for the publication of new regulations. This heavy-handed psychology of "getting them before they know what has hit them" gravely undermines our trust in government and the stability of all social institutions, including the academy. It offers nothing but a bureaucratic morass as a replacement.

In this vein, we find ourselves spending much time and effort second-guessing new regulations and trying to limit our overall costs by purchasing an ounce of prevention now. No review of this nature would be complete without a shaggy dog story, and we have our own. Our treatment of animals in our medical research laboratories is regulated by the U.S. Department of Agriculture under P. L. 89–544, the Animal Welfare Act. We recently constructed animal holding facilities as part of our new basic medical sciences complex on campus. Although it did not appear in the final Act, our veterinarian noted that Agriculture officials had supported draft legislation which would have required building runs for canine exercise. We discovered that if the Act were ever subsequently amended to require such facilities, we would face very expensive building modification costs. Thus, as a preventative measure, and at no small cost, several runs of inefficiently utilized interior floor space were added to the original construction plans!

While this has been a somewhat tentative review of types of costs we as a university face because of, or in spite of, government regulation, we hope that our sentiments and experiences are of interest to you. In taking all of this in summary, we would make a modest proposal: that no regulatory agency be allowed to increase its emission of hazardous regulations until it has first conducted a cost impact study and published a budgetary protection plan.

A View from Capitol Hill

Robert C. Andringa
U.S. House of Representatives

Let me just take a moment to assay what to my mind is the most promising feature of this conference, the demonstration of interest on the part of a faculty organization in the major issues of higher education. At least from the perspective of Capitol Hill, we seldom hear from or get involved with the faculty and we need more of it. I mention this even though your particular organization, the University Centers for Rational Alternatives, has the mistaken notion that "rational alternatives" have any place in this peculiar city. I do not really mean this in an absolute sense since in fact, Dr. Chambers who described his problem with canine runs could indeed adopt a more rational alternative by hiring college work-study students to walk "experimental pets" outside on the street. It seems evident from speaker to speaker as we move along through this conference that educational decision-making and the rules made by the government are primarily political. Although based on what is perceived to be true, personal judgments seem to weigh far heavier than any set of facts that has won consensus and has been accepted as objectively true. So I too offer some perceptions based on seven years of work with the Education and Labor Committee in the House of Representatives of what is, and a little of what might be, concerning the topic of this panel.

First, it is unfortunate but true that government action of some sort was necessary to ensure that certain fundamental values of our society were reflected on our campuses and throughout society. Higher education did have the chance to correct some of its sins. But even after they were brought to light, higher education appears to have done little on its own to effect significant change. The focus of my comments is not limited to Civil Rights or Affirmative Action. It bears rather on the general state of affairs that has come about in response to the over four hundred separate categorical programs Chester Finn mentioned in his remarks. In most of the discussions I have participated in here in Washington on regulations, the focus has been only on *dollars*. And for this approach there is actually very little sympathy I can detect on Capitol Hill. In fact the cost, amounting to only one percent, of the various regulations might seem like a bargain in the eyes of many. In my mind, however, the real cost of federal regulation, which is more important and fundamental than expenditures of money, is the greater threat to our tradition of higher learning. That cost and the problem it generates is not well understood on Capitol Hill, but the message is beginning to get through. It is a message that sounds surprisingly similar to the one coming from small business and other more regulated enterprises in the country protesting the burden of regulation.

Decision-making in the regulatory process is extremely diffused. I am told that a modest regulation change in an office of education program must be approved by twenty-three different offices. The authority for regulation-writing is generated by dozens of congressional committees enlarged by at least twenty-five executive agencies. No single law or executive order is going to reduce by very much the total impact of such a process. As the complaints arrive in Washington you will observe that almost every politician in both branches of government responds with sympathy. All bemoan federal red tape. Most are today "down" on "big government," but the problem is always "the other guy." No one admits that *his* committee or *his* program is superfluous, overexpanded or overbearing in any way whatsoever. This reflects the fact that congressional committees and executive agencies function quite independently of one another. No one is charged with even thinking about the extent of the total federal interface with higher education, not to mention the costs of overlapping and duplication and their nuisance effects. Thus, any one in higher education who complains about Washington or Congress or the Administration expecting government to respond to the academy's problems often reflects a lack of understanding about how things are done at the federal level.

I have sensed that most of us at this Conference really support the positive motives behind most federal regulations. The problems fall into several subcategories. I list some here. We need different strategies to deal with each of them.

First, there is the mistaken notion that a person's inner attitudes and feelings towards his fellow men or women can be fundamentally altered by threats of external force coupled with examples of punitive action for noncompliance. I suggest we need to explore what the actual effects of these approaches have been more realistically than we have in the past. Second, there is the tendency of any administration to attempt to reshape, by regulation, laws passed by Congress that do not conform with the Administration's original policy views on that issue. This tension between the two branches often leads to exciting combats between the bureaucrats and the staff on the Hill, but it does ultimately hurt the regulated. Third, is the mistaken attitude that someone in Washington can anticipate every small detail of how any goal should be carried out in over five thousand very different institutions. Fourth, we witness the lack of coordination among regulation writers and implementational agencies. Fifth is the trend of regulations in recent years to assume guilt on the part of all target institutions resulting in regulatory overkill. This creates an emotional backlash that sometimes inhibits rather than advances the original purpose of the law or the regulation. Sixth is the problem of promulgating regulations that government has no possible way of enforcing. The result is that it leaves government with even less credibility than it does with respect to those it is attempting to regulate. Seventh, higher education has failed to make a convincing case for separate and unequal regulations in contradistinction to the regulations applicable to other segments of society. Granted that regulations unique to higher education or to a particular segment of higher education cannot be justified in all situations, but it seems reasonable to me that an excellent case can be made for them in some. Eighth and finally, is the political problem of attempting to revise or cut back excessive regulations through legislation when such regulations deal with minority rights, women's rights, safety or pay of employees, equal opportunity for the handicapped or other emotional issues supported by highly vocal advocacy groups. Most members of Congress will tell you privately that regulations in these areas, almost always, exceed the scope and detail of the law. These members understand very well what they voted for. But to go out front with any proposal that could be interpreted by the vocal interest groups involved as lack of *total* committment to their rights, or, at least, to their interests, is begging for political trouble. Most members will say: "Who needs it!"

The federal government has in the past few years tried to respond to the problem of government by regulation. Just a few examples which came out of our Committee and which were developed primarily under the leadership of Congressman James O'Hara who has been chairman of the Subcommittee on Post-Secondary Education. We developed a requirement that regulations appear in the Federal Register as Proposed Rules so that the public could have adequate time to comment. We then arranged to subject the proposed regulations to possible congressional disapproval within a certain time period before they took effect. However this device has never been invoked to date. More recently, in the 1976 amendments we have written legislations more specifically trying to lessen the opportunity for bureaucratic interpretation. Also, within the executive branch, recent HEW initiatives to seek broader public input into the whole rule-making process, through notices-of-intent, raise the same issues. The new problem may be, I suggest, that as agencies feel compelled to include in the final regulations answers to the hundreds of public comments, the total amount of regulations will be increased and not decreased. In closing, and speaking as only one member of the congressional staff, I readily concede that solutions to the multiple problems we are discussing would be immensely facilitated if the laws on which most regulations are based could be more clearly written and thoughtfully developed. Let us hope that this will be a topic for a future conference.

GOVERNMENT REGULATION
AND ACADEMIC FREEDOM

Government Regulation
and Academic Freedom

William J. McGill

President, Columbia University

In his annual report of 1926–27, President Nicholas Murray Butler advised the Trustees of Columbia University of a painful truth already quite well-known to them. The task of formulating the University's budget for the year ending June 30, 1928 had proved to be one of "exceptional difficulty and embarrassment." Expenditures for University operations were anticipated to be $8.6 million. The budget would be in balance if the general income of the University apart from gifts and endowments were as large as $6.2 million, but the most optimistic income estimates yielded only $5.8 million. Hence the president contemplated the embarrassment of an operating deficit in the 1927–28 academic year amounting to more than $400,000. Butler, making full use of the pious language which university presidents reserve for the most painful financial moments with their trustees, observed that "the estimated deficit was kept even at this very large sum only by declining to make appropriations urgently asked for and really all but necessary for the effective carrying forward of the University's work."

Having used nearly the same rhetoric last May to divert a new generation of Columbia Trustees from the stark reality of a projected operating deficit in 1976–77, I can appreciate Butler's embarrassment as thoroughly as I can savor his faultless display of presidential legerdemain in slipping a bad budget past a skeptical board. It is almost as though nothing had changed in the last fifty years at Columbia. But closer observation reveals that a great deal has changed. The essential circumstances governing that change have brought us together in this conference to discuss the proper role of government in higher education.

The budget which I expect to bring to the Columbia Trustees next April will forecast university expenditures in 1977–78 approximating $230 million. Roughly $70 million of that figure will be generated by the university's instructional activities. Another $70 million will come directly from the federal government via programs of research support and student aid. An additional $25 million of our budgeted expenditures will come to us from New York City and New York State. Substantial portions of this funding have their origins in federal programs.

Nicholas Murray Butler's budget for Columbia University in 1928 had no government money in it at all, whereas nearly one-third of my budget in 1978 will be paid for in Washington. During the last fifty years we have entered into a remarkable partnership with the federal government. In so doing we and government have managed to create an extraordinary educational enterprise contributing greatly to the advancement of our nation. The partnership has fostered standards of excellence in colleges and universities across the nation unmatched elsewhere in the world. It has generated an almost unbroken sequence of American accomplishments in science and in the arts since the Second World War. These achievements have projected our country and our educational system into positions of world leadership. I need not belabor this sophisticated audience with the obvious caveat that this major accomplishment did not happen by accident. It was built out of the brains and the labors of extremely capable men and women working cooperatively over many years to create an educational system that has now trained increasing numbers of even more capable men and women. The evidence of success is clear as the Nobel Prizes begin to roll in, and as our remarkable economy manages to adjust to the rigors of a hostile world environment in which we can no longer claim to control a significant portion of the resources consumed by our industry and by our standard of living. Our technology continues to be the marvel of the rest of the world, and of course it has been built upon a foundation of higher education.

In comparing Butler's budget of 1928 with Columbia's budget forecast for 1978, I should also note that the 1928 expenditures in each of the traditional major categories of expense are now multiplied by a factor of about twenty. The last fifty years have not produced a major expansion of the university either in its student body or its faculty. We have gone from about 12,000 students and 2,000 faculty in 1927 to about 16,000 students and 3,700 faculty in 1977. The very large increases in our dollar expenditures are due chiefly to the inexorable force of currency devaluation over the last fifty years. Endowment earnings are systematically eroded in times of inflation by the operation of what seems to be an economic law affecting institutions dependent upon the delivery of costly professional services. Investments tend to increase in yield at a rate determined by inflation in the productive areas of the economy, whereas a university's operating budget grows at a substantially higher rate since costs of professional services cannot be controlled by enforced productivity changes. This means that in times of inflation endowment income grows more slowly than operating expenses.

The financial pressures experienced by Columbia during the last fifty years have forced us to search for new sources of current income. Accordingly our partnership with the federal government was not entirely voluntary. The more than twenty-fold inflation of our basic costs over the past fifty years, coupled with the inability of our endowment to keep pace, led us to turn to the government for financial assistance. During the 1950s Columbia University crossed a fundamental threshold that will determine the basic structure of the University for at least as long as we are alive. In this period and for the first time in our long history, a yearly infusion of federal resources became absolutely necessary for our operation and for our survival. It is a fortunate thing that Columbia's emerging need for sources of revenue over and above tuition and endowment earnings happened also to coincide with the federal government's decision to turn to the major research universities for a unique kind of public service. We were given stewardship over the nation's expanded commitment to basic research and advanced teaching. The threshold was passed in 1957 when the Soviets launched their Sputnik beeping to the world its message of technological superiority. After Sputnik our involvement with government initiatives in higher education, and our dependence on federal funds for expansion of our facilities and our mission, was such that no major American university would ever be the same again. On our side at least the new federal partnership was born in part because of serious financial needs and in part because of understandable aspirations to excellence. Despite our ancient charter, and despite our reputation as one of the world's great independent institutions, Columbia University is no longer a truly private university. We are now acutely and critically dependent on the federal government not only for roughly one-third of our annual operating budget but for the sustenance of the intellectual activity of perhaps half of our faculty. In this respect we differ only in trivial ways from the fifty or so other large universities in the United States, both public and private. There is no substantial qualitative difference between Columbia, Berkeley, and Michigan, for example. Each of us holds substantial private resources, and each of us is also critically dependent on major federal support to insure the quality of our scholarly activities. Berkeley and Michigan happen to go to their legislatures annually to meet the costs of faculty salaries and to maintain their physical plants. Columbia passes most of such costs through to its students in tuition charges. The difference does not seem to me to be crucial in defining the style of operation of the three universities. Each of us functions in essentially the same way and none of us could survive in anything remotely resembling our current configuration without a transfusion of resources received each year from the federal government. Columbia ranked seventh in the nation in the dollar amount of federal support in 1975, whereas Berkeley ranked eleventh and Michigan twelfth.

I have offered this somewhat unusual treatise on the elements of modern university financing as a preliminary argument in order to make clear the vulnerability of the nation's major univerisites to currents of change in federal policy. President Nixon was not misdirected in threatening to cut off federal grant support for MIT when he became furious with the policy advice given by MIT's president. Mr. Nixon was angry enough to want to destroy MIT, and in his own inimitable fashion he chose the surest and deadliest way of doing it. Fortunately no one else in the government took him seriously. His intemperate outburst illustrates more clearly than any reasoned argument how vulnerable large universities have become to federal economic attack. We are totally dependent upon the cooperative efforts of an enlightened citizenry and wise public officials for providing the necessities of political freedom and assured financing on which our stability rests. Nicholas Murray Butler could plan Columbia's activities in 1927 with evident disregard for the impact of federal support on his University. Butler's successor in 1977 is virtually obsessed by the problem. That has happened not just to Columbia but to every major university in the United States during the last fifty years. It is, as I have said, a fundamental change and there will be no turning back.

Have we in fact traded away our political freedom for federal dollars? There are now insistent voices in the academic community claiming that this is really what has happened to us, but a more temperate analysis suggests that the partnership between the federal government and American education was not only inevitable but has proved to be immensely beneficial to most universities. No institution can afford to build and equip the major instructional facilities or to design and implement the advanced curricula demanded by the march of human knowledge without going heavily into debt. The cost of educating a medical student in the United States is now in excess of $20,000 annually. Would it be better to pass on such costs to students in heavy tuition charges or should the government be asked to share the burden with us? It is claimed that we should not have first-class science facilities and modern instructional programs in American universities or that we should not educate medical students because we cannot afford to do so without federal assistance. That is the dilemma. The angry voices in the academic community, claiming that we have sold out our academic freedom in pursuit of federal dollars, seem nevertheless determined to enjoy all the benefits of federally supported educational excellence. They want their chief administrators to increase federal economic assistance and at the same time to eliminate federal oversight of colleges and universities—no minor accomplishment!

Nothing draws American academics to the barricades more readily than threats of government interference with the internal affairs of a faculty, or attempts by public officials to limit what a faculty might think or teach so as to conform to political standards of orthodoxy. I have spent all my adult life in universities and have experienced a great deal, yet I continue to be amazed at the way in which even I can become stirred by struggles involving academic freedom.

For three years the University and I waged a bitter struggle with the Soviet Union in order to secure an exit visa for Vitaly Rubin, a Soviet professor of Chinese language and culture, permitting him to come to Columbia in order to take up an appointment as a visiting professor. The Soviet government refused on the ground that Rubin was the possessor of state secrets. We were outraged to see a fellow academic refused the privilege of a visiting appointment at Columbia because his government had subjected him to such a ridiculous political test. Then suddenly last June we were notified that Rubin was free. When he arrived at Columbia in September, I wept openly to think that our public struggle had not only restored Vitaly Rubin's academic freedom but had given new hope to countless unknown professors elsewhere in the world laboring under the cold scrutiny of oppressive governments.

When I was a graduate student at Harvard, I experienced the chill engendered by Senator Joseph McCarthy's merciless public handling of a fellow graduate student whose crime happened to be that he believed in Marxism. It was frightening to see close at hand the damage to one individual's life caused by an irresponsible public official interested largely in personal publicity.

Years later when I became Chancellor of the University of California, San Diego, I found myself jousting with the American Legion, the people of San Diego, the California legislature, and even the Governor, as they all sought to force an aging Marxist philosopher, Herbert Marcuse, from his post on our faculty on the ground that his teaching posed a danger to the community. The memory of Senator McCarthy made me very difficult to deal with on that occasion.

At Columbia in 1971 I experienced the threats and insults of the Puerto Rican Independence Party as they sought to prevent Arturo Morales Carrion, then a visiting professor, from teaching his classes on Morningside Heights because they disagreed with his version of Puerto Rican history. Professor Morales Carrion taught his classes protected by security guards, but he taught them. He was recently elected President of the University of Puerto Rico. We now laugh about the incident because it is his responsibility to defend unpopular professors just as I once had to defend him.

These academic freedom battles were easy because the offenses were gross. The imperative need to resist incursions on the freedom of a teacher in his classroom was perfectly clear to everyone. The heavy boot of oppression was evident and no great qualities of mind were required to detect it. One needed only the courage to resist. And of course over the years we have managed to win most of these struggles. American public officials and crusading groups now rarely attempt to interfere directly in faculty appointments or in classroom and laboratory activities. They have found the American academy to be both explosive and persistent when our academic freedom is challenged. Hence, most of our current efforts are directed at recalcitrant officials in the Soviet Union, in South America, and the Middle East.

Our dealings with the federal regulatory establishment pose a much more subtle set of questions. We are struggling not with political zealots but with bureaucrats, ordinary government employees carrying out what they perceive to be the requirements of public policy. In order to understand whether or not this bureaucratic environment offers a genuine threat to the freedom of the academic community, we need to look more closely at the nature of the regulatory process.

The topic of federal regulation is now almost a commonplace gripe among executives attempting to manage enterprises subject to federal regulatory control or dependent on federal resources. There is no doubt that such regulation has been accelerating with unusual rapidity during the last decade. During a recent session of the American Assembly at Columbia at St. Louis, the banker Leonall C. Anderson noted that the Federal Register, where agencies publish their regulations, had grown from 3,450 pages in 1937 to 35,591 pages in 1973, 45,422 pages in 1974 and 60,221 pages in 1975. Not long ago a business colleague pointed out to me that during the past year Congress enacted 402 laws, whereas in the same period 7,496 new federal regulations appeared. The sheer expansion of the regulatory framework attested to by these statistics is both astonishing and worrisome. What began at the turn of the century as a somewhat hesitant attempt to control public utilities and other monopolies, has become in our time a vast legal and bureaucratic apparatus for the public management of nearly all forms of commerce, universities included.

No experienced university president would think of criticizing a process that has liberated America's minorities, protected our consumers, and provided a standard of living for American workers unequalled elsewhere in the world. Clearly this socially oriented regulation of business has strengthened our society and buttressed it against revolutionary pressures inherent in the growth of industry. A well-established body of law implements the regulatory process. It has been studied and shaped by our law schools and political science departments over many years, but administrative law tends to be less well understood by faculty in other fields. Most of the rest of us tend to confine our interest in the law to the Constitution and the Bill of Rights. Clearly that is not a sensible way to deal with regulation. Constitutional doctrine is not entirely relevant to regulatory practice.

As I have suggested, federal regulation is hardly an unmixed blessing. Among other things it has sponsored a formidable bureaucracy in Washington and in countless other outreach offices. This bureaucracy supervises vast programs of salary and wage administration, personnel

management, equal opportunity regulations, pension rights and retirement benefits, health and safety regulations, expenditure audits, rules on
accounting, record keeping, and reporting of commercial transactions.
The list grows longer every day. Today any enterprise dependent on
federal funds must, as a matter of course, organize itself to furnish a
continuous flow of documentation to regulatory agencies in any of these
areas. The paper flow is truly stupendous. I would estimate that Columbia
University spends easily in excess of $1 million each year just in meeting
its various federal reporting obligations.

We must also be prepared to submit to the quasi-judicial judgments
of the regulators in disputes that are bound to arise from time to time in the
conduct of our activities. During the past five years, for example, we
have been in periodic difficulty with the Office of Civil Rights of the
Department of Health, Education, and Welfare on the adequacy of
Columbia's Affirmative Action Program. After much public trauma a
major submission was made by the University in 1972 and eventually
approved by HEW. Last June we received a notice from the agency
disallowing our 1972 Affirmative Action Program and calling for improved data based on recent changes in regulations as well as new
guidelines governing the submission of such plans. The letter of disal-
lowance was accompanied by a long and carefully drawn document citing
the deficiencies in our plan of 1972. This kind of problem no longer
throws us into panic. We have tried to organize ourselves to achieve
affirmative action compliance via the development of a modern personnel
administration under the direction of an experienced Vice President for
Personnel Management, but the effort has taken a great deal of money as
well as a great deal of our attention, and it is still by no means complete.

Recently we were sued by a group of thirty of our employees,
university maids, who charged that we had entered into an illegal labor
contract with a union because the distinction between janitors and maids
provided in the contract was a form of sex discrimination. On this ground
we were charged with various offenses and violations of the Equal Pay
Act. Actually, of course, we were not sued by the Columbia maids but by
two very able young lawyers who sought to represent the maids against
Columbia and thereby to project themselves into national prominence. I
was particularly privileged in this case to be sued personally by two
successive Secretaries of Labor who joined the maids in their action
against the University. In such matters one cannot make basic mistakes,
although I suppose I can always show my grandchildren the legal papers
in which Secretaries Brennan and Dunlop take dead aim at me.

Fortunately we won the case in court. We had originally sought to lay off the maids in order to reduce our building maintenance budget by $100,000. At the conclusion of the litigation we found that there had been no layoffs and the legal costs of our defense exceeded $50,000. The principal outcome of the suit was that our labor contract was modified to provide for "light cleaners" and "heavy cleaners" without distinction as to sex. I do not see it as a great intellectual or administrative advance but that seems to be the way in which the Department of Labor wants it, and our policy is to keep Columbia out of trouble. Evidently any administrative initiative that begins as an attempted expenditure reduction of $100,000 and ends with not only no savings but an added $50,000 in legal costs is hardly the way to administer a university in today's hazardous environment. I will not make that kind of mistake again!

Currently a large number of women employees, including many faculty, have filed a complaint with the Equal Employment Opportunity Commission charging the university with maintaining a discriminatory pension benefit plan. Women employees with the same salary history as male employees nevertheless receive smaller monthly retirement payments because their expected lifetime is greater according to insurance actuaries. The problem is that Columbia does not administer the retirement plan at all. We subscribe to the TIAA-CREF program which has been offering retirement benefits to university employees all over the country for years predicated on the principles now under challenge.

The action is directed against the university rather than TIAA-CREF because we could have elected to purchase added benefits at our own expense, assuring equal retirement payments to men and women. Our lawyers tell me that the Department of Labor treats the TIAA-CREF retirement plan as acceptable whereas EEOC does not. The university is thus caught in the middle of a regulatory dispute between two federal agencies.

Finally, I will mention that two years ago, a letter of complaint written by a graduate student to a local congressman led to an in-depth investigation of Columbia's Chemistry Department by OSHA, the federal Occupational Safety and Health Administration. What happened was that a senior member of the Department of Chemistry contracted cancer and died. In cleaning out his laboratory, the Department discovered a low level of residual radiation from several bottles of radioactive salts left on the laboratory bench. This was reported routinely to the University's radiation safety officer. There was no problem and there never was any danger, but a physics graduate student who had been sponsoring political

147

demonstrations against his Department claiming their involvement with the JASON group of the Department of Defense, found out about the incident and reported it to OSHA and also to his congressman. He warned of a radiation hazard in the Department of Chemistry at Columbia. The congressman did what he had to do in the circumstances—he passed the complaint off to OSHA. The next thing we knew we were being investigated. Of course, it all came to nothing, but for awhile we were very worried about and very busy with the formalities. In fact, the entire affair could have been settled by a phone call to a responsible administrator or the Chairman of the Chemistry Department, but things seldom work out that way in areas subject to federal regulation.

These few incidents will suffice to show the character of the regulatory process as it is currently being experienced in colleges and universities. The list might have been amplified one hundredfold but I have spared you a full accounting of audit disputes, IRS investigations, Labor Relations Board rulings, and other common problems. Each of the matters I have cited suggests a special difficulty to which we might address ourselves constructively as we consider what might be done to diminish the adversary character of regulation of universities. The basic issue of academic freedom seems to me to be closely related to the adversary approach taken by the regulators.

University people accustomed to thinking in terms of constitutional protections find the Federal Register to be quite a revelation. It is, as I have said, a set of published standards describing in legal language the manner in which federal agencies will interpret and enforce the titles of legislation that require supervisory activities by the government.

Typically such legislation will state a requirement in the form: "No funds appropriated under this act may be disbursed to educational institutions which as a matter of policy do such and such"—for example, "which bar military recruiting on campus." The entire requirement may be set down in no more than ten lines of legislation, but the pertinent regulation will then often develop the federal agency's interpretation of the meaning and scope of the legislation in several thousand lines of detailed controls. The now well-known rules governing Title IX of the higher education amendments of 1972 are a good example.

One of the major features of the regulatory process is that regulations are typically cast in such a way as to place the burden of proof of good behavior on the defendant institution, reversing the ordinary requirements of legal procedure. This means in effect that every silly claim is investigated seriously and a great deal of time must be devoted by both agencies and universities to the handling of frivolous and trivial complaints. As a consequence the regulatory agencies find themselves buried beneath a paper mountain of ultimately worthless allegations. The incident at Columbia in which a graduate student's complaint about a radiation hazard in the Department of Chemistry led to an OSHA investigation illustrates this difficulty nicely.

It is a situation which cries out for the concept of an administrative action threshold placing an important part of the burden of establishing the seriousness of a complaint on the complainant himself. Federal agencies should be prepared to exercise their power only in the most serious matters.

Presently there seems to be no effective review mechanism governing the correspondence between the regulatory language and the intentions of Congress in framing legislation. Thus, for example, we have recently seen the ridiculous circumstance in which the President of the United States was forced to intervene personally to deter HEW from prohibiting father-son affairs in school districts on the ground that they constitute a form of sex discrimination barred by Title IX. Certainly this is not what Congress intended. There is little doubt that congressional review of regulations would avoid their misapplication to cases having little or no merit and there is no doubt at all that such congressional review can be carried out.

Congresswoman Edith Green wrote a provision in Title IX of the Higher Education Amendments of 1972 requiring that the text of the proposed regulations be specifically reviewed and approved by the Congress. It was an extremely good idea. We cannot guarantee that Congressional review would control the growing numbers of questionable regulations, although I believe that to be a likely consequence if the review were carried out broadly. More important, in my judgment is the fact that congressional review and supervision of regulations would assure the correspondence between regulations and congressional intent. Thus we might put to rest one of the most frequently expressed complaints about the federal bureaucracy, namely, that it is a unique form of government by the nonelected.

One of the first tasks to which the new administration should address itself if it intends to limit the almost cancerous growth of regulatory initiatives by government, ought to be the maze of bureaucratic conflicts and overlapping jurisdictions that have developed around the important social legislation of the last two decades. The case of Columbia's women employees charging a discriminatory pension plan under guidelines provided by EEOC offers a good illustration of the problem. Columbia's administration relies on guidelines followed by the Department of Labor, and it is plain that the two federal agencies seem to be in basic disagreement on what constitutes sex discrimination in retirement benefits. A university cannot act in such circumstances without inviting attack from one aggrieved party or another. In this instance it is women faculty who filed the action, and it is EEOC that is pursuing it. If we or TIAA-CREF were to move to unisex mortality tables in determining our pension benefits, we would almost certainly invite suit by male faculty who could claim that they were being forced to pay for extra pension benefits for women. In this claim they would appear to be supported by the policy of the Department of Labor.

As we deal with the government on matters of affirmative action in employment and promotion, universities must work with the Office for Civil Rights of the Department of Health, Education, and Welfare and the Office of Contract Compliance of the Department of Labor. These two agencies appear to coordinate quite well but when compliance disputes develop, their staffs have been known to give different brands of advice, forcing universities to follow two different tracks of conflict resolution among the federal departments.

And of course, it is well known to this audience that an employee charging race or sex discrimination in employment has almost unlimited recourse to advocacy of his claim by a veritable maze of city, state, and federal agencies. Few of these agencies recognize the jurisdiction of the others. I know of at least one case at Columbia in which a terminated member of our research staff took his case to all four jurisdictions (including EEOC) during the last five years. It pains me even to think of the money expended in unnecessary legal costs attributable to the necessity of responding to the same charges in multiple jurisdictions.

I have sought in these remarks to address myself to what I take to be the real problems, and not to stress the familiar litany of complaints asserted by university people in response to the federal requirement for submission of goals and time tables for increasing the utilization of the so-called protected categories in university affirmative action programs. Columbia University was one of the first to come under federal scrutiny in 1971 because of the inadequacy of its federal reporting on matters of affirmative action. We said then that we were willing and anxious to meet federal regulations on affirmative action. The fact is that we believe in equal opportunity and we acknowledge the ugly history of discrimination in the United States. Of all the institutions of society, universities should be prepared to exercise leadership in the national commitment to break down race and sex discrimination in employment. Our problem was the inadequacy of our data analysis. We sought promptly to correct those deficiencies. Accordingly, Columbia was one of the first universities to achieve a federally approved affirmative action plan in 1972. There has never been any attempt by the government to treat the goals and time-tables we submitted as though they were contractual obligations. We have dealt with HEW in good faith and the agency has dealt with us in the same way. On the essentials of affirmative action we agree with the intent of the law and the regulations. We see such matters as issues of moral principle and we are committed to lead in breaking down all vestiges of discrimination in America.

The major problems associated with affirmative action plans seem to me not to be in the area of academic freedom but in the rigidity of the regulations themselves. In 1972 several of us made urgent representa-tions to the Secretary of HEW, that the use of principles identical to those applied earlier with business firms would wreak havoc among us. The regulations required that responsibility for employment policy be highly centralized in the personnel management function. Any university, as we all know, operates best on a loosely coupled collegial organization in which each academic unit is primarily responsible for supervising its own conduct. If the president of the university were to attempt to dictate enforcement of affirmative action in tenure actions by departments, it would be a certain prescription for campus warfare. Yet the regulations are written assuming such managerial control. We suggested to the Secretary of HEW that special guidelines should be developed after consultation with universities on the specifics of such problems. To the great credit of HEW this was done, but there was very little give and take between the universities and the HEW regulators in the development of the guidelines. Our goal of working closely with federal agencies in the development of practical and enforceable guidelines could not be real-ized. Of course, the agencies are faced with continuous political pres-sures from representatives of the so-called protected groups. Regulators cannot appear to be in league with universities or subject to the charge that they have entered into cozy agreements which have the effect of perpetual employment discrimination. This has always been the dilemma of regulatory bodies. The adversary polarities in society prevent regulatory agencies from working closely with the institutions they regulate. For instance, several of us have sought to point out the scientific inadequacies in the so-called utilization analyses in affirmative action plans. Members of protected categories currently employed are compared with expectations based upon random sampling from a pool or universe of qualified potential employees. Underrepresentation is treated as an inadequacy to be corrected by setting appropriate hiring goals. The problem with this argument is that it assigns spurious precision to the discrepancies which every student of probability theory knows to be subject to random fluctuations. There is a well-established body of knowledge for making valid estimates in the face of random fluctuation, but it does not appear in the mechanics of the regulations. They will therefore be viewed skeptically by knowledgeable university people, but any attempt to introduce probability theory at this point would no doubt lead to a political struggle on the ground that HEW was becoming soft on enforcement at universities. The regulators have their problems too.

We have urged HEW to develop a graded series of sanctions for dealing with noncompliance. At present affirmative action regulations are written at the maximum level of enforcement. You must comply or face a cut off of federal funds. Clearly a university with a faulty personnel management system or inadequate data reporting should not be placed in the same jeopardy as a state which creates publicly supported private academies in order to avoid desegregation. Yet the regulations provide no flexibility for dealing with minor inadequacies or limited noncompliance. One entrenched and misguided department chairman can bring an entire university under federal threat. It would be more reasonable and perhaps also more just if federal regulators could direct their pressures pointedly at the malingerers.

Certainly it is the case that the regulatory code makes the power of federal agencies very great in relation to the recipients of federal funds. The only prudent course for institutions dependent upon federal funds is to attempt to comply with all applicable regulations and stay out of trouble with the government. This, however, implies a parallel obligation on the part of government to review and supervise its regulatory code in order to insure that it accords fully with the intentions of Congress.

Similarly the government must act to minimize the regulatory burden by eliminating jurisdictional and policy ambiguities among federal agencies in the enforcement of regulations.

Finally, the government, having established a public policy in the form of laws we are all obliged to accept, must make a determined nonadversary effort to work closely with regulated institutions in order to insure that the mechanisms of regulation are reasonable, just, and flexible.

A recipient of federal funds who feels himself mishandled by a regulatory agency can always take his complaint to court. But this involves months and sometimes years of litigation. Columbia's dispute with its maids illustrates this dilemma. It is cold comfort to discover at this end of a long court case that you have won your point at the expense of very heavy legal fees. Few people prefer to go broke in a just cause. Such disputes never should be in court. They should be brought to a negotiated peace in some alternative form of dispute settlement matched to the subtlety of the issues involved.

Last spring the Chief Justice of the United States appeared before a judicial conference in St. Paul honoring the 75th Anniversary of Roscoe Pound's famous 1906 address to the Bar Association on "The Causes of Popular Dissatisfaction with the Administration of Justice." He observed that the federal courts were heavily overburdened, and much too taken up with procedural and jurisdictional disputes. He urged the removal from the adversary courtroom process of a variety of personal disputes: divorce, child custody, medical negligence, probate among others, in the hope of creating a more effective and a more responsible legal system.

It saddens me to observe that the United States has drifted into an unparalleled growth of adversary struggle. The emerging social order appears to be one in which policy at all levels is forged out of the struggle of narrowly based constituency groups at war with one another, each pressing for its own special interests. One aspect of this struggle is the remarkable recent growth of federal initiatives in regulation. I believe it to reflect activist political philosophy that seeks desirable social goals by direct intervention into the operation of society's institutions, rather than by the patient application of social incentives. The impact has been stunning, and the protests over government by a bureaucratic elite rather than by elected representatives appear to be growing. Presidential candidates now campaign vigorously against the bureaucracy, but no President has been able to mold it to his policy or to limit its growth.

It is time to pay some attention to this problem. Federal regulation, if carried out fairly and responsibly and if aimed at genuine abuses, is a clear necessity in a free society. Twenty years of experience with Amer-

A Response to
President McGill

Allan Bloom
University of Toronto

My first reaction to President McGill's presentation was that one must be something of a madman to undertake the governance of a university in our time when a university president must appeal to so many contradictory and strident inconstituencies that it is almost impossible that he be coherent, let alone that he be able to pay attention to the primary business of a university, which is education. He has my fullest sympathies, but I also must begin by saying that I belong to one of the difficult constituencies.

What I found unsettling in this paper is that President McGill does not say anything about what distinguishes a university from other organizations which do business with the government. He merely assures us that the university is just fine—doing what it ought to do better than ever, turning out Nobel Prizes as Swift turns out sausages—and that Columbia at least has a President who will defend academic freedom, standing on the barricades to protect the university from a (rather unlikely) unfriendly incursion of the type familiar during the McCarthy era. Now I would have to insist that the university is not all right—that it is in very poor condition; that there are very present threats to the academy which are not of the old kind, and that the lack of definition of what we are about manifest in this paper is not a result of President McGill's failings—or those of his paper—but reflects the fact that the university is in disarray, has lost its sense of purpose, a loss partly due to the relations with the government which have grown up during these last years. There can hardly be threats to the integrity of an institution which has no character; we have no standard by which to judge what is an encroachment. Or, in other words, the greatest threat to the university is the university's loss of purpose, for it does not know what to resist nor can it demand respect from society for the respectable things which it represents. In our current situation those of us who wish to resist the embraces or threats of government are reduced to the *noli me tangere* bitchiness of a virgin in a liberated age when the value of what she is protecting has lost its evidence. The posture does not lack nobility, but better grounds for it are needed.

I hope I will be forgiven the recitation of a few banalities which, for all their banal character, nonetheless are in need of constant repetition. I fear that they will put me in the camp that President McGill thinks to be intemperate: the university can claim a right to special consideration and special status—to academic freedom as opposed to citizen freedom, to exemption from the regulation to which all other institutions are subject, to a right of self-government or autonomy—only to the extent that it is genuinely dedicated to the knowledge of the permanent concerns of man as man, not to the fragments of man that we find in this time in this place, concerns which every decent society must respect and which its particular needs are likely to cause it to forget. Whatever is directed to public utility—even if it be so important as a cure for cancer or the weapon which might ensure our survival—can legitimately be regulated by the society which it serves. Only the consideration of the things which society must serve, as opposed to those which serve it, belongs to the sacred sphere. The pursuit of truth is not a sufficient definition of the university's goal; General Electric and Sharpe & Dohme are interested in truth too. It must be pursuit of the important truth, the quest for knowledge of the first causes of things, of God, of the nature of man and his duties, of the good life. Only those disciplines whose primary goal is the clarification of these questions belong to the core of the university; it can tolerate peripheral disciplines which feed off of it, but it cannot tolerate the periphery becoming the center. And this is what has happened, in part due to the federal money which has poured into the university since Sputnik. The university today has no visage. Liberal education has no meaning. University education can now be defined only as what is given in a university—a university is a university is a university. The studies which inspire a liberal education are ever less weighty in the university, and their quality is ever thinner. The tradition which kept the perennial questions before us has lost its authority and is fading. Students can hardly conceive that the university years could be devoted to learning how to reflect on the good life. We now have a generation of students which hardly reads at all, let alone reads important books. And the university does not encourage them either to identify, study or love important books. Surely liberal education and what it means is not a primary concern of the administrators who are—in general—not liberally educated men themselves. If the university ought to encourage and protect studies and men which civil society does not characteristically encourage and protect, then it is not now doing its job.

The ideal of the university should be the theoretical life—a life always threatened by society's need for self-deception. If Toqueville is right, the theoretical life is most of all threatened in democracy—a regime particularly attentive to, nay, founded on, men's desire for well-being, hence more dedicated to utility, theory's enemy, than any other regime. Men in democratic society find it hard even to recognize the motives of a man like Pascal, let alone emulate them. Archimedes so despised his own great engineering exploits that he wanted all traces of them destroyed. Such is the theoretical man. If such men and such thought are essential to the fullness of man and of human life, the university's task in a democracy is especially difficult, although it is in itself clear what that task should be.

Again, Toqueville distinguishes two forms of oppression—hard tyranny and soft tyranny, the former direct, external, using force, imprisoning and killing, but causing only fear, not inner acquiescence; the latter, unbending the springs of the mind's action by taking away all hope of resistance, giving the appearance of morality to what oppresses it, a tyranny operating by public opinion, gradually uprooting all grounds of principled opposition and all sources of hostile inspiration, one which takes away freedom by suppressing awareness of the alternatives to it, by narrowing the horizon instead of trying to get men to stop looking. It is this latter tyranny which is more endemic to democracy; we are rather good at handling the former kind: McCarthyism was of that variety and such are the threats about which President McGill spoke. But we are not so good at dealing with the soft tyranny: it comes from within; it is disguised in principles we think we should favor; its proponents are people like us. This is the threat we are now facing. We have had in the course of this conference two examples of the way in which this form of oppression operates. Yesterday Dr. Tollett suggested that anyone who raises questions or doubts about affirmative action is a racist. This was a mode of intimidation, and an attempt to limit free reflection and discussion. Several of us reacted by trying to persuade Dr. Tollett that we are not racist. The intimidation worked. Then we had the edifying experience of seeing a young bureaucrat, Mr. Gerry, whose office has kept the universities in fear and trembling these last years, sermonizing us, using as his text John Rawl's book on justice.* A superficial interpretation of a superficial book about justice seems now to be canonic for government of universities. Universities used to be places where various profound notions about justice were studied and reflected on. Mr. Gerry apparently had no idea that his views are questionable and that the imposition of them on the universities would be destructive of the most important function of the university. If we combine the positions presented by Tollett and Gerry, we will see that fear and ignorance concerning the fundamental questions is the result of the current atmosphere.

I am, therefore, profoundly in disagreement with President McGill on affirmative action—which in its source, its intention and its effect belongs to the increased pressure to intellectual conformity which has been at work in the last twelve years, the Berkeley wave, the successor of the Sputnik wave. I gather President McGill would like to consign this discussion to "the familiar litany" as opposed to "the real problems," not something we need to discuss—it has been discussed so endlessly and it arouses so many passions. His reasoning is as follows: we are all against discrimination; affirmative action fights discrimination; therefore we should all be for affirmative action and get on with our business. It is our moral duty. The university should fight discrimination; in his paper this is the only statement of a common purpose for the university which I could discover. It should be pointed out that moral commitments can be the most effective way of undermining the good conscience of open-minded reflection and that the university should be careful about making moral commitments other than those immediately connected with its end. They are the disguise in which popular prejudice can enter our sanctum.

Mr. Gerry spoke extemporaneously and submitted no manuscript for publication.—*Editor*

The historical background of academic freedom is the struggle of the men of the enlightenment to shield philosophy and science from religious intolerance. That was a great threat to our understanding of things and that threat has been largely dissipated. There are threats characteristic to every regime, and it is against them that we must be particularly vigilant, which is difficult since we are not likely to identify them, and opinion refuses to recognize them. Oppressive oligarchies are likely to fear democracy, and democracies truly threatened by mob rule are likely to suspect an aristocratic party. To return to my beloved Tocqueville, the dominant, unquestionable principle of modern democracy is equality. If we are to be intellectually free we must think about it, even call it into question, certainly examine its meaning, its reasonable applications, its strengths and weaknesses. But precisely that is what is difficult: such investigation arouses indignation which feeds the priests and vigilantes of democracy, and since we in the university are good democrats, it gives us a bad conscience. The university rebellions of the 60s were an attempt to impose a radical levelling egalitarianism on the university and force it, the most independent of institutions, into the system of public opinion and transform it into an instrument of social change. And the fact that the participants in those rebellions marched under the colors of the principle to which we all adhere is why we responded to it relatively poorly as opposed to our response to McCarthyism. Now affirmative action is but the bureaucratization of the academic pathos of the 60s, somewhat as the Olympian gods were, as some ancient writers indicate, but dead barbarian tyrants, who after having committed atrocities like castrating their fathers, migrated to heaven to persecute mankind from there. The thought behind affirmative action originated in universities; and the view that universities are nothing but microcosms of a larger prejudiced society was first revealed in that period. Just as a charge of heresy was a potent weapon in the hands of fanatics, hypocrites and the ignorant, so are the equivalent charges of racism, sexism, and elitism. It is questionable whether universities should not, at least in some sense, be discriminating; they certainly should preserve the powers of discrimination and the awareness of just distinctions among men and things. It is, moreover, a long way from identifying the unjust forms of discrimination to agreeing that affirmative action either recognizes them or is the proper social policy for righting the wrong; and the distance is even greater between the latter assertion and the notion that it should be applied to

159

universities or that there has in recent times been serious discrimination within the universities. Without developing this theme further, the price we pay in intellectual timidity for accepting this nonsense is immense. The whole business constitutes a new kind of intimidation and regulation, a breach of our principle that intellectual merit is the only thing we consider, and that only we are the appropriate judges of it. It is a continuous affront to the universities.

The special character of our current situation was brought to my mind by President McGill's referring to his defense of an old Marxist against a nasty local reaction in San Diego. At about that time this old Marxist joined in the authorship of a book that attacked the very principle of academic freedom, a book that is not uninfluential in universities. This was really something new. There were in the past professors in whose heart there was no real love of academic freedom, but they always paid lip service to it or engaged in casuistries which implied its acceptance. But now in the name of the movement, in the name of commitment, it became possible to reject academic freedom. This aging Marxist saw that the conviction is no longer there and he could get away with it. Marcuse is original in nothing, but this he did not get from Marx. Here he is but the child of the greatest philosophical intellect of this century, who in 1933 told a German university that it must commit itself to the National Socialist movement; in fact that it was no longer a decision to be made because "the youngest part of the nation has already decided." The exhortation was not an accident due to political innocence or moral vice, but a conclusion of his meditation on science and reason altogether. His thought, domesticated and made compatible with the left, is more and more our thought—manifest for example in the modish critique of objectivity. The doubt about the possibility or desirability of science or knowledge of the good or values undermines the conviction which is the heart of the university's enterprise. A pincers attack—constituted by German philosophy and American egalitarianism—is besieging the universities. This attack is making the university's public position untenable. On the one hand nihilistic doubt; on the other hand assurance that we are the first to know what justice is.

President McGill ends with a lament about the cancerous growth of adversary relations in our society. I could not agree with him more. But again its source is in large measure in the universities—both in the view of man and his relation to his fellows fostered by much of contemporary social science and philosophy, and in the university's failure to provide a living model of a community based on a true common interest and on motives other than gain or glory, which separate men. Such a model is the true service a university can render to a society and is a source of humanizing inspiration. The leaders of universities must look to restoration of the university in this sense as their primary goal and then tell the government what they need and what the government should not ask of them.

Opening the Academic Gates

George W. Bonham
Editor-in-Chief, Change Magazine

As this UCRA symposium has so amply demonstrated, it has grown increasingly difficult to keep one's usual temperance in talking about the federal influence over higher education. As the most recent presidential campaign made so clear, both American liberals and conservatives now consider governmental concentration excessive and arbitrary, and this new if slightly curious coalition holds no less true in academic life.

My own convictions on the matter, not to speak of sympathies, lie much closer to that of President McGill than Professor Allan Bloom. Surely, in terms of what now matters in the academy, there must be equal respect for the service of pragmatism as well as for human ideals. We all wish for a more perfect society, but Dr. McGill must daily deal with its imperfections, while Professor Bloom has the enviable luxury of cerebrating about such deficiencies without jeopardizing the functions of his job.

Some of our present arguments over government interference, I submit, are best left on grounds that have less to do with principle than with making the kinds of sociopolitical arrangements which will more likely tend to the social priorities of this society. How to do this without needlessly treading on the rights and dignities of its citizens and its institutions? This is the nub of the issue. It would be hard to find in the Constitution any provisions which would warrant much of the federal oversight of American institutions, academic or otherwise, the exception surely being the concept of equality under the law. But even here, there exists no legal basis for insisting on numerical goals. The fact of the matter is that the federal government now spends $15 billion a year on and in higher education. Somehow, these expenditures must and should be reasonably accounted for. Still, as John Gardner observes, academics used to expect the government to put the money "on the stump," and no questions asked. Now there is moss on the stump, and the temptation is to say, in Kingman Brewster's words, "now that I have bought the button, I have a right to design the coat."

As President McGill reports, Columbia University next year expects to receive about $95 million from various governments. This is well over a third of his total budget. He, and the many other college and university presidents like him, will face his share of justified governmental requests, as well as his share of inanities and sheer stupidities, which, I regret to say, seem to be part and parcel of modern life. The trick is to survive, sustaining the university's essential principles of its domain, and ameliorating the excesses of government and litigation to the extent these efforts are felt to be tolerable and affordable.

Unfortunately, unlike business corporations, academic institutions cannot pass on the survival costs of litigation and bureaucracy. This is where the insistence on principle must invariably be weighed against the fiscal investments in such principles as a function of rising tuition costs. Were it not for the particular cost quandaries of modern nonprofit institutions, I would find it hard to make a distinction between the institutional rights and responsibilities of a university and that of any other major American institution. Some academics still prefer to view the university as a special and unique preserve of Western culture. But the basic social functions of the universities have changed, as well as their external social environment. The rights of faculty are more likely to be preserved these days through the mechanisms of the law than through tenure. There is no question in my mind that new social contracts in terms of the rights and protection of citizens, as developed by our elected officials, should apply to academic institutions as clearly as to AT&T and the Federal Trade Commission. To argue that the universities continue to be some special sanctuary is also to argue for the special privileges once accorded to the academic guild. I doubt that such special treatment would any longer be tolerated by the majority of Americans.

As part of a long editorial last year on "Government and Academic Vitality," I became much concerned about the demonstrable arbitrariness of certain government bureaus, more egregious perhaps at the state than at the federal level. I was also struck by what seemed a growing mindlessness among academics to turn antibureaucratic and anti-Washington, when, only a decade before, these very same people had importuned Washington to act and intervene in behalf of a new "Great" or "Fair" Society. The academics' laments were more characteristic of our most vocal free enterprisers than of thoughtful and analytic intellectuals, whose first concerns, one assumed, were social and not private advancement.

Few men and women in academic life would in fact argue with the social intent of present-day legislation, but only with the manner in which the intent of that legislation is carried out. This difficulty of excessive zeal, one needs no reminding, is now an *American* problem, not only an academic one. The complaints of academics in this sphere are no more or less justified than those of city and local governments dealing with Washington, of school districts or of business corporations or voluntary hospitals. This ought not to make anybody feel better, but it is a part of the larger American anatomy which needs to be dealt with, and dealt with by the public at large.

With very few exceptions, academic institutions could not survive without the strong presence and support of federal, state, and local governments. In a recent publication on federal government reorganization, the Carnegie Council on Policy Studies in Higher Education shows eleven pages of tiny-type listings of government agencies which now carry on some form of education programs. If the federal support of higher education were to be divided among every student now attending a college or university, the stipend would come to $1,500 each, or nearly $24,000 for each college faculty member. It is strange, after all these years of enormous growth of the higher education enterprise, triggered in large part by federal and state governments, that faculty on the whole still know and care so little about the political consequences of this growth, and its parentage.

The university administrator is damned if he brings in the money ("he's just a moneyman anyway") and damned if he doesn't. He is a philistine if he addresses the local banker's club, and a carpetbagger for his frequent flights to Washington. Only rarely does he seem to uphold the high principles of truth and honor and uncompromising scholarship, which may make an academic leader worthy of faculty support. These circumstances of academic schisms are somewhat overstated here, but they illustrate how poorly equipped most academic institutions are in dealing with the issue of governmental incursions in a fastidious and, one hopes, somewhat unified manner. One must seek alliances in these circumstances, and argue out such matters with thought and discretion. One needs not be reminded how difficult it is to contain and reduce bureaucratic enterprises, in opposition to creating new ones.

Against my better judgment, I shall finish these remarks on one aspect of affirmative action and the governmental interest in this matter. One slips here almost instantly into quicksand, for almost everything about this subject can be readily misunderstood and misinterpreted. To equalize life opportunities for all human beings is above all a matter of the heart and mind. Only later does it become a matter of the law and culture and history. I cannot agree with Kenneth Tollett that to be against affirmative action is necessarily to be a racist. As Andrew Young has so well demonstrated, the word has lost much of its past precision, and probably ought to be used less and not more. One can be against affirmative action (and goals, if you will) and believe in the absolutism of demonstrated merit, whatever one happens to measure. I think this is an arguable position, and one ought to be able to do so without having the baggage of racism thrust on one's back.

I choose to make the point on less eclectic grounds. I believe that it is absolutely necessary to bring American blacks into the mainstream with as much dispatch, and haste, as this is possible. It has been long enough. If selection to academic posts and entry into undergraduate and graduate schools were so scientific and numerically pure as is often made out, a case for sustaining such standards could possibly be made. But no such scientific measure does indeed exist, nor does the academic profession have a particularly good record for providing equal access and equal opportunities. The classic academic predilection against women need not be recited here, nor the dominance of Anglo-Saxon tonalities on most American campuses. As a majority American, I find it far easier to live with preferential admission goals than will those black persons who must come in under those special programs, knowing full well that they have not quite made it under their own steam. Like the symposium speakers, I would have preferred not to see the *Bakke* case come to the court at this time. But now that it is there, I would hope that heart and mind will be triumphant, and not the cold, if principled, calculations of the pedants. It is a false principle that they are pursuing. Opening the academic gates will not be the end of Athens, and it could significantly contribute to the healing between the races.

THE UNIVERSITY AND STATE: CLAIMS AND EXPECTATIONS

The Limits of Governmental Regulation

Robert H. Bork
former U.S. Solicitor General

It is instructive that colleges and universities have recently become so concerned about the intrusion of the federal government into what they had thought until lately were their private concerns. The title given this afternoon's session—"The University and the State: Claims and Expectations"—not only shows that we are seeking to define the proper role of the federal government with respect to higher education but suggests that we do so because we sense that the state has already seriously overstepped the area of its legitimate concern and that much worse is in prospect. I think both the diagnosis and the prognosis are quite correct.

What is not correct, and what I have heard in the pronouncements of university presidents and perhaps read in some of the papers presented here, is the thought that the federal government makes a unique kind of error when it undertakes to regulate universities, or that universities are so different and more subtly complex than other institutions that regulation is bound to be uniquely destructive when applied to them. None of these things is true. What we are witnessing is a more general political phenomenon in which government regulation expands to control the decisional processes of all institutions in the private sector, and the effects of overregulation are quite as pernicious for other private institutions and, indeed, for state and local government.

The peril of our time, and of the time that stretches ten or twenty or thirty years ahead of us, is that expressed by Walter Bagehot: "The characteristic danger of great nations, like the Romans and the English, which have a long history of continuous creation, is that they may at last fail from not comprehending the great institutions which they have created."

We seem to be courting that danger. It is not merely that we have failed fully to comprehend the great private institutions of our society— universities, corporations, the free market, and the like—but that we have not understood with any degree of sophistication the limits of government and the inherent and inescapable nature of bureaucratic regulation. The dominant strains of opinion at the moment appear to be egalitarian and legalistic, joined, rather ominously, to a simplistic view of the society and its possiblities for improvement. The claims and expectations of government with respect to all institutions, of which universities are merely a subset, grow out of this moralism and the belief that law can effectively guarantee fairness in every relationship.

These trends in ideas about society and government tend to produce what Robert Nisbet calls the twilight of authority, which is a decline in the authority and autonomy of institutions. It is customary, almost obligatory in Washington, to lay the decline of governmental institutions to Watergate or Vietnam, but it clearly began before either of those events had any substantial impact upon public opinion, and those occurrences would account for the unpopularity of only a few major institutions. But the phenomenon is far more widespread. It is as though over the past few years the American institutional landscape has been flattened. The most cursory look around shows that. Have the universities gained or lost in authority and autonomy in the last decade? Have the major corporations gained or lost? Have political parties gained or lost? The answer is clear in every case: they have lost authority, autonomy, prestige, and power, they have done so precipitously, and the trend promises to continue.

Authority is deeply resented in any form, and the universities, long perceived as elitist and authoritarian establishments, are natural targets for those riding a new surge of egalitarianism and populism. Not long ago—when most of us were students, in fact—the university turbulence and destruction of both property and academic standards of performance that we saw during the late 1960s would have been unthinkable. And though the worst of those times are over, it is clear that the university communities have not by any means completely restored their standards, that their morale has been damaged, perhaps permanently, and that some continue to be unable to respond with authority to fresh disruptions, particularly if they come from the left. Indeed, the autonomy and self-governing capacities of universities are now so little thought of that not only legislatures and federal agencies but courts are willing as never before in our history to scrutinize every exercise of discretion. One incessantly sued college president reports that his mother now refers to him as "my son, the defendant."

That this is occurring is undeniable. That it is a general movement affecting all institutions seems equally clear. What may not be evident is why universities in particular have proved so vulnerable and why they have not resisted and do not resist more vigorously and effectively. Should they continue to fail to do so, not only the universities but all of society will be the losers. There was a time, it should be remembered, when it was believed that safety from a powerful state at the service of mass opinion lay in the strength of intermediate institutions, like corporations and universities, that could be relied upon to resist the intrusion of the state. Everybody is quoting Tocqueville these days, and I would refrain were he not so pertinent, even though in this context he also appears so mistaken.

Aristocratic countries, he said, abound in powerful individuals who cannot easily be oppressed and "such persons restrain a government within general habits of moderation and reserve." Democracies contain no such persons, but their role, Tocqueville thought, may be assumed by great private corporations and associations, each of which "is a powerful and enlightened member of the community, which cannot be disposed of at pleasure or oppressed without remonstrance, and which, by defending its own rights against the encroachments of the government, saves the common liberties of the country."

In our time the great private corporations and associations have not played the role assigned them. The question why they have not is well beyond my topic, but it may be worth examining briefly some of the specific reasons why universities have proved both docile and vulnerable to political and bureaucratic encroachments.

The first reason, of course, is simply that as never before higher education is dependent upon federal money. That is true in part because of the higher costs government has forced upon the universities, but it would be true in any event because of higher costs and the inability of higher education to take advantage of management techniques and mechanization that are available to private industry. With federal money there inevitably come attempts at federal control. That is a firm rule of government, and no one need not be shocked by it.

But it would be possible for universities to rally more effective political opposition to control, at least to minimize and contain it, had they not damaged their own images so badly in the recent past. While university spokesmen talk of the indispensable role of the university as the base for disinterested scholarship and impartial attempts to understand our world, the universities sometimes behave in ways that belie the image. I would not be misunderstood. Much disinterested and brilliant scholarship takes place in universities. But much takes place that is by no definition disinterested, brilliant, or scholarly, and those activities frequently occur in public and make the newspapers. So it is that when our spokesmen talk of the scholarly ideal, the public thinks it knows better.

It is, moreover, apparent to everyone that university faculties—particularly in the social sciences, humanities, and in the professional schools having relation to public policy—are, to greater or lesser degree, politicized. The causes of the phenomenon are no doubt quite complex, but the fact remains that the faculties of many of our most prestigious universities are perceived and, worse, are perceived correctly, as well to the left of the national political spectrum. It is also apparent that political conclusions are often presented dogmatically and as though they were the result of scholarship, even when it is plain that they are not. Universities are thus seen not entirely as bases of dispassionate analysis but also in large measure as inculcators of political values, and political values of one type. Institutions so perceived are obviously in much poorer position to resist governmental regulation on the ground that their scholarly independence must not be compromised.

Universities also did incalculable damage to their public reputations by their reactions to assaults during the time of student turmoil. Faculties and administrations frequently seemed to compete to see which could give in to irrational and anti-intellectual demands more rapidly. The message to the public was that the universities themselves were not really serious about the values of intellectual excellence and independence they professed. Observe the popularity of S. I. Hayakawa for standing against disruptions and imagine what were the feelings of the public about those university presidents and faculties who chose to run with the student radicals and to match their rhetoric as a mode of appeasement. The opinions formed then persist.

There is, besides, a pleasure which is nonetheless real, even if perverse, in seeing elitist institutions scream when the remedies they have prescribed for others are applied to them. I don't know how many times I have heard that sentiment expressed in government. But it is certainly true that the academic branch of the intellectual community has strongly supported political control of the other institutions of our society, programs of affirmative action that turned out to be quotas, governmental direction of institutional purposes, and so forth. The academic world, speaking generally, has been actively hostile to the claims of other nongovernmental institutions to autonomy in the name of greater efficiency that benefits society. The result is not only that many today take pleasure in the plight of academics forced to swallow their own medicine but also that the public philosophy of dispersed authority has been undermined and ridiculed by intellectuals who now invoke it for their own benefit. It should not come as a surprise if that invocation is met with a smile.

Once all the resources and institutions of a society are seen as assets to be used by government to satisfy politically defined wants, there is no particular reason why government should not decide it wants short-run scientific results for immediate application rather than basic research; and there is no particular reason why government should not use its grant money to influence curricula so that the large numbers of students the universities and colleges now take may find "education" more entertaining and less arduous. We may argue the wisdom of each of these political wants separately, but we have lost, in large measure through our own efforts, the indispensable presumption that the decision maker should be the institution concerned rather than the government.

I make these points not because I take a gloomy pleasure in saying that the universities asked for it, though it is in some measure true that I do and they did, but because I think the universities' fate inseparable from that of the rest of society. It is simply unreasonable to suppose that general political and social trends will affect every institution other than the university. We will certainly share a common fate.

This is not a counsel to despair, or at least it is not intended as such. Nor is it a counsel to abstain from all but the largest political efforts. General movements are influenced by innumerable small victories and losses over details. There is, therefore, every reason for educators to make their case publicly, to use such political influence as they can muster over the details of political regulation, and to try to educate the president, the Congress, the courts, and, perhaps most importantly, the federal bureaucracy about the ways in which universities work and the harm that is done to them as organisms by well-intentioned efforts to make them perform in ways that are perceived as fairer.

Since it is true that government does not understand universities or the mode of abstract intellectual endeavor, it is important that universities make an effort to understand the nature of bureaucratic government. Bureaucrats are as well-intentioned a group as I have ever seen, but they move according to bureaucratic imperatives of which they are not even aware. We tend to create a new bureaucracy for every principle we wish to enforce. That means every such organization has one principle: health; saftey; clean environment; racial equality; sexual equality; whatever. No single principle is fit to live with. At some point every principle becomes too expensive in terms of other values to be pushed further. But most of us would recognize the stopping point much sooner than would an equally intelligent person whose career is defined entirely by the single principle, and so bureaucracies thrust on past the balance point to produce results that are disastrous to institutions and processes that depend upon a balance of principles.

Bureaucracies produce more laws than Congress does. Their ability to do so is considered their virtue, for we now regulate so many details of a complex society that our elected officials cannot begin to cope with the decisions that must be made. The matters are now so complex that congressional oversight is defeated, and inded the effort to follow the bureaucracy is now so far beyond the politicians' capacities that Congress has created enormous staff bureaucracies of its own to watch the other bureaucracies. The result is not congressional oversight but bureaucratic oversight. And each bureaucracy is specialized by principle. It is not very surprising, then, that regulations are imposed upon the society which, taken one by one as legislative proposals, would not have the slightest chance of enactment by Congress or of escaping a veto by the president.

These considerations suggest to me that universities cannot simply rely upon educating the bureaucracies; they must, if they wish not merely to survive but to survive as vital and autonomous intellectual centers, make the case against any additional regulation and seek to roll back much that now exists.

The first and foremost expectation of government with respect to universities, the expectation that should override all others, is that they continue as independent institutions. Growing regulation is incompatible with that expectation and the public case can surely be made by the most articulate group in our society.

It would help if the universities were publicly more assertive. There is in much of the rhetoric coming from university leaders today a defensive note with an unattractive whining undertone, partly, one supposes, because they are aware that they seek an autonomy not granted to others and which many of them have vigorously opposed granting to others. If the society does not understand higher education and research and their needs, it is also true that universities have too little troubled to understand other institutions and their needs. Universities and higher education, for example, are not more complex than corporations and the economic marketplace, and the case against the politicization of the former is really no stronger than the case against the politicization of the latter.

The difficulty is that when we discuss the claims and expectations of government with respect to higher education, we are bound to take account of the political-intellectual atmosphere in which government frames those claims and expectations. It is demonstrable that government has come to believe in its own superior competence and morality and has, as a consequence, undertaken controls that have made economic markets and social processes work less well than they otherwise would. Why should anyone expect that government would suddenly become more modest about its righteousness and abilities when it turned to higher education? That suggests to me that the fate of the universities ultimately depends upon whether the large intellectual class they house comes to understand the institutions of our society or continues to press for statist, central control in all areas but their own.

*   *   *

POSTSCRIPT: The case may be hopeless. In the discussion that followed this and the other talks, a prominent educator-administrator said government had to understand that university faculties were selected on the principle of excellence and that this principle distinguished professors from garbage collectors, whose selection, one gathered, may properly be governed on grounds other than excellence. I was struck not only by the persistence of the claim to university uniqueness but to the apparent use of garbage collection as a metaphor for the activities of the rest of society.

Governments and Universities

Edward Shils
University of Chicago

The activities of the human race may be seen as a triangle. At one angle are those devoted to keeping the physiological organism in being through the gratification of the practical needs of food, shelter, clothing, move-ment, etc. They do this through the collection and cultivation of plants, the mining of minerals, the hunting and catching of wild and edible creatures, the husbanding of domesticated ones for food, traction, the use of animal skins and spun and woven fibers, etc. These activities are susceptible to specialized performance and to coordination into a division of the labor that serves the gratification of these practical needs, although often in a very roundabout manner. At the second angle are those activities addressed to the understanding and interpretation of the vicis-situdes and enigmas of man's existence on the earth and in the cosmos, perceiving and assessing the principles and powers that govern human actions and achievements, individual and collective. The activities that attempt to find the meaning and the laws of existence, in large and in small, that attempt to make sense of the world and men and their history are also organized into elaborate institutional forms that are capable of specialization of performance and coherence through a division of labor with unity, and they are sustained by deep and subtle traditions. The third angle subsumes those collectivities that permit and preside over the gratification of physiological, cognitive, and spiritual necessities, that maintain and increase order by regulating conflicts and enunciating rules. These include families, villages, tribes, municipalities, nations, and states.

Governments—legislators, civil servants, judges—universities, churches, the ownership of land, buildings, and machines, the learned professions, and the military together form the center of society, which is a loose agglomeration; they are attended to and deferred to; they preoccupy minds and attract aspirations; they exercise authority and play a dominant part in the allocation of resources and rewards.

The agglomeration of the constituent parts of the center is never wholly harmonious or in an easily stable equilibrium. Each of the constituent elements has its own pattern of values elaborated through long tradition and nurtured within specialized institutions. These traditions are not mutually exclusive of each other in their ends. These traditions contain ends that, although compatible and even mutually affirmative in particular points and on occasion, are not identical. Within the center, the various constituents may be in relationships of superordination and subordination, of consensus, compromise, and conflict.

Governments and churches have coexisted in changing relationships with each other for many centuries. Between theocracy at one rare extreme and real caesaropapism at the other no less rare extreme, with the earthly ruler being effectively and not just nominally the head of the state-religion, there are many intermediate points. At present, the relationship between these two central institutions in most liberal Western societies is the far-reaching factual separation of church and state. The state does not intervene into the internal government of churches, it does not attempt to regulate their doctrines, it does not subsidize them, nor does it demand particular services from them. The churches are almost as separate from the state as they could be. They do not claim that the government should use its powers to require that all members of the society subscribe to their particular religious belief; they acknowledge the right of the government to conduct educational and eleemosynary institutions without their own participation. It is true that a complete separation is not attained in any country: the remnants of caesaropapism remain, for instance, in Germany and the United Kingdom; the property of churches is exempt from taxes on real property: in the United States monetary contributions to churches—as well as to educational and charitable institutions—are treated by government as permissible deductions from taxable income. Furthermore, churches are not interested only in the next world. They have always attempted to give ethical guidance to the earthly conduct of their own members, and they have almost always judged the conduct of their earthly rulers. As the preoccupation of the churches increasingly embraced the affairs of this world, the churches became assessors of the moral condition of society, and this too forced them into contact, often censorious, with the government of their societies.

A complete separation of church and state is impossible; so is a complete and harmonious fusion. So too is the complete and harmonious subordination of the church to the state. The same limits obtain for the other institutions of the center. As long as each has its own sphere of activity, and as long as each cherishes its own ends and values, complete harmony between them seems out of the question. Yet they exist in the same society; they are parts, however different from each other, of the same center of that society. They are bound to each other by all sorts of ties of mutual dependence. Nonetheless, despite all these traditional and inevitable interdependencies, liberal Western societies in the latter part of the last century and the first half of the present century have tried to establish a very considerable degree of pluralism in the relations of the different sectors of the center.

From positions of subordination or dominion, the churches were equally removed by the increasing religious neutrality of the states and the universities. The universities enjoyed, within the limits set, the various national traditions and arrangements that obtained in this time; a fairly far-reaching separation from the state. Both churches and universities appeared to be at the same rung on the ladder of autonomy from the state. The churches, however, were moving in the direction of greater separation from the state; the universities were on the verge of a movement towards a diminution of their autonomy. The churches were acquiring greater autonomy as governments became more indifferent to matters of religious belief; on the other hand, the relations of government and universities have become denser and more multifarious because secular knowledge has come to be more highly regarded by governments. Governments have come to believe that secular scientific and scholarly knowledge are pertinent to their own purposes and to the ends they have in view for their societies. The beliefs that scientific and scholarly knowledge such as is pursued in universities is instrumental to the achievement of the ends of economic prosperity, social justice, and

179

military effectiveness, and that the possession of such knowledge should be made available to individuals so that they may increase their incomes and elevate their social status, work against a separation of government and universities comparable to the separation that has come about between governments and churches.

In societies where universities and churches were once allied to each other, the separation of church and state has also been concomitant with the separation of church and university. The close ties which once bound the church and the state have been relaxed while the ties of state and university have been tightened. The separation of church and university was a necessary condition for these two simultaneous and opposite movements.

The universities are not the only arrangements dealing with cognitive tasks, any more than governments are the only institutions concerning themselves with practical tasks. Churches and monasteries, academies, research institutes, and independent private foundations for the pursuit of scholarship are among the variety of institutions devoted to the pursuit of learning. Universities have emerged triumphant over all these alternative arrangements for learning during the course of the past century and a half. The prominence they have achieved in consequence of that triumph has made governments more demanding for their subordination. There is a principle of division of labor among institutions implicit in the ends which each cultivates, but there is also potential conflict among these sets of ends. This division of labor may be so organized that it does harm to one or the other partners of the division, or to the others and to the larger society and culture of which they are parts. Each, regarding exclusively its own interest, may frustrate its own intentions and do damage to the other institution and to the larger whole. Such a situation seems to have developed in recent decades as the demands on governments, and the aspirations and self-confidence of government officials, have grown. Politicians and civil servants have come to think of themselves not only as the ultimate arbiters whose task it is to confine conflict within the bounds of the political order, but also as the agents of substantive values. The prudential American concept of "a compelling state interest" that permits the substantive values of institutions to be overriden is indicative of the tendency of the state to regard its own substantive ends as more central than those of all other sectors of society.

The effective equilibrium between universities and governments, which prevailed in most Western countries for about three-quarters of a century up to the 1930s in some of them and later in others, now seems to be under stress.

The relationship between universities and government must be restudied in a wide historical context and with a fresh appreciation of the contemporary situation. There is a pressing need to reconsider what each owes to the other, and what each owes to values inherent in its own distinctive nature and not necessarily harmonious with the values of the other. The objective should be a "constitution of university and state according to the idea of each."[1]

I

The government and the university each owes to the other the acknowledgement, and the performances corresponding thereto, of their distinctive and different obligations to the well-being of their society, their culture, and their civilization—three things which are by no means identical. Government is not coterminous with society; the well-being of society is not always, even in the welfare state, what government decides is the well-being towards which it should strive. The purposes and the values of the various sections of society are never exhaustively protected or pursued by governments, although certain illiberal governments pretend to be able to do so and actually do. Government has many specific purposes that are legitimated by its service of the purposes and values of the individuals and institutions that make up their society, and by its service of the value inherent in that society and its culture. A government may protect the framework of society, it may enable its constituent institutions of society to pursue their respective and distinctive ends. But governments also have purposes of their own which may result in the benefit of particular groups or the realization of a particular form of society. In the advancement of the purposes which are its own, it may attempt to bend the constituent institutions of society so that they will move towards the fulfillment of these purposes.

The values of universities are inherent in their existence as universities. Those who enter them without the deliberate intention of subverting them accept, in varying degrees of awareness, a commitment to these values. The basic commitment inherent in the activities that constitute universities is a belief in the superior value of some cognitive beliefs over others and of some modes of acquiring knowledge over others. The task of the university is the cultivation, extension, and transmission of knowledge as valid as the human imagination, reason, memory, and observational powers can make it. If it does not do that, then it falls short of being a university, even though it carries the name of a university. From this end derives its other activities such as training for the professions where such knowledge is a necessity for effective practice. However devoted many of its members may be to "service" and "practical relevance," there is a particular, pervasive, elusive quality which universities generally seek to have or claim to have. This quality is the furtherance of the acquisition and wider possession of truth—of valid and important knowledge—about "serious" things.

There are many academics who profess to scorn such a formulation; others are outrightly hostile to it, and still others point to higher educational institutions that seldom give explicit thought to such an end. Nonetheless, I think that throughout the academic world, there is a sense that dedication to the acquisition of truth is where universities started from, and that most other things universities do should be derivative from that standard. Despite numerous deviations and shortcomings, this interest in what constitutes a university is apprehended far more widely than among a few idealists who are opposed to the idea that the university should be an intellectual "resource station" for the practical purposes of government, of society as a whole, or for particular groups in society.

The general acceptance of this criterion is evidenced by the recognition of a hierarchy, or as it is called, a "pecking order" among universities. It is recognized in society more widely than in the academic world. The fact that so much lip-service is paid to the standard of being a "great university" and of "the obligation to adhere to the highest standards of scholarship and teaching," shows how widely this standard is accepted, both inside and outside universities. Some institutions of higher education approximate this ideal more closely than others. The state of morale of university teachers depends on some measure of observance of this ideal. Where the discrepancy between the ideal and the reality is seen to be great, university teachers become embittered and demoralized and immerse themselves in rancorous and aggressive disputes.

The quality of the society is believed by many persons to depend on the presence of the institutional embodiment of this ideal. Quite apart from the long-term practical benefits that do in fact often flow from the cultivation of this ideal, its denial of this ideal by the "practical" elements of a society in time leads to a brutalizing of that society. A society without learning, like a society without religion or art would be a society of brutes, however comfortable and well-managed. Even bureaucrats and utilitarian and hedonist philosophers would quail at such a prospect. Totalitarian ideologists and military dictators do not seek the obliteration of learning from their higher educational institutions but neither do they care to maintain a pluralistic society.

There are countercurrents to the foregoing. Some persons would say that any institution which calls itself a university, e.g., "The University of Islam" in Chicago, is a university or that any institution that receives a charter from the state as a university or that is established by the state is a university regardless of what it does when it acquires the legal right to use that name. More common and more influential have been those who assert that universities are justified not by their dedication to ideals of truth and scholarship but by their relevance to the practical undertakings of society as presently constructed and in their likely future. They cannot see much sense in the study of "useless" subjects. The ideal of a university whose curriculum centers around the study of "useless" subjects is preposterous to them; they believe that universities should be subservient to the powers in charge of the practical tasks of society, and ultimately to "the people."

There is still another countercurrent of criticism to the university as an institution of learning that is rather close to the criticisms by the proponents of practicality. It emanates from the critics who charge the universities with being aristocratically indifferent to the needs and interests of "the people." In the United States where this criticism of the universities for "elitism" became most vehement, it was originally espoused by anticapitalistic, antibourgeoisie radicals. Nonetheless, it is closely akin to the populistic, practicalistic criticism of politicians, businessmen, and publicists who were not at all radicals. It is not that the latter day critics of the "elitism" of the universities think that they should teach practical subjects exclusively. Their objection places more weight on the fact that the learning pursued in the universities which they condemn, is in its essence not accessible to everyone or is of no interest to everyone. This objection to the allegedly "aristocratic" character of learning is coupled with the "practicalists'" criticism of the "elitist" universities on the grounds that they are "irrelevant" to the tasks of transforming society in a socialistic, populistic direction. The "practical" bourgeois, populistic, and radical critics of universities all seem to believe—although they have never worked their ideas out in any clear form—that societies should be homogeneous in their culture, and that there should not be any differentiation in the quality of culture. The idea of a pluralistic society is fundamentally alien to them.

Nonetheless, the criticisms of the ideal from the practical and popular standpoints and the numerous divergences from the ideal within the universities themselves do not annul the actual existence of the university as a place where, in addition to much else, the ideal is cultivated. The universities that are most esteemed, and the university members who seek to conform with the ideal or standard associated with that status do things that other institutions cannot do to the same extent. They contribute to the deeper understanding of the universe and of man and his works, they train students to do so, and they educate young persons up to the highest level of such understanding. This is one of their main justifications for existence and this is why they are esteemed by so many persons. It is one of the main reasons why they have been supported.

Now it is true that this kind of learning, which is the constitutive idea of the university, has not always been practiced in universities. Universities that have not cultivated this kind of learning have not been esteemed; and at the time, the most active and deepest life of learning went on among private scholars or in monasteries or at royal courts.

There are very few private scholars any more; there are very few royal courts, and they are not major patrons of learning; and the monastic orders could represent, if they were intellectually active, only a very small part of the range of learning. At their present level of sophistication it is difficult to conceive of science and scholarship being carried on as amateur enterprises. They are too intertwined with expensive equipment, large libraries, seminars, students, research assistants, and colleagues to revert to their old form. Learning in its present form requires universities. If the universities exclude it, it will languish and the universities themselves will become something very different from what they have been during the better part of the past century and a half.

Learning is a phenomenon which emerges in every differentiated and literate society. It is an emergent property of the social life of the species, like speech in the individual human organism. Like the economic life of the species, it has come to have an institutional organization that performs the function in a way no individual, unaided by institutions and traditions, could ever do. It is a function which has its own exigencies and laws, just as an economic system has. It has inherent in itself a disposition towards autonomy, but it is not and cannot be wholly autonomous.

II

Universities are not and have never been self-supporting institutions. They have never received payments for their services which were adequate for their maintenance. Greatly esteemed though they have been for their cultivation, pursuit, and transmission of knowledge of the most fundamental and serious things, universities would not have received as much support as they did over the centuries had they not also supplied certain services to the society from which they received their support. The service they rendered was to train young persons for the direct performance of certain vocations and duties.

There are practical activities with high intellectual components of knowledge and skills, mastery of which must be acquired by systematic and disciplined study. The practice of medicine and the practice of law—the traditional learned professions—were among the earliest and most important of these. The cure of souls and their preparation for redemption also fall into this category—a profession in which the practical and the spiritual meet. In the course of the nineteenth and twentieth centuries, the number of occupations with high intellectual components increased; the amount of scientific knowledge incorporated into the practice of the traditional learned professions was vastly expanded. Warfare became more scientific in the sense that the production of munitions and weapons was progressively infused with scientific knowledge. Industrial and agricultural production incorporated scientific knowledge into their procedures. Governmental administration purportedly became more scientific. Record keeping and accounting, necessary to all large organizations, have acquired a more scientific character; social work, librarianship, the detection of crime, and other police work have also acquired intellectual components they did not have in the middle of the nineteenth century. The design and construction of buildings, roads, machines, factories, etc., have all been subject to the same scientific influence. The kinds of knowledge their practice requires and their spokesmen desire as necessary in the training of their practitioners are the kinds of knowledge discovered and taught in universities.

The numbers of persons in these new or minor professions has increased, as has the number of such occupations, and they are now regarded as more important to society than in the past. Their practitioners certainly regard themselves as more important than they used to be and as more entitled to deference by others. Two of the important grounds for this claim are that their practice is grounded on scientific knowledge and that that knowledge has been acquired in universities and has been certified by them. Universities have had assigned to them the power to legitimatize the standing of a profession and its practitioners and it has been thought by many that they alone are uniquely qualified to do so. It has not always been so.

Universities have been esteemed in society because they have been the place where knowledge of "serious," fundamental things was discovered, interpreted, and taught. By a circular process they have also been esteemed because they have been progenitors of the professions and occupations that were closely associated with authority and "serious" things like justice, order, life, and death. In consequence, universities have been regarded not only as a link with the order of serious things through the understanding of their nature, but also because they were linked to the most esteemed roles of their respective societies by the training of their incumbents—and their offspring.

III

Universities were supported by churchmen partly because they were institutions that trained for the superior levels of correct understanding of the world central to a Christian civilization or the service of the church. They were supported by princes partly because they trained lawyers, civil servants, physicians, and clergymen for the service of the state, society, and church—and later teachers for the advanced secondary schools—all of which the prince and his government needed for the good order of society. The universities were supported by the state and by private persons, including ecclesiastical patrons, also because intellectual learning as such was esteemed. In the United States, the state universities were supported by the citizenry and by the state governments for all these reasons. In addition, they were esteemed because they placed opportunities for the acquisition of learning and for entry into the socially superior and more remunerative occupations within the range of a larger part of the population than had been the case in Europe. These various grounds for support could coexist because their corresponding functions could be pursued simultaneously in the same institutions. The universities could serve both the demands of learning and the demands of their society for learning at the same time. There was sometimes a tension between the cultivators of these two kinds of learning in the university, not least in the United States where the practical learning of the universities received more attention than elsewhere.

There was an unwritten, unspoken concordat between the universities and the government which maintained this balance. The universities performed the service of training for certain professions that the government regarded as necessary and desirable for its own purposes, as well as those of the society for which it was the custodian. They had this while they cultivated serious learning in a dispassionate way. Governments—and private patrons in the English-speaking countries—supported the universities for these reasons, although they placed the greatest emphasis on the training for the practical-intellectual professions. It was in general accepted without question that universities had tasks apart from the training of young persons for the learned professions and for the service of church, state, and society. Learning as such was esteemed as intrinsically valuable, just as the religious knowledge and ritual of the churches were intrinsically and unquestionably valuable. The universities received and they gave. What they gave was a service that they could give because of their unique possession of advanced knowledge.

The universities were placed in a position something like that of the churches. They were regarded as something very different from business firms or voluntary associations. They were clearly different from political parties or political associations. In certain important respects they were placed apart from the everday life of society. They were not instruments of public policy. Where they served ends contributory to public policy, they were welcomed and encouraged; they were not to be coerced.

Even in the practical United States, the universities were supported by state governments in the Middle and Far West and by private patrons, because they pursued knowledge in a selfless and dispassionate way. It was accepted that they had to have an internal life of their own, led according to their own standards. Despite the university laws laid down by the German states or by other countries where governments promulgated the constitutions of their universities, efforts were made to assure that the universities would have a realm of autonomy of decision and action, in which they could apply their own standards and act in accordance with their own traditions. Even in the time of the *Obrigkeitsstaat* a sphere of autonomous action was respected by the government. Although professors were civil servants with legal status that entailed rights and obligations of loyalty, they were basically not under the command of the minister or his highest officials. This was what was meant by *akademische Lehrfreiheit* and *akademische Selbstverwaltung*. Comparable principles were not formulated in England because universities were not creatures of the state. Although chartered by the state they were self-governing bodies with a much wider range of autonomy from the state than their continental counterparts. In the United States the situation was not fundamentally different from that in Great Britain. The American pattern was formed in the traditions of Oxford and Cambridge, qualified by the pattern of the colleges of the free Church which had lay governing bodies. The state universities also adopted the institution of a lay governing body so that it was not a part of the executive branch of the state government. In both the state and private universities the principle of the autonomy of the university *vis-a-vis* the government was respected in principle. In fact, the state universities, wishing to remain on good and fruitful terms with the state legislatures, made concessions by providing courses of study and research schemes that would be pleasing to public and political opinion. In the private universities there were not the same pressures on the substance of teaching and research. In both the state and private universities in the United States, the autonomy of universities in matters of appointment was infringed upon when from time to time teachers were dismissed or threatened with dismissal because of their radical political views.

The structure of university government in the United States was a product of this acceptance of the autonomous character of the state universities. They were not governed by the department of education of the state, nor by the state legislature but rather by a board of regents, popularly elected or appointed by the governor, that intended to act as an autonomous body. In this respect they had the same position as the court of a modern British university. Both were lay bodies like the boards of trustees of the American private universities. They were expected to act as buffers to prevent damaging collisions between the universities and the external world, governmental and private. They were also expected to exercise a custodial solicitude over proceedings within the universities. As the present century moved forward, the lay governing body of the university—both the private and the state university—has left the internal affairs of the university more and more to the president, deans, and the academic staff, out of a recognition of the rightness of academic self-government. (Within the universities, authority has in fact evolved more and more from the central administration to the academic departments, although legally the board of trustees is the ultimate governing body.)

There are many qualifications to be made in this account of the written and unwritten pacts between the universities and government in the United States. Before the Second World War these pacts were sometimes violated by trustees and regents and sometimes by legislators. Most of the infringements touched on the right of the universities to make appointments—particularly reappointments and promotions—in accordance with their own criteria of academic achievement and promise, while the lay authorities insisted that radical political views should be regarded as disqualifications. Such cases were not numerous however. In matters of syllabi, examinations, degrees, research programs, and in appointments, apart from those in which radical political views were involved, governments remained as aloof as the lay governing bodies. Many changes have occurred since that period.

In different legal settings the Continental universities also developed a considerable degree of autonomy. In appointments the final authority rested with ministers of education, acting on the recommendation of faculties. In most cases, the recommendations were accepted. Although the content of syllabi and qualifying examinations for candidates' entry into the professions (*Staatsexamen*) had official status, they were largely made up by professors; examinations for degrees were entirely in the hands of academics. Syllabi were oriented towards professional requirements in those courses of study that were preparatory to the practice of the profession, but since these were mainly in the hands of academics, the syllabi were also. In those subjects in which students were not preparing for the "state examination," the professor was entirely free to teach those parts of the subject that he himself thought most pertinent to the attainment of a high standard of scholarship. On the Continent as in the English speaking world, the marking of examinations has been exclusively a matter for the academic staff. The same has been true of programs of research, although as particular research schemes became more expensive, the autonomy of the university was limited by the readiness of external patrons financially to support a particular kind of research. Even there the various institutional arrangements that were invented in Great Britain, Germany, and France, provided for the decisions to be made by juries of qualified scientists who were usually academics. They were not necessarily from the same university as the applicant, but the decision remained generally within the academic profession and thus represented some adherence to the principles of academic autonomy.

IV

Throughout the Western world, a strain has arisen in these traditional patterns of relationship between government and universities. The cognitive expansion of recent trends has been accompanied—when it has not been caused—by the belief that knowledge of the systematic empirical scientific subject matter, such as is sought and transmitted in universities, is of instrumental importance in the pursuit of the ends of government, armies, private and public economic enterprises, schools, and many other institutions. Governments have also acquired through popular desire and consent, greater powers than they have ever exercised before, and they also believe in their own competence. There has also arisen a greater desire in the populace for higher education as a path to higher culture, social status, and monetary returns. Western governments have taken upon themselves the responsibility for the realization of these ambitions. These increases in the activities of research and instruction have enlarged the financial burdens on universities and governments that have on the whole been very forthcoming in meeting most of the demands for increased expenditures. In consequence of all this, universities have become much more visible. Governments are now very much more aware of them than they have been in the past, and are demanding more of them. One result is that governments are now much more concerned with and inquisitive about the affairs of universities.

Long before the disruptions of universities by agitating students and their followers, there was much talk about the new tasks of universities. In Great Britain and the United States, reports on the need for more "scientific manpower" and the increasingly munificent governmental subvention of scientific research in the universities, led the universities to be used primarily as instruments for the service of government policies.

In Great Britain the autonomy of the universities has been respected more than in the other Western countries. This was due largely to the traditions established by the University Grants Committee, which made block grants to the universities for them to spend in accordance with their own conceptions. Meanwhile the universities had become almost wholly dependent on the central government for their financial resources. Private philanthropy, private industry, and municipal government support had dwindled below the level required to meet the rising expenditures needed for conducting university functions under existing conditions. Parliament became more concerned and restive about the universities. As a result the University Grants Committee was detached from the Treasury which had been its only representation to the government, and added to the Department of Education and Science, which already possessed a more direct control over the polytechnic stratum of higher education. The accounts of the universities had within the preceding decade been opened to inspection by the Comptroller and Accountant-General, a relationship that had for several decades been successfully resisted by the University Grants Committee. Most recently, a private members' bill to amalgamate the polytechnics and the universities into a single unitary system of higher education was narrowly defeated.

The *Wissenschaftsrat* in the Federal German Republic was a new step into the relations between government and the universities. Universities had never been the concern of the central government in Germany. Neither the imperial nor the republican government had concerned themselves with the affairs of universities; the National Socialist regime was the first German government to give attention to the universities—with damaging effect. The Federal Republic returned universities to the care of the states but it created the *Wissenschaftsrat* which had only advisory powers. Nonetheless the Federal government soon entered into university affairs more directly through a system of grants for capital construction. This in itself did not infringe on the powers of the states, but it did establish the central government as a potential force in the life of the universities. The next step was taken with the preparation of the *Hochschulrahmengesetz*, which laid down the pattern for the university laws of the states that had previously been sovereign in this matter. Meanwhile, most of the states had enacted university laws that changed the composition of the governing bodies of universities to include substantial representatives of students and nonacademic staff. One by-product of this has been a pronounced tendency for the new governing bodies to make recommendations for appointments on political grounds. The state governments have felt it incumbent on them to reject some of these recommendations on the grounds that the nominees were disloyal to the constitution. Laws have been enacted prohibiting appointments to the civil service—which include university teachers—on grounds of disloyalty to the constitution.

In the United States the greatest changes have taken place through the entry of the federal government into the relationship with universities. There had been a thickening of relationships during the First World War, but after that war the situation returned to what it had been previously. The previously existent situation had been one in which there was practically no active connection between the federal government and the universities, other than the very restricted ones contained in the Morrill Act and the relations between the Department of Agriculture and the state agricultural research stations that were often connected with state universities or agricultural and mechanical colleges. State and private universities received no grants of any sort from the federal government; they performed no work contract for the federal government. Education was not a "state-subject." The social legislation of the federal government was very limited and did not impinge on the university.

In the Second World War the universities were drawn into corporate relationships with the federal government through the acceptance of contracts to conduct certain research projects on behalf of the federal government. Various parts of the Manhattan Project were conducted by universities on contract with the federal government and under the security restrictions of the armed forces: the Radiation Project was much the same in this regard. The universities undertook to house and provide instruction for various parts of the Army Specialist Training Program.

After the war, the first impact of the federal government was through the "GI Bill of Rights" which, by providing tuition fees and maintenance for veterans of the armed forces attending universities, caused the size of the student body of the universities to expand rapidly. The Office of Naval Research continued to offer contracts to the universities to "perform" research; the Atomic Energy Commission did the same. The Department of Defense and then the National Institutes of Health and the National Science Foundation, when they appeared on the scene, awarded grants, let contracts, and provided postdoctoral fellowships. Grants and contracts also enabled universities to provide scholarships and research assistantships to graduate students in the natural sciences.

In pursuing this course in relation to the universities, the federal government was not developing anything new. The system of grants for "project research" had been developed in a very rudimentary form by the Bureau of Mines during the First World War, then by the National Research Council and the Rockefeller Foundation in the 1920s and 1930s. The provision of fellowships was developed by the Rockefeller Foundation and the National Research Council in the first decade after the war. The letting of contracts was of course a very old procedure for the purchase of goods and services by governments from private suppliers. The only innovation of the more recent period was that universities became "contractors" like any commercial or industrial firm, which undertook to manufacture military aircraft or to supply typewriters or military books in accordance with agreed specifications and for an agreed payment.

The government has from time to time promoted the teaching of particular groups of subjects, such as oriental languages or medicine. Its interest in the teaching of undergraduates has been restricted to particular subjects for designated periods. It has made funds available by grants and loans for the payment of fees in connection with undergraduate and graduate studies. It has generally promoted the increase in the number of students and the size of the universities.

The federal government has never attempted to support universities in the way in which British and Continental governments have done. It has avoided doing so because it moved into relations with universities in a very piecemeal fashion, and because to do so would immediately raise very difficult political problems. There are more than 1500 degree-granting universities and colleges in the United States; they vary widely in quality and it would be invidious to discriminate among them. It would moreover rouse legislators to look after the interests of their constituents whose interests and desires would undoubtedly bear little connection with their intellectual merit. But there is a more fundamental reason. It is that the federal government, despite all these programs, does not have what can be called a genuine policy with respect to universities. It has rather intended to achieve certain specific ends for which a number of separate, overlapping policies in the universities are regarded as appropriate instruments.

The federal government in the United States works on an unspoken assumption of the self-maintaining existence of the universities. It is not concerned with the maintenance of the universities; it accepts the fact that they are already there and that it may purchase resources from them at marginal cost. Its various policies have not been accompanied by any reflection or sense of responsibility to the source of the services. It is like a tribe at the level of a hunting and gathering mode of life; it looks upon the university as an already existent resource that came into being without its support and that will go on existing without its support. In viewing the existence of the universities, the government regards them as an instrument to be used for particular purposes as the occasion arises and to be set

193

aside when the occasion passes, as institutions that will continue to exist from their own resources and always available to supply services at marginal cost, when they are so desired.

The government has not developed the concern for the ecology of universities that it has developed for lakes and fishes. It regards the university as a stream which runs on of itself, available to it for particular purposes but of no concern aside from those purposes. It takes no more responsibility for the maintenance of the university than a factory owner, before the period of "environmental" legislation, took responsibility for the replenishment and purity of the stream. As in other spheres of activity, the government of the United States is living beyond its means but manages so far to escape the consequences by consuming the capital accumulated in the past and the capital being accumulated for the future. It is using the capital accumulated by generations of scientists, scholars, and teachers and public and private patrons without any thought for the maintenance and renewal of that capital except sporadically and incidentally to its own purposes.

The Continental and British governments, whatever else they may do, take responsibility for the entire university and at the same time do not demand so many particular services from it. In the British universities Lord Rothschild did attempt to transform a part of governmental support science into a controlled relationship between "customer" and "seller" of scientific services, but that pattern has not come to dominate all of the relationships between government and university in Great Britain.

There is, however, a qualification to be made in this account of the federal government and the universities in the United States. Although the federal government treats the university as it would any other contractor who looks after his own interest and charges accordingly, it has subtly managed to change the nature of the contractual relationship. Whereas traditionally a contract stipulated the good or service to be received, the quality, quantity, time of delivery, and the payment to be made, the government of the United States has now set certain extracontractual conditions to which the contractor must adhere.

Henry Maine's interpretation of legal and social history as a transition from "status to contract" was long regarded by social scientists and historians as touching on a significant difference between modern and premodern societies. The new policies of the government of the United States represent a divergence from this theme. A contract now comprises something outside the terms of the goods or services to be delivered and the consideration offered in return for it; the contractor has now to exhibit qualities which have no connection with the goods or services. In the years immediately after the Second World War, the federal government introduced into its contracts a stipulation regarding the loyalty of the contractor and his employees. In a limited number of cases this stipulation was roughly reasonable where secrecy was necessary; in many cases it was simply irrelevant to the goods or services to be "delivered," which was not bound by the requirement of secrecy. Nonetheless the precedent was established. The contractor had henceforth to abide by conditions external to the substance of the transaction fixed by the contract.

This obligation to affirm loyalty to the government and constitution was of no practical value to either party to the contract; it was only humiliating to academics and academic administrators to submit to it, but since it was a condition of receiving funds from the government for specific purposes, it was accepted. It was easy enough therefore for the federal government to extend the extracontractual condition in the contract for other moral purposes. The contractor had henceforth, as the insistence on loyalty became less pressing, to employ a staff of a given ethnic composition. This innovation in the relationship between the federal government and its contractor originally was not intended to apply to universities. But as the contractual idiom had prevailed in the purchase of services and the rental of facilities, such as buildings and laboratories from universities by the federal government during the Second World War and then persisted thereafter, universities became contractors like any others.

There are however considerable differences between universities as "contractors" and other contractors. These are not just differences in the nature of the "service" provided. They also lie in the capacity to bear the costs of the government's demands. The federal government's social policies, which intend to promote the welfare of the mass of the population, entail the provision of employment for blacks, Puerto Ricans, American Indians, Latin Americans, and women, and the keeping of records to prove that this is being done up to the required standard. The increased payment of taxes for old age pensions, compensation in periods of unemployment, occupational safety and health, environmental protection, and conformity with minimum standards of wages and hours are also required of universities, just as they are for any private business corporation.

The costs of giving statistically persuasive assurance to the government of "equal employment opportunity" and equal pay are not compensated by the federal government. These costs must be met from revenue derived from student fees, the interest on endowment and gifts, and by restraint on the increase of the salaries of their teaching and research staff; the acquisition of books and journals by the library and costs of the extracontractual conditions make the burden all the heavier.

Private business enterprises that have these various charges upon them by the federal government can ordinarily transfer any additional costs of doing business to the consumer by raising their prices. When such a private business enters into a contractual relationship with the government, it does so on terms that will meet all of its costs, including the costs of capital equipment, and provide a profit. Universities have never covered their costs and cannot cover their costs from revenue resulting from the sale of their products. They cannot pass the additional expenses—both those involved in the contract and those that are generally applicable to contractors and noncontractors alike—imposed by government to anyone except their students and their academic staff, and by drawing on their endowments. They can increase the fees they charge their students, and they can reduce the scholarships available to them; if they are private universities, they can endanger their continued existence by "pricing themselves out of the market" and by liquidating their endowment. They can also allow the salaries of their teachers and research workers to remain constant and thus fall further and further behind the inflation of prices. They can reduce the purchases of books for the libraries and otherwise dilute their quality. Even if universities were not subject to contractual conditions of their agreement, the governmentally engendered inflation would be a burden on them. The costs of the extracontractual conditions make that burden all the heavier.

When the government makes a contract with a private firm, the firm includes in its charges provision for the payment of dividends to its shareholders in return for the capital that they have provided. The federal government in dealing with universities makes no provision for the reimbursement of the capital used in the fulfillment of the contract. Charges for "overhead," about which the government is very grudging, do not take into account the uses of capital by which the government benefits when it enters into a contract with a university.

The capital of a university is much more than its physical plant or its library; it is also more than the stock of knowledge and skills that its academic staff members bring to their tasks. It includes the zeal for discovery, the moral integrity, the powers of discriminating judgment, the awareness of important problems, and the possibilities for their

196

solution that their members possess. These are qualities of individuals, but their stable persistence depends on the existence of an academic community, within departments and faculties in the university as a whole and in the academic community at large—within the boundaries of the country and internationally. These refinements of intellectual sensibility depend on the presence of like-minded colleagues and students, not just within the academic person's particular field of specialization, but over a much wider range.

It is true that it is difficult to apprehend the subtle intellectual product arising from the presence of other persons with similar outlooks and similar propensities. It is nonetheless this presence which keeps these propensities and outlooks alert and constant. The community of scholars who are teachers and investigators at the same time is constituted by these alert and constant propensities and outlooks. The community of scholars who are teachers and investigators at the same time is constituted by this mutual influence and by the identifications formed in consequence of it. This intellectual community and its traditions are what makes the physical plant, the library, and the laboratories and the individual members of the university into a university. This is one of the factors that has made universities so successful in the quest for knowledge and in the induction of young persons into the intellectual and moral culture, which the universities at their best can offer.

When it lets a contract or awards a grant for the performance of a particular piece of research, the government is receiving therefore more than the particular activity of the particular persons who receive the money it pays to the university. The government is receiving the benefits that have come to the recipients of its grants or contracts from the presence of many other scientists and scholars, young and old, students and teachers who, separately and all together through the course of their lives, have sustained and incessantly refreshed the atmosphere that each member of the university inhales. Without a stringent standard, without an alert curiosity, without the sense of the urgent importance of discovery, a scientist or scholar, even with a great stock of knowledge of the "relevant literature" and with great ratiocinative capacity, cannot accomplish very much. These dispositions must be kept intense and vivacious. To attain and maintain them at this high level, the presence of colleagues and students with a similar intensity or vivacity is of the first importance. Of course not all colleagues and fellow students are equally weighty; those who are superior contribute more to put the rest of them on their mettle; and there are always some who are resistant or impermeable. But the difference between better and less good universities is that the former have a smaller proportion of their members in the latter category.

All of these considerations should make sense even to persons who think strictly in economic terms, who think that capital should, at the very least, be maintained and that a wise policy of investment would set aside earnings sufficient to maintain the inheritance of capital from which future earnings are to be drawn. Such considerations are no more than an argument that the market must set the price for a good that will cover provision for the replacement and renewal of the capital that has gone into its production; otherwise the good will disappear from the market. It will not be brought back into the market by an increase in price because it has grown over a long time and cannot be re-created by deliberate policy. It can only be maintained if the conditions for its existence are maintained. Its growth and present existence are the result of congenial external circumstances and internal processes and inheritance. They are the products of autonomy with a beneficent matrix.

The long-term interests of government—and of society, if we assume that the interests of government and society coincide, which is by no means self-evident—would be advanced by a policy of action towards universities that acknowledges that universities are institutions of advanced learning with their own distinctive and autonomous traditions. Such a policy will accept that universities have the tasks of discovery and transmission of new and important knowledge, of educating young persons highly enough qualified to assimilate that knowledge and training for the practice of professions that demand the possession of that kind of knowledge for their effective practice, and of training young persons to appreciate and carry on the search for new knowledge. This reasonable policy would accept that the performance of these main tasks presupposes the existence within the university of an ethos that prizes the intrinsic value of such learning. It is primarily in such a setting that the intellectual curiosity necessary for the practical application of knowledge or the acquisition of new knowledge to be used for practical ends can be inculcated and sustained.

These things are the root of a university. A government that wishes to continue to collect their fruits will conduct itself so that the root is not starved. A proper division of labor between universities and government is one that would enable the universities to perform their distinctive tasks and not simply act as an instrument for the execution of the tasks set to it by the momentary or even enduring demands of governments.

Universities have another task which is not met by the fulfillment of their obligations to government and society. This is the obligation to understand what the world in its manifoldness is about. By this I do not mean primarily the understanding of the contemporary world or modern society. I will not say that the universities are identical with churches, but they have much in common with the church in a society of believers. What the universities discover and teach has a status approximate to what the churches have preached. The churches are to be esteemed not because anthropologists say that all known societies have had religious beliefs and a cult of transcendent things; the churches are to be esteemed because what they teach is right and necessary for human beings to know. The understanding and acceptance of the divine order is the obligation of human beings in societies in which that order is acknowledged. The understanding of the world up to the edge of the understanding of divinity is the obligation of the university. The monastic community was—and is—the place for those persons whose need to acknowledge the divine order and to live in accordance with it was the highest possible in existence in this world. The university is the place for those who search unremittingly for the rational understanding and appreciation of the order of this world, and for those young persons for whom that search is an essential component of their lives. The fact that not everyone wishes zealously to lead such a life or is incapable of leading such a life is not a criticism of its value. The fact that not all academics are desirous or capable of leading such a life is no criticism of the idea of the university or of the academic ethos which is central to it. The fact that not everyone cares to or is capable of becoming a creative artist or writer or cares to contemplate the works that such artists and writers produce is not a criticism of art or literature. A society without art, or one indifferent to art and literature of a kind that has no use but which is superior to entertainment, is an impoverished and unworthy society. The same may be said of a society which is indifferent to the achievement of an ordered, rational understanding of the world.

The coincidence in the same place and in the same institutions of the search for an improved rational understanding of the world and the acquisition of understanding that has practical utility sometimes renders it difficult to distinguish these two great functions of the university. At the

199

same time the dependence of the latter on the former renders it necessary to see that they are different things. A wise policy would see to it that the former is as necessary as the latter and that the latter could not exist without the former. This should be a fundamental article of the new constitution of state and university.

V

In contributing to the support of universities the federal government of the United States disregards but takes advantage of all this. It "buys" specific services: particular pieces of research and particular "training programs." It pays for the time of those who work directly on its projects; it pays for equipment and supplies. It might also pay for the space it uses and for the administrative expenditures connected with the project. It does not pay for the cost that has gone into creating and maintaining a high level of academic morale, or for maintaining and creating the academic ethos, which is under present circumstances a precondition for understanding and its growth. It is at present obtaining those benefits without charge. It exploits them and does not replenish them; indeed, it runs them down. The system of "project-grants" and "contract-research" has disaggregated the universities of the United States during the period of great expansion. It has led to the self-centeredness of individuals and a disregard for the claims of the institution and of the obligations of membership in it or, as some sociologists have put it, to "placing identification with one's profession above identification with one's institution."

The federal government of the United States by its mode of support for particular activities in the universities has been treating central parts of the universities as a "free good." It does not pay for what its "contractors" or its "principal investigators" receive from their presence as teachers and students in the university and in the national and international community of universities and the knowledge that enters into their service for government and society.

The federal government does not pay for the most fundamental part of what it receives, namely the effect of the long tradition of the universities' devotion to the discovery, interpretation, and teaching of fundamental knowledge about serious things. It is this interior life of the university, this devotion to knowledge as intrinsically valuable that gives intellectual substance to the pursuit of knowledge about things that are of practical importance. Without that intense intellectual discipline and devotion, which is sustained by the tradition interior to the university, there would not be the scientific probity and exactingness and the intellectual sensitivity which goes into research with practical ends in view.

VI

At the beginning I spoke about "a new constitution of universities and state appropriate to the idea of each." The idea of the state is the concern for and protection of the good order of society which includes the material well-being of its members, their diligent support of themselves and their families through paid employment, justice in their relations with each other and with authority, etc. Government is not everything in society, it is not the "be-all and end-all" of society. It is not the church and it is not the university. The church has almost wholly been deprived of its provision of welfare services and the university, on the contrary, has had more and more tasks assigned to it for the provision of specific services required by the purposes of government.

The cultivation of learning for the purpose of the understanding of the order of nature and of humanity and its works has not, like religious beliefs, been declared a "private" affair. It has however been rudely classified by economists as a consumer's good. Others wishing to praise it, classify it as an aesthetic good, like the ballet or the performance of a string quartet. Still others disparage it as "elitist" or as the useless preoccupation of the occupants of an "ivory tower." The government refuses to acknowledge it as such and supports only particular research projects and training programs "related to national needs."

The government, insofar as it is not using something of the greatest value at no charge to itself—the cost of the capital being borne by state governments and private patrons—is doing so "on the cheap." It is not paying for what it is getting; it is rather demanding and obtaining a great deal more than what it pays for. It is using up and not renewing the intellectual capital of the universities by making their circumstances more straitened than they have been. It is proceeding blithely to starve the goose which lays the golden eggs, assuming that there are others who will breed more geese and who will feed them. It is going further than this and insisting that the universities appoint their staffs with regard to racial and sexual characteristics of candidates, instead of attending to excellency by intellectual criteria. As a result the intellectual capital of the universities is further depleted.

The universities of the European continent have not been faced with this problem, since there their governments take responsibility for the mass of the total budget of the universities. The dangers they face from their governments are however not unlike those faced by the American universities. In Sweden, the central government aims to turn the universities into institutions integrated into the labor market. Their functions, according to its intentions, will be to train students for particular professions and occupations. In effect places of learning will be closed. The other Continental universities have not gone this far in explicitly depriving the universities of their autonomy by making them subservient to the presumably predictable future demand for persons to engage in particular professions and occupations.

The hardest blow that a number of Continental governments have struck against the continuity of the intellectual traditions of universities has been through the provision in the new university legislation for the participation of academically and intellectually unqualified persons in the deliberations and decisions regarding academic appointments. Whereas in the United States, in the pursuit of the ideals of equality and justice, the federal government has imposed sex and race as criteria to be taken into account in appointments, the Continental governments have unthinkingly promoted the application of political criteria. They have done this, in the name of democracy, by aiding the entry into governing bodies of nonacademics, mainly students, whose interests are primarily, if not exclusively political. In consequence, particularly in the Federal German Republic, a number of universities have appointed to their teaching staff persons whose interests and intentions are preponderantly political— usually in a radical direction—rather than intellectual and academic. Thus the interior life of the university is turned into an extension of the political arena.

In different ways, therefore, the equilibrium between government and universities has been out of balance. The universities have been in varying degrees forced to renounce their particularity as institutions of learning and are being made into instruments of governmental and political interests which have their centers of gravity outside of the academic sphere.

A new "constitution" that reasserts the rights and obligations of the universities and of the earthly powers at the center of society is needed. The terms of a new "constitution" must be expressed in words of a general form. It would not even be desirable, at present, to formulate them precisely, even if that were feasible. I begin negatively with the acceptance of the proposition that things will never go back to what they were from the late nineteenth century until the Second World War. It must be accepted that governments and private institutions will continue to regard scientific knowledge as important to them for the construction, assessment, and execution of their policies. For the foreseeable future, government will not be able to have all the scientific research it desires done in governmental research establishments. Even if it could and wished to do so, it would still not be able to dispense with the capacity, distinctive of universities, to do research of high quality on fundamentally important problems and for the inculcation into young persons of the result of that research and of the ethos that is necessary to it. Furthermore, universities will continue to be dependent on governments for financial support to do the research which they wish to do. Unless research were to become as inexpensive as it was a century and a half ago—which is most improbable—universities will remain dependent on governments and, to a smaller extent, private business enterprises and persons for the support of that scientific research. The chances for a "disestablishment of science, " which would leave scientists just as well-endowed as they are now, but wholly free of any obligations to government or industry and equally free to pursue only their own interests whatever they might be, become slight to the point of being negligible.

For the foreseeable future, the universities will therefore be under obligation to perform much research in which government has an interest. The universities will continue to be under obligation to train young persons for the learned professions, both the traditional ones and certain newer ones, which have a genuine need for genuinely scientific and scholarly knowledge, such as universities are uniquely qualified to provide. At the same time the universities should be freed from the pressure to accept contracts for the execution of "crash programs" devised by civil servants or the staffs of legislators to provide short time definitive solutions to evanescent problems or to problems which cannot be definitively "solved," and certainly not in a short time. Governments should refrain from tampering with the mechanisms of academic appointment.

The "new constitution of state and university" is not going to be wholly new. Much of the "older constitution" should be retained or be restored. Certain features of the older pattern have been gradually displaced with very few persons being aware of what was happening. Both academics and governments must once more recognize that universities have ends which are not identical with those of government, that are in themselves as valuable as those of government, but are also necessary preconditions to the realization of the ends espoused by government.

Governments must abandon the belief that universities are extensions of the spheres of government and politics. The definitions of the right relationship in this absolutely crucial matter is not easy. A total separation of the proper sphere of the universities from these spheres is impossible as well as undesirable. But the far-reaching assimilation of the universities into those spheres or the movement towards that condition observable in the United States, Sweden, or other countries of the European continent should be halted. It should be halted because the general direction of this movement is clear. In all countries including Great Britain the governments have been bringing the universities increasingly into a subordinate position. The particular modes of subordination and encroachment vary however from country to country; they vary in accoradance with the traditions of the earlier constitutions of university and state. A new constitution would have to have, in addition to a common preamble of principles, a separate text for each country, which takes into account the tradition of that country and the particular setting within which the principles would have to be realized.

The principle is that of a division of labor in the cultivation of the plurality of ends to be sought in a good society. The division of labor should not be one which is organized for the realization of a single end. A good society has a multiplicity of good ends which are not identical or even harmonious with each other. Among the obligations of the institutions that pursue their several ends, one of the most important is the appreciation of the ends inherent in the existence of the others. An adaptation of the principle laid down in Matt. 12:21 "to render unto Caesar the things which are Caesar's and unto God the things that are God's" is necessary. Upon the universities this imposes the task of finding the right combination of obligations within and obligations without. Upon the world of government and society, it imposes the task of defining what it is entitled to ask of and receive from the universities, and what it must recognize as due to the universities in their own right.

NOTE

1. See Samuel Taylor Coleridge, *On the Constitution of the Churches and State according to the Idea of Each* (London: William Pickering, 1839).

A More Balanced View

University of California, Berkeley

I found much to agree with in both of these presentations. But in their different ways each presents a fairly bleak picture of our present situation; and I want to begin by discussing some of the bleakest elements of each. It seems to me that Mr. Bork perceives us as institutions dominated by politicized academic departments full of left-wing professors who are busy screaming that the government should impose regulations on other institutions in society that we wish to be exempt from ourselves. In his own words

> It is apparent to everyone that university faculties, particularly in the social sciences, humanities, and in the professional schools having relation to public policy, that those faculties are, to greater or lesser degree politicized. I do not want to make too much of the point, and the causes of the phenomenon are no doubt quite complex, but the fact remains that the faculties of many of our most prestigious universities are perceived and, worse, perceived correctly, as well to the left of the national political spectrum. It is also apparent that political conclusions are often presented as though they were the result of scholarship.

Furthermore I detect a distinct note of pleasure in his observation that these same left-wing professors are extremely upset that the onerous burdens they wish to be placed on other institutions in the society are placed on themselves. Again in his own words,

> There is, besides, a pleasure which is nonetheless real even if perverse, in seeing elitist institutions scream when the remedies they have prescribed for others are applied to them.

Now I want to suggest that the picture he has of American academia is for the most part mistaken. In major universities (with some notable exceptions), politicized left-wing departments presenting ideological results as unbiased scholarship, are extremely rare. One of the striking things indeed about American universities in the seventies is that, unlike many German and French universities, we did not emerge from the sixties with permanently politicized faculties or student bodies. Professors do indeed vote "to the left of the national political spectrum," or at least *on* the left of that spectrum, but that is not at all the same as being politicized and doing ideologically biased left-wing research. That we are perceived as having the features he cites may indeed be a problem, but that is essentially a problem in public relations, and in public image management, something we have never been very good at. However his claim that this public image is accurate, is, I believe, mistaken.

Professor Shils as always presents one with more ideas than one can really comment on or even come to grips with, but there is one implication in his talk that I want to contest at the outset. I am not at all sure that he intended it, but someone might take his position to imply that our universities might be perhaps better off if we had less money or at any rate less federal money; that perhaps many of our problems would be solved if we did not have quite so much in the way of federal research contracts. I think that federal funding of university research projects is on balance one of the great strengths of the American university structure, but it does create problems: that in fact is why we are here—to discuss how the universities can get the money from the federal government and still cope successfully with the problems.

Let me start the discussion of that on a positive note: it seems to me there are several things to be said on behalf of the American university system that have not been said yet. First of all, it is probably not an exaggeration to say we have educated a higher percentage of the population to a higher intellectual level than any other contemporary society, quite possibly than any society in history. Now, we are all familiar with the horror stories of American education: we all have Ph.D. students who do not know the difference between "like" and "as" and do not know that *i* comes before *e* except after *c*. But granted the horrible gaps in the mode of sensibility that we have imparted, nonetheless we have made some impressive educational achievements. A second achievement I think is worth mentioning is that the research level of what goes on in our best universities in many subjects is probably the best in the world. Indeed, internationally an interesting thing has happened: the direction of cultural impact is now going not from Europe to America but from America to Europe. My university, as I am sure is true of most of yours as well, is each year visited by sizable numbers of people from Germany, Benelux, Scandinavia and yes, even England, and France who have got a year's grant to come and study the most advanced work being done in their subjects; because in most of the subjects I am familiar with the best work is being done in the United States. And incidentally even the professional publications, the articles and books published in the fields that I am most familiar with, in philosophy and linguistics, are distinctly superior to what was being published as recently as twenty years ago. Many articles that would have been accepted for publication twenty years ago would not be accepted now, because they would be regarded as technically inadequate.

If this optimistic news that I am now recounting were all that needed to be said, we wouldn't be here today; so let me tell you some of the problems we are facing, particularly in relation to the government. I'll be extremely brief because some of these points have been touched on before. First, there is the spread of governmental bureaucracy generally and we are now feeling its effects in the universities. We are now feeling the impact of that basic principle that Mr. Bork referred to, namely, that where there is government largesse it seems to be almost inevitable that there is an attempt at government regulation. Furthermore, as part of our inheritance from the sixties we are becoming more accustomed to the adversary style of conflict resolution in the universities. Somebody said in one of our proceedings that that was a fault of the universities; I think that if one had to place the blame it is the fault of the lawyers. I think ours is an excessively lawyer-ridden society and culture generally, and the legalistic model of conflict resolution is one that has pervaded the universities. Now another difficulty we are facing, which has been mentioned briefly, is the spread of egalitarianism in the ideology of the government and the society at large. The elite universities are in a weak position to cope with this. We are by our very nature elitist in the sense that we believe that education is a matter of achieving some kind of excellence, and that varying degrees of excellence are achieved by people depending on their innate abilities and the amount of effort and training that they put into their work. I think that what we are seeing in the affirmative action issue, for example, is one of those long-term trends in America where there are oscillating swings between periods of emphasis on achievement and periods of emphasis on egalitarianism. I hope in fact that the wind may now have started to blow the other way, in the direction of achievement. The noises coming out of HEW seem to me not as frightening now as they were a few years ago.

Now, in the face of these pressures coming from outside the universities, let me mention some of the internal weaknesses that we have in coping with them. First of all, I mentioned government bureaucracy but it seems to me our own university bureaucracies are very much out of hand already as well. I don't know how many of you have been university administrators or department chairmen but if you have, you will have been subjected to a remarkable amount of sheer administrative guff that goes across your desk in the form of detailed regulations about how this and that is supposed to be done. And all of this is quite apart from the various problems about affirmative action that we hear so much about. It seems to be something we have to live with as our own larger universities get ever proliferating bureaucracies. I saw some figures the other day that I can hardly believe, but I will tell them to you so that you can disbelieve them as well. It was published in one of the papers in the Bay Area that the University of California, that is all nine campuses of the whole statewide system, has 25,000 academic employees. But the figure for nonacademic employees was 55,000: more than twice as many nonacademic employees as academic employees. Now it is not just that the tail is wagging the dog, but that the dog is really getting crowded out, and it is easy to lose sight of what the enterprise is all about. With the endless proliferation of miscellaneous employees, you get unionization and you get job security arrangements and so on, so that it becomes a permanent fixture of our academic scene that we have vast so-called "support services." We are a bit like the army in Vietnam where it took eight men to support one combat soldier, and much of the administrative effort is concerned with the supporting services.

Another problem that goes deeper was again touched on briefly but I want to say a little more about it. Various people have said that we have lost our sense of mission. Well in a way that is true, but in a way it isn't. What has happened, I think, is something like this. We have lost a sense of our teaching mission and we have increased our sense of our research mission. I am talking now about the leading universities in the country. The best professors in these universities do have an acute sense of what they are trying to do in their respective disciplines. And they are quite articulate about what their objectives are in these disciplines. But for the most part, they do not think of themselves as primarily dedicating their work to their particular universities. Rather, they address an international clientele of fellow specialists in a more or less narrow discipline; and the good ones, as I said earlier, make excellent contributions to their disciplines. But if you ask these same professors, what do you think the educational mission of the university is, and what is your mission in education or your mission in undergraduate education, then the answers become much more feeble. And indeed operationally one might say it often appears to be the case that the educational mission as far as undergraduates are concerned is to see as little of them as possible, ideally not see them at all. That I think is a serious problem. It isn't that we have lost track of what intellectual values are, but many of the best professors have lost track of what the ideal of educating the young is; and I do not see any solution to that problem in the short run.

Related to that problem is the next one: there is really a remarkable shortage of educational leadership in this country. I would like, for example, to know the names of the ten great American educators of the present era. More and more university presidents are chosen not for their vision of what higher education can be, but for their administrative skills and their skills at milking more money out of legislatures and alumni. The acute emphasis on our research mission (and I'm not knocking it, I live by it, I think it is important and indeed in my view, it is our greatest achievement) is combined with a sense of confusion about what we are trying to do in education and indeed what the institution, as an institution, is trying to achieve. And that I think is a more significant weakness than the fact that we have a few politicized sociology departments which give us a bad image in Washington. I think our failure of educational nerve is a much deeper source of our ineptitude in meeting the assaults that the university is suffering from the federal government.

In our negotiations with the government, in our dealings with the government, what sort of stance should we adopt? We are told in the excellent paper by Mr. Finn, that there are about fifteen billion dollars a year in federal funds going to the universities in one way or another, and in fact I think a great deal of the credit for the research achievements of American universities is directly tied to the support that universities get from the federal government. A great amount of really excellent research is financed by the NSF and other government contracting agencies. It's perhaps true that, as Professor Shils says, they don't pay enough overhead (though incidentally until recently we got quite a lot of overhead at the University of California, we got something like 29 percent routinely on research contracts from the government); but at any rate, it is important to us that we continue to receive funding for research; and though there is a lot of useless research that goes on, there is a lot of excellent research as well.

The first principle we should adopt in our dealings with the federal government is to avoid the assumption that somehow the more onerous forms of government regulation are inevitable and unavoidable. After all, we have already in our dealings with the government several models of satisfactory relationships. For example in my dealings with it, I have not found the National Science Foundation at all politicized or unreasonable; and indeed quite striking instances of its flexibility and the flexibility of its sister agencies are readily available. A friend of mine who is one of the most articulate and insistent of left-wing spokesmen in the United States has continued over the years to rail against the government in no uncertain terms; yet I am always amused to see at the front of his professional books a short acknowledgement of the sources of his support: it is an interesting list—the National Science Foundation, the Office of Naval Research, the U.S. Army Signal Corps, the U.S. Air Force, and their kindred like. Now I regard it as a credit to these agencies, and a credit to him, that for purposes of his professional research, which is of high quality, his various left-wing activities are regarded as really quite irrelevant. I think the government has a healthy attitude toward his case, and it is certainly a stance of political neutrality that government financing agencies should be encouraged to adopt generally.

Could we have and should we work toward a variation of the University Grants Committee in this country? It appears to have worked well in Britain, or at least it appeared to me to work well when I lived and taught in England, and the forms of government distribution of money that we already have in such agencies as the NSF are not totally unlike the UGC in that they work for the most part on intellectual criteria, free from political interference. Still it is not clear whether we could maintain that quality in decision making if we changed the principle of federal financing from contract grants to block grants. Since we are not likely to be able to count on the continuation of the best principles of the operation of the NSF in any extended government operations modelled on the UGC the question still remains, what other principles should we adopt in our dealings with the federal government?

Another principle we should adopt—and here I agree with Mr. Bork entirely—is that we ought to fight the regulations. We ought to fight them much harder than we have been fighting them. The usual response of university administrations under pressure from the federal government with threats of economic retaliation if they do not comply, is simply to give in. They gave in to the Pottinger syndrome at HEW with effects that were disastrous in the short run and very difficult to overcome in the long run. And it is very important to spell out those effects with some care so that we are not in the position of appearing to be opposed to greater minority employment in the universities. As a former department chairman with a fair amount of experience in dealing with affirmative action programs, I found two really bad effects of "Affirmative Action." First, the operational meaning of affirmative action programs as they are practiced at present is that you are supposed to discriminate against white males. No one ever says it that way in so many words, but that is clearly its meaning. There is no way that it is possible to discriminate in favor of some selected person or group without discriminating against some other person or group. The way it works in practice is that if you cannot produce a so-called minority person to fill a vacant faculty position it is regarded as somehow a failure on your part. At best you did not work hard enough, at worst you are somehow or other racially or sexually biased. A very common experience I had a few years ago was to call other department chairmen who had vacancies at other universities to recommend one of our graduate students, and to be told "No, we need a woman for this position," or "Haven't you got a black person you could recommend for the slot?" And if one points out that such remarks imply a policy that is clearly unconstitutional, one is usually told that the department in question is under a lot of pressure from the administration to meet their affirmative action goals, which are of course in effect quotas.

Now a second feature of the affirmative action program is really as bad as the first, though it has received less publicity. The sheer onerousness of the procedures, the sheer amount of bureaucratic red tape that is necessary to justify a nonminority appointment becomes in a way a kind of sanction. A department like ours that announces a vacancy is likely to get three hundred or so applicants. The regulations require us to state in writing for each applicant we did not hire why he or she did not get the job, and if we hire a white male we have to be prepared to demonstrate that he was superior to all of the "minority" applicants. Now the sheer amount of faculty and administrative time necessary to do all of this make-work constitutes a very effective form of pressure to practice discrimination against white males. The twin evils of affirmative action go hand in hand to produce a situation where the official rhetoric of affirmative action is that of increased opportunities for previously "disadvantaged" groups but the actual facts are that the policy amounts to discrimination against a prominent minority, viz., white males.

We have talked a lot about affirmative action but that is not the only area in which we are having trouble with the federal government. There is another thing looming on the horizon that may be quite unfortunate. For many years the government did not insist on the full horror of government accounting procedures for university contract research. They are now beginning to do that. And I don't think many professors realize what that is going to mean. I think it is unnecessary for the government to do that. The present situation is not as if somehow or other it has been suddenly discovered that a whole lot of professors were busy embezzling research funds. When, for example, did you last hear of somebody fleeing to Mexico with his NSF grant in his pocket? That is not a real problem. It is rather that in the secular amoebalike ooze of the bureaucracy it just seems somehow odd that these guys shouldn't be filling out the same kind of forms in the universities that they're busy filling out in the commerce department. So a whole lot more forms have come in. I think, again, it's not just a matter of having more work to do, it actually alters the quality of intellectual life.

Another principle I would like us to adopt in our dealings with the government is to make quite clear the special characteristics of universities as explicitly as we can. No one says that universities are absolutely unique and that they share no characteristics with other institutions in the society; obviously there is a continuum between universities and other institutions. But it seems clear to me that the government often proceeds on false premises in dealing with universities. For example when it comes to affirmative action they assume that there is a pool of people who are qualified in virtue of their training to be professors of philosophy in Berkeley, and that this pool has a certain ethnic makeup; and they cannot for the life of them see why our department does not reflect the ethnic makeup of that pool. Now the assumption on which we proceed is that no one is in that way "qualified" to be a professor of philosophy in Berkeley, anymore than anyone is qualified by his training to be the starting quarterback of the Redskins or the winner of the Nobel Prize. It is simply not the case that there are a whole lot of people that are "qualified" and you can go get any one of them. In fact, what we are trying to get is the absolutely best person available and often the best person available is not good enough. The premises under which we are operating, in short, are that we are trying to maintain and if possible improve very delicate standards of excellence. Now this is simply unintelligible to the people we have been dealing with in HEW. In our terms most of the people who have Ph.D.'s in philosophy are hopelessly "unqualified" to teach in our department. Philosophy, as is true of most really serious disciplines, is a bit like bullfighting: it is very hard to do it at all and almost impossible to do it really well.

To conclude, I think our ability to fight the regulations is going to involve us in a much greater commitment to presenting a unified front than we have done in the past. The amazing thing about our dealings with the Pottinger people from HEW was not in what they insisted on. Their demands seem to be part of the *Zeitgeist*. The amazing thing was the fact that the universities did not present them with a united front. HEW picked us off one at a time. Why didn't the leading fifty universities in the United States get together and say "O.K. this is going to be our position on this particular issue"? What the government did was go to Berkeley and then Columbia and others and literally pick them off, one university at a time, so they never really had to face a united front. In fact the entire university system is in this together, and we are likely to be facing continuing attacks on our autonomy. In producing a sense of common problems and common interest I believe this organization could play a crucial role.

They should be more different, but they are not. Especially important is the fact that in any view that a government official is likely to have of the universities, universities are not likely to be seen as different.

You may have heard the government people use the word "interface." They "interface" with each other and with spokesmen of interest groups or associations or institutions all the time. And, I ask, what *face* do government officials see when they "interface" with university spokesmen? In my experience, the spokesmen of higher education who are in Washington or who come to Washington and "interface" with government officials are indistinguishable to the eye of government officials, with rare exceptions, from any other lobbyists or special pleaders. They do plead for advantage, after all; they plead for special interests, and they present no visible basis for a claim of difference or superiority. They plead the private interests of students; they plead the private interests of faculty members; they plead the private interests of those who have projects or contracts that they want to negotiate; and they plead the interests of institutions.

When I was a college dean, I was in a long negotiation with students and faculty over the question of whether grades should be dropped or somehow modified. Their argument was, briefly, that if the college was, as it claimed to be, a community of learners, then grading was a jarring irrelevancy in the serious business of studying and learning together. Much of the faculty, and some students, on the other hand, argued that the grades were really necessary for the business of the college in certain practical external ways, and also for the serious internal objective of maintaining standards of excellence. We got nowhere in the dispute, because there was much merit on both sides, until finally one faculty member said, "Grades are only one more manifestation of the fallen nature of man." And that ended the deliberations, and the grading system remained unchanged. The problem of universities, and of their relations with the government, and the problem of regulation, are I think, clearly powerful manifestations of the fallen nature of the universities.

The lack of integrity, that is, the lack of principle that unifies an educational institution—even accepting the distinction that Professor Searle makes that that lack is especially evident in the teaching aspect of the university—that lack of integrity, I think, is the manifestation of the fallen nature of the universities. It is visible; it is massive; and it is seen by the government officials. And, therefore, they *know* that there is no reason to treat the "lobbyists" for higher education differently than they

216

treat other special pleaders—livestock associations, labor unions, soy-bean growers, or any other professional and trade associations who come to them for special advantage.

For these reasons I have no *lofty* advice for you. I have only what I would call bits of rather lowly advice. The higher, more interesting advice, to seek first to restore the integrity of our universities, would be, to a certain extent, a fruitless exhortation. Not wholly so, but largely so. I will limit myself, therefore, to what I think are less interesting kinds of advice, but not fruitless. Many times yesterday and today it was pointed out that affirmative action regulations, and especially provisions that use the phrase "goals and timetables," stem from an Executive Order, and that there is no legislative ground for them. That is, since 1965, when the phrase "affirmative action" was first used in the Executive Order, until now, almost a dozen years later, Congress has never acted. The phrase, "goals and timetables," as was said a number of times, does not occur in the Executive Order, and there is no evidence to think, and no reason to believe, that goals and timetables were envisioned by the people who issued the affirmative action Executive Order.

In all this time, if you think of the volumes of regulations, if you think of the countless pages that have been put out in affirmative action plans of different universities, all stemming from these regulations, and then remind yourself that they don't even have the status of a presidential order, but only a departmental order, and that in all this time Congress has never acted, I think you will see that there is an opportunity for the academic spokesmen to hit hard at the legitimacy of the affirmative action regulations, especially all those things having to do with goals and timetables. If any of you have any influence with the Carter administration (I assume I have none), I think that's the thing to hit. Let the argument be made that *this is a matter that Congress ought to deliberate.* Let the Congress hold hearings. Let the people affected, now, with a decade of experience, come before them and explain to them why they think these things ought to be incorporated in law, or why they should not be. And let the Congress deliberate, let them vote on it. If they pass a bill, let them send it to the president for his consideration and, possibly, his signature. But why not have a law on the matter, instead of what now has only bureaucratic standing?

There was one repeated factual error in President McGill's talk this morning. He said, in several places, that with regard to affirmative action his university tried to act in accord with the intent of Congress. Congress has not expressed its intent, or anything else, on this subject. There are all sorts of things that are close to it, of course, but there is no legislation on affirmative action and goals and timetables applied to university faculties, and I think that is something that should be put on the congressional agenda.

The second bit of advice I have is that you not be too easily reassured. (Allan Bloom and I have an unspoken agreement that no reassurance should be left untouched.) Professor Searle tried to reassure you that the bureaucrats may not go unreasonably far in their efforts to regulate. I think that's a false hope, and I think that the tendency to regulate will not diminish. Let me give you an example which I hope will horrify you, which very few people know about, which apparently is not yet being acted upon although it now exists, but which, when acted upon, will dwarf affirmative action programs. The Internal Revenue Service has a bureau for Exempt Organizations. They are the ones who issue certificates of tax exemption to deserving institutions of all sorts. Without such a certificate a school is not exempt from taxes, and gifts made to it are not deductible. Every university and college, of course, has such a certificate, and could not survive without it. IRS audits such organizations every year. There are, of course, numerous regulations that must be complied with in order to get, and then continue to hold, a tax-exempt certificate.

The Exempt Organizations division recently issued racially nondiscriminatory policy regulations applying to private schools: not just higher education, but every private school from nursery school on up through graduate school, of every sort. The regulations are quite lengthy, quite detailed, and there are burdensome reporting and record-keeping requirements. Private schools are also required to advertise their nondiscriminatory policy. The requirements apply to every private school, even if it is not a federal contractor or it does not participate in federally supported programs, or receive any other kind of benefit.

The underlying principle is the assumption that tax exemption is a benefit bestowed by the government. I won't elaborate the dangers in that principle. The regulations have some connection with a federal court decision, *Green* v. *Mississippi,* but when this set of regulations had not yet been published in final form in the Federal Register, I complained that this was being done without cause, that there was no requirement on them to put out these regulations, that Congress had not acted. And the reply was that a court decision required it of them. When my office (I then served in the White House as Special Consultant to the President) looked into that, unfortunately too late, because the regulations were already in the Federal Register by then, it became clear that the court's order applied only to private schools in Mississippi, where many private schools had been organized for the purpose of escaping desegregation orders, and in other states that had had a dual school system, and therefore have a "similar badge of doubt."

The IRS, on that basis, put out regulations that apply to *every* private school throughout the United States without exception. And when my office raised the question, and showed that the court order was limited to schools with a history of racial discrimination, the IRS no longer said that they were "required" to do it by the court order, but said only that their new regulations were "in accord with" the court order in the case in Mississippi.

Now I don't know how strenuously IRS auditors are applying the new regulations, but the sanction is a powerful one anytime they choose to use it. If it's found that, in one way or another, a school has not complied with the record-keeping or reporting or advertising or other racially nondiscriminatory policy regulations, the penalty can be withdrawal of the tax-exempt certificate. In addition, remember that there is no exception because, to the best of my knowledge, there is no private school in the United States that can survive without a tax-exempt certificate. In short, these regulations have unbounded extension and can inflict unlimited punishment. So much for any hope of diminution of the bureaucratic tendency to regulate wherever one can imagine it, and even to extents that cannot be imagined.

My final bit of advice. I saw many different kinds of groups while I was in the White House, coming to plead for support and for funds, mostly funds, for support which almost always took the form of money. You can imagine, especially since the government runs at a great deficit all the time, that any request for money is regarded with some skepticism. What seems to be clever ingenuity to those who come to make their plea is really just tiresome repetition to those who have heard a similar story, over and over again, from every kind of group. There were special pleas by organizations that had gone to a great deal of trouble to get the ear of the President, who would come in to the Cabinet Room with ten, twelve, twenty of their spokesmen with the President, people from appropriate agencies, depending on what the subject matter was and, of course, people from the Office of Management and Budget. The most successful presentation I heard, and that was unusually clever, was by a group of scientists—I'm not sure, I think it may have been the National Science Foundation's council. They never mentioned money. They spent the entire time describing to the President some of the interesting projects that were being undertaken by their organization, or with the support of their organization. For example, they described in some detail what is known now about the crust of the earth, something about the plates and how the plates move, and the friction where they overlap and rub, and what that tells us about the location of minerals, the genesis of earthquakes, and all sorts of other things. The President was fascinated and so were the others present. They concluded, in effect, by saying, "Mr. President, we wanted you to know what we do." And that was it. And they got an increased grant when the matter came up because weeks later the President could say: "I remember them, they really do important work."

That's my last bit of advice, and it's not trivial. To the extent that the spokesmen of higher education can come before government officials and show them, in an honest and meaningful way, that they really speak for something special and vital in our society, and different from all the other organizations and special pleaders, to that extent—and to that extent only—can they hope realistically to be treated differently.

The Grant, the Scholar and the University Community

Charles Bazerman
Baruch College, CUNY

At this conference speakers such as Dr. Finn and Dr. Powell have amply demonstrated the kinds of problems, confusions, and distortions that affect the university when there is a large infusion of federal grant money; their discussion necessarily required the distance of administrative abstraction. But certain related questions are best approached in a personal, introspective way: these are questions of what happens to us as teachers and scholars when we are put within sniffing range of these grants. As a junior faculty member interested in literature and the teaching of writing at a large urban university, I have observed and felt some of the temptations arising from the presence or potential presence of grant money. Although the particulars of the experiences that have given rise to the following comments must remain buried, I suspect the experiences are common enough for everyone to fill in his or her own examples.

The minor bendings of purpose and perception that arise from knowledge of potential grant money, even though they may appear to be only matters of personal conscience, are worth considering for their effect on the university, for the community of any academic institution depends on the day-to-day relations—written and spoken—between and among faculty and students. If anything changes what we talk about and where we go for answers; if our normally confused and obscurely directed discourse is obscured and deflected even more; if our human, and therefore curious, motives and relationships are made even more curious—then we should inquire into the effects lest those fortunate conjunctions of thought that result in new knowledge and learning become attenuated further. "The atmosphere which each member of the university 'inhales'" is not just a precondition for the production of that knowledge which the government wishes to purchase, as Dr. Shils points out, but it is the mode of existence for the university.

Grants at their best do provide the means for scholars and researchers to pursue projects they would not have been able to pursue otherwise, at least not without the care, thoroughness, and methods that a grant makes available. In my own areas of interest federal money has made possible definitive editions, allowed the collection of extensive data concerning the development of the writing process in students, and given writers the time to realize their designs. We have all seen the direct good that grants make possible.

An indirect, but significant, effect of grant money is that it encourages the creation of many unsuccessful proposals. The lure of a grant has been known to mobilize those who might not otherwise have found a focus for their work and thought. In the hope of some largesse from above, they start to define their problem, plough through the literature, and start to perceive what it is they need to know. Their grant proposals may be lacking in many ways and ultimately may be rejected, but, as I have heard many times, "the process was an education." Grant writing, as any form of writing, helps to clarify and develop thought.

I am often amazed by the power of the distant possibility of grant money to mobilize some of the most stagnant of colleagues. And this is not even money they can put in their pocket; at best they might gain summer pay or release from teaching. Yet we have all heard the size of a grant request being used as a sign of puissance, a boost to the ego, and a measure of one's value to the institution. There is security in knowing you bring funds to your school rather than being just a ward of the payroll office. Through the grapevine, usually an indicator of our pettier motives, the size of a grant request is reported with more emphasis and interest than the whys and hows of the project. That human beings are fascinated with money is nothing new; what is new is that large amounts are only a proposal away for people of our profession, people whose complicated responses to money have been complicated further by a long history of relative poverty. Though this effect of grant money to move souls may be unpleasant to contemplate, if the result is to gain action where there was none, the effect seems benign.

The problem is not that scholars are drawn to activity, but that those who would be doing something are encouraged to work along lines not the most likely to lead to their goal. I have seen this diversion operate in a number of ways.

First, the possiblity of a grant fevers the mind with grandiosity. The small, immediate task is left untended, and we move instinctively toward the larger issue or the certitude of large amounts of data. This often goes hand in hand with the ancient way of avoiding action: we do not know enough yet to act. As true as that excuse may be in some circumstances, I have seen reasonable small-scale research projects dropped, narrow and possible essays never written, administrative arrangements put off, and simple tests never drafted while awaiting resolution of some larger issue on the far side of some rainbow. By the simple equation that grant equals money equals answers, the task at hand is not faced, effort goes into a grant proposal that may well not be accepted. Even if the grant is accepted, it may not provide the answers hoped for or needed. Though nobody's intention was to table anything, an issue is lost in further study.

Even for those issues where further study is advisable we must ask whether the kind of study encouraged by grants is likely to produce the best results. In the fields I know most about, the most fruitful lines of work usually involve little more than time, a library card, some colleagues and students to talk with, blank paper, a typewriter, and lots of coffee. But of course this is not what tends to be rewarded or supported, so there is a multiplication of projects using inappropriate techniques, turning the arts of reading and understanding into gross quantifiable measures of particular tropes with little regard for context, import, nuance, or purpose. In order to become more grantworthy (that, by the way, is a very interesting new term in the English language), research in writing has tended toward the most easily identifiable elements of grammar and style, particularly as practiced by those at the lower end of competence. The traditional methods in both areas involved studying what was most idiosyncratic and original in the most individual of writers; since the products of such writers are such intricate webs of ways of meaning, gross quantifiable features will not tell you what you want to know and will not help your students appreciate what is best.

These two temptations to less fruitful modes of inquiry and action are exacerbated by the usual interest of grant-giving agencies in research of practical use, which is immediately transferable to other institutions and situations. The local considerations and interests of researchers must be hedged by considerations of exportability. One can understand the agencies' desires to get their money's worth and not to support irresponsibly idiosyncratic private projects; however, stipulations on grant offers ultimately do tend to reshape disciplines. Such shifts, as that in the teaching of writing from that which is most unique and masterful to that which most have already mastered, may be quite salutory, but they should not go unmarked and unexamined.

Other disciplines must meet the criteria of grant research more easily with less distortion of method and interest, but even there a further complication enters in: the perception of how one must write a grant in order to succeed. I have no specific knowledge of how grants actually are awarded, but I do know the way my colleagues talk of grant writing. Since one is selling a pig in a poke, the promise of a project with results still distant, one tries to appeal to the prejudices, as one perceives them, of the grant-giving agency. No matter how high-minded one is, this extraneous factor enters into the original design of research. The formula usually goes like this: One wants to propose something recognizable (that is, it must resemble earlier work in the field to show that the proposal is sound) yet recognizably different (so that the grant givers will not feel the proposal is redundant). The element of fashion has much to do with what is recognizable and recognizably different. One is led not just in theme, but also in acceptable variations. In this way the agency becomes more than just a silent partner from the earliest days of the project. It is difficult enough for innovation to flourish when any academy exists, but the situation is made far worse when the researcher must trim his plant while it is still a seed. Nor is the innovator the only one who suffers; unless one grafts an obviously different idea onto a traditional approach, the value of one's work may be missed. The art of attractive promises is different from the ability to produce interesting and significant results; that these two arts are always compatible is questionable.

Of course, as serious scholars it is our own personal responsibility to wend our way down the path of truth, avoiding digression, temptation, and the designs of power; our self-esteem often hangs on our ability to sort out appropriate lines of inquiry and to disdain lesser considerations. However, we must look at this matter as more than a test of our own virtue, for in certain atmospheres we tarnish more easily. And when the tarnish is covered over with the appearance of national purpose, the cumulative effects on the institution may be considerable before they are noticed. Let me suggest a few of the places where the effect may become noticeable: First, when we discuss our work with our colleagues, we tend to discuss what is foremost in our minds. What happens to our discourse when grant obtaining becomes a major concern? Second, with our students we share not just the content of our current intellectual concerns, we share our methods and our selves as models. Our concerns, our manner of talk, our ambitions, our dispositions, our reading, and our writing are the means by which students come to know our disciplines and the human meaning of those disciplines. What effect does our grant orientation have here? Finally, insofar as grant obtaining is a sign of instant recognition, based on promise rather than proven accomplishment, and grants, once obtained, become a source of power, how does this affect relations among colleagues, the academic pecking order, and ambitions?

For all these considerations, grants serve many useful functions, and I am not suggesting cloaking ourselves in white robes and abjuring the money. It is for those with more understanding and control of the situation than myself to take such matters into account when they draft new ways of distributing the largesse in a manner that will most benefit learning, knowledge, and their own particular practical purposes. As for myself, I will keep looking to see if something I want to know corresponds to something grant-giving agencies will support. I don't think I am the only one haunted by this vision of funding.

pursuit of science should be free"—enshrined in the not very democratic Prussian Constitution in the nineteenth century—the very fact that these interventions of government were widely regarded as violations of academic freedom testifies to the strength of the principle.

The situation is no different with respect to American higher education. The absence of genuine academic freedom in most American colleges and universities until the twentieth century was more the consequence of religious than political intolerance. By the latter half of the twentieth century the principles of academic freedom and the recognition of the relative autonomy of the university became, so to speak, the common law of the academy. The dogma that those who underwrite the costs of university education control in any significant way its character, could hardly be squared with the fact that in the area of private university education the most common criticism among the donors to universities, who are drawn mainly from the business classes, has been that classroom instruction as well as faculty judgment has not been objective or neutral with respect to the free enterprise system but, on the whole, aggressively and pervasively hostile. It is widely alleged that the academy has adopted an adversary posture to the business values of our culture. Despite these criticisms, universities have properly refused to accept benefactions tied to any provision requiring that certain doctrines or practices be upheld or decried. This consistent policy has been accompanied by a rise in contributions to the private universities from the private sector of the economy.

Surprisingly, the more significant threat to the autonomy of the university in recent times has come from the state, specifically from governmental agencies and the courts. This has developed in consequence of measures adopted for the laudable purpose of making *access* to higher education more universal and at the same time preventing invidious discrimination against qualified candidates for admission and teaching posts on grounds of race, sex, religion, or national origin. It is sheer demagogy to maintain as some partisans of preferential hiring have done, that criticism of some of the methods and measures imposed by governmental agencies is merely a rationalization of racial prejudice. Those who ask: "What is all the shooting about?", and insist that "government intervention has been advancing equal opportunity in education" seem blind to an obvious fact that should have given them profound concern in the light of their own professions. They have willfully ignored the fact that the abuses of the original Executive Orders, on which affirmative action programs were based and which have led to preferential hiring, deny "equal opportunity" to those who are the victims of preferential hiring. They systematically confuse the goal of "equality of opportunity" with the achievement of "equality of result," regardless of relevant differences in merit.

Before discussing some questionable aspects of government intervention, it is necessary to state briefly some underlying assumptions of my argument. I do not believe that a valid case can be made for the absolute autonomy of the university, however its academic mission be defined. The university is not exempt from the laws of the democratic community, nor can it be indifferent to the assessment of reflective ethical judgment to its aims and practices. The community which supports it is justified in expecting the university to fill a social need and purpose in the same way that the community expects a medical school to fill the social need to improve, by its research, teaching, and clinical practices, human health. The academic mission of the university is, broadly speaking, to inquire, publish, and teach the truth as its qualified faculty members see it in the arts, sciences, and humanities. In doing so, the university performs a social function and social need of the first importance in any civilized community. The recognition of that social function is justification enough for the community to support it. The university may, of course, take on *voluntarily* other social functions at the request of the community and its representatives, provided they do not interfere with the adequate performance of its central mission.

The community is under no legal obligation, and, depending upon costs and its other pressing priorities, under no moral obligation to underwrite or support the university. Members of the academy as citizens enjoy the same equal rights of other citizens to press their claims for educational priority, but as democrats they must submit to the arbitrament of the political process even as they agitate for a wiser policy. Once, however, the community through its authorized representatives has granted educational support, it has no moral right to dictate how the professionally qualified educator should carry out his task. The educators themselves are under a moral obligation to resist the infringement of the state on their professional prerogatives. This sometimes requires sacrifice and courage. But in situations of conflict the willingness to defend the academic mission is the measure of professional integrity.

It is surprising how often this simple but basic position is disregarded. It is disregarded both by those who make an absolute of university autonomy and who demand that decisions concerning it be exempt from considerations normally pertinent in the allocation of a community's resources, and by those who, accepting the relative autonomy of the university, are prepared to subordinate and compromise standards of professional integrity in order to receive continued funding. To bring the matter home in relation to some recent issues, we may apply these principles to the establishment of schools of medicine. The decision of a state university, for example, to establish a school of medicine, which is a notoriously costly operation, cannot and should not be effected without legislative warrant. There may be good and sufficient reasons why other programs should receive precedence. Since resources are always limited, the legislative decision to underwrite alternative programs and to reject the proposal to establish the medical school must be accepted as legitimate even if it is deemed unwise by educators and physicians and made an issue in the next electoral appeal to the citizens. But once the school of medicine is funded, it would be utterly intolerable for the legislature or the executive or judiciary to lay down directives on what constitutes a proper medical education, what subjects should be taught, how they should be taught, the criteria of qualification for admission and graduation, and what medical doctrines or theories should govern instruction.

Decisions on these matters are the exclusive province of the faculty of the medical school. This does not mean, of course, that the faculty is free to do anything it pleases in this area. If any specific practice violates a constitutional right, if there is discrimination not on the basis of one relevant standard of fitness or merit, applied equitably to all, but on the basis of race, sex, religion, national origin, or any other criterion unrelated and irrelevant to the purpose of medical education, the community through its representatives is justified in intervening. The law of the land must be upheld in every domain. The university is not a sanctuary for those who run foul of it. The contention, however, that a law of the land has been violated by a medical institution must be established beyond reasonable doubt or on preponderant evidence by those making the charge. The institution must not be expected to shoulder the burden of proof that it is innocent of wrongdoing. That burden must rest upon whoever makes the allegation of guilt.

Recent educational history is replete with illustrations of the unjustified intrusion of organs of the state into the academy. Congress and legislative bodies have not been the chief governmental bodies guilty of such practices, but the federal and state bureaucracies, most notably the Department of Health, Education and Welfare, and the Courts. A few illustrations should suffice. Not so long ago, a student won reinstatement to the George Washington University School of Medicine from which he had been expelled by its Evaluation Committee by a vote of thirteen to one, on the ground that for two successive years he had done academic work "of marginal quality." The student in question had done poorly in his second year, and had failed in one key course. The Committee on Educational Evaluation reviewed his case, decided to give him "a second chance," and permitted him to repeat the year. This meant that he would be repeating courses he had already, even if barely, passed, thus having an additional opportunity to increase his standing. He was placed under close faculty supervision by a faculty member of his choice, someone whom he regarded as most sympathetic to him. He was explicitly warned that he would be treated in "the most harsh fashion"—tantamount to declaring he would be dropped—in the event that his academic performance continued to be of "marginal quality."

At the time of this compassionate treatment by the Evaluation Committee, the student raised no questions about what work of "marginal quality" meant, or what its criteria are. Although the phrase had been used and acted upon by the Committee in the past, no *formal* definition was ever formulated or agreed upon. The logic of the concept is like that of a "borderline" case, a "twilight zone" which in the nature of the case defies precise definition although there is little difficulty with their operative use. Nonetheless, when the student was dropped from the rolls, he sued in the courts for reinstatement. Incredible as it seems, Chief Judge Harold H. Greene of the District of Columbia Superior Court ruled in the student's favor, and ordered him reinstated at the University where he is now a third-year student. Because there was no fixed definition of "marginal quality"—this student who placed 142 in a class of 151—at his second try!—and 151 in a class of 151 in behavioral science (facts known to Judge Greene), was held to be the victim of arbitrary action by the faculty.

If anything was arbitrary in this situation, it was the judge's action. For it was a clear violation of the faculty's right to set academic standards and revealed an egregious ignorance of traditional scholarly practice in most educational institutions.

It is noteworthy that the student did not claim that he was dropped because of racial, religious, or sexual reasons, or that he was discriminated against on personal grounds, or that he was denied due process and hearing. All he claimed was that the action was arbitrary, despite his

record, and the judge upheld him. The reasoning—or rather the rationalization of the judge—was as specious as it was educationally unwise:

> What this medical school may not do—any more than any other
> institution, public or private—is to enter into a contractual arrange-
> ment with an individual upon which that individual reasonably
> relies, and then provide, to the individual's detriment, its own
> subjective interpretation of the agreement after the fact and without
> prior notice.

One rubs one's eyes in disbelief. There was no contractual arrangement with the student of the kind implicit in accepting his tuition and
offering him educational services. The Committee could have dropped
him at the end of his second year without giving him a second chance.
There was no question but that the Evaluation Committee was to be the
judge of what constituted "marginal work." Every teacher knows that
except when he or she is dealing with sharply defined extensive magni-
tudes that can be compared in an exact quantitative way, there is a
penumbral area that shades off from satisfactory work. When thirteen out
of fourteen faculty members, whose *parti pris* on any personal or constitutional ground has not been established or even alleged, agree that a
student is unfit or unqualified, it is hard to understand on what grounds
they can reasonably be taxed with making an arbitrary judgment. Most
awards of fellowships, most prizes in essay contests, are made on the
basis of criteria much more vague and ill-defined than those followed by
an Evaluation Committee on the relative standing of students. In many
situations when individuals are placed on probation for failings of a
personal and intellectual nature, there are no fixed rules on which the
individuals can rely, or if there are rules, they are not always necessary or
sufficient, and do not exclude consideration of relevant data that do not
come under the rules. Judgment is made usually of the situation as a
whole. In the case in question, the student was not told to do his best, and
that his best would see him through. He was told to do his best and that the
Evaluation Committee would then judge. They found that his best was
simply not good enough. If an action is arbitrary when it is done without
"reasons," we must conclude that on this score the expulsion of the
student was not arbitrary because all thirteen of those who voted against
him could have given reasons even if it turned out that they were not all
identical. If an action is arbitrary when it is done capriciously, then the

action against the student was not arbitrary, since he was warned. The action against him was not out of the blue or animated by any persecutory zeal.

There are a number of other illustrations of judicial intervention into the educational process which reflect either judicial arrogance or ignorance of the requirements of scholarship. In some jurisdictions judges have attempted on various grounds to determine the conditions under which permanent tenure in a university is to be earned. Where a university department hires someone to teach, permanent tenure cannot be automatic. It must be acquired after a certain period. Normally good teaching and publication are necessary conditions. But they are not always sufficient. Some judges have held that the burden of proof must rest with the department that does not grant permanent tenure to show that the individual to whom it has been denied has not earned it, that his performance is not satisfactory, etc. But this overlooks what is or should be the chief consideration in granting permanent tenure, viz.: What decision will be for the best educational interests of students and the furtherance of scholarship in fulfillment of the institution's academic mission? A person may be a good teacher, a passable scholar, and a collegial asset but still not good enough for the best interests of the department, the subject matter, and the students as a whole. Someone else may become available who can fill an important educational need of the department—say, mastery of a newly opened field—and whose seminal contributions already give promise of even greater things.

By all odds the greatest threat to the educational autonomy of the university has been the HEW guidelines interpreting the provisions of the Executive Orders outlawing discrimination on grounds of race, sex, religion, or national origin. These guidelines prescribe numerical goals and timetables by bureaucratic decree. Evidence of invidious discrimination is inferred from statistical frequencies in racial and sexual hiring incommensurate with statistical frequencies in those regarded as potentially utilizable. Good faith efforts to achieve these numerical goals must be manifested to the satisfaction of the bureaucrats of HEW. Scores of cases have been documented in which reverse discrimination has been practiced against young white males and sometimes against members of minorities in behalf of other minorities. The arguments, and the relevant data, have been developed elsewhere but here I wish to consider the narrow question of how, not the policies of affirmative action, but the

233

practices of preferential hiring, of numerical goals, and quotas, that violate proper principles of affirmative action, have invaded an area in which the university must enjoy autonomy to fulfill its academic mission.

To begin with, and the point cannot be repeated too often, the principles of affirmative action, as formulated in the Executive Order 11246 as amended, forbid all invidious discrimination in employment practices by government contractors of any kind. This is the law of the land. If an institution wishes to forego profiting from any contractual relationship with the government, it would still not be free to discriminate invidiously on grounds of race, color, religion, sex, or national origin in its hiring practices, for this would run foul of the Civil Rights Act of 1964 and of the Fourteenth Amendment to the Constitution as interpreted by the courts.

From a purely educational point of view, there is no justification for any kind of invidious discrimination of this sort even if there were no pains or penalties imposed for the practice. For the academic mission of the university requires that the best qualified persons available should be selected. In addition, on moral and political grounds, every citizen who is a member of any sexual, religious, ethnic, or national group has a justified grievance against any educational institution engaging in invidious discriminatory practices. Since such institutions profit directly by the tax support of the community or indirectly in virtue of their tax exemption, why should his tax contributions underwrite institutions that discriminate against his kind?

It is one thing to support the principle of affirmative action so construed and quite another to impose numerical goals or quotas on universities. For with respect to admissions and hiring, this intrudes into the province in which, until now, the academy has jealously guarded its prerogatives. The saddening spectacle of the capitulation of great universities to HEW demands for numerical goals and time schedules in the hiring of faculties on which their academic future depends can be attributed to an erosion of commitment to the pursuit of excellence if this jeopardizes income. Only recently has there been some principled opposition on the part of some medical schools at the federally mandated requirement that they accept a government set quota of American medical students who have enrolled and completed a period of study in medical schools abroad. Led by the Johns Hopkins University School of Medicine, almost a score of university affiliated medical schools are up in arms

234

against this attempt of the state to dictate the criteria that should govern the selection of students. It is notorious that because of the incomparably higher level of educational instruction, evaluation, and certification in American medical schools as compared with most European countries, students who study abroad are overwhelmingly among those whom American medical schools have already rejected as unworthy of admission. Rather than permit them to enter through a back door, the institutions in question have decided to forego government support to the tune of approximately a half million dollars in each case. Although the medical schools are permitted under the amendment that contains this provision to prescribe the successful passing of a qualification test as a necessary condition of acceptance, they have refused to yield, and there is an excellent likelihood that the amendment will be repealed. This makes quite mystifying the support by some of these schools, as this is being written, of the racial quota system for the acceptance of students at the Medical School of the University of California at Davis which is the focus of the Bakke case and, in the case of their associated liberal arts colleges and graduate schools, preferential hiring practices that seek to fulfill numerical goals that cannot be normally implemented without reverse discrimination.

One of the arguments heard in the Bakke case is that universities should be permitted to make their own determinations about admissions even when they are recipients of grants for medical education from the government. It is very odd, however, that those taking this position do not protest the guidelines laid down by HEW which impose numerical goals and time schedules, actually good faith efforts to achieve quotas, as a necessary condition for receiving federal funding in any contractual relation with the government. And this despite the fact that these directives violate the letter and spirit of the Executive Order 11246 and Section 703 [j] of Title VII of the Civil Rights Act of 1964.

The ill-considered legislation that set quotas for acceptance of American medical students now studying abroad was motivated by kindly concern for the future of the approximately six thousand persons who fall in this class. But it does not justify undermining the relative autonomy and morale of the medical schools. The altogether laudable zeal to eradicate all vestiges of invidious discrimination in higher education, and to provide equal opportunities and access to colleges and universities, does not justify the abandonment of one relevant and equitable standard, regardless of its components, for admissions, hiring, promotion, and other educational practices.

Recently, some administrators and educators have indicated that when it is available, they preferred private to state support for educational purposes on the ground that grants from private sources do not require tremendous clerical burdens and are not subject to the controls imposed by the Department of Labor's Office of Federal Contract Compliance. This is quite understandable but as the costs of higher education mount, it is wishful thinking to expect American universities, with the exception of a small number that are highly endowed, to survive without increasing amounts of government support.

Even highly endowed private universities, in virtue of their tax exemption, cannot shake themselves free from the potential incubus of an overregulation that threatens in some areas their hard-won traditional relative autonomy. Independently of their current resources, the universities of the nation must develop an informed and continued concern in the educational moves of the government. They must act in concert to guard the educational mission from the fallout of general legislation not directly aimed at them. The pending legislation outlawing mandatory retirement at sixty-five is a good illustration of a law, which, whatever can be said for it in some areas, may be prejudicial to the best interests of institutions of higher education and, to that extent, to the nation itself, if no provision is made for the exemption of relatively high-paid tenured professors who suffer no hardship on their retirement.

It may be that to preserve the integrity of the academic mission, the university may have to divest itself of new departments and divisions, and return to the lean days of the past in which scholars led lives of genteel poverty. Even if they were to end up this way, it is not a sad fate. It would be preferable to capitulating to unreasonable government intervention for the sake of a bloated affluence. But these do not exhaust the alternatives. Courageous faculties supporting courageous administrators, and prepared if need be, to make temporary sacrifices, can successfully resist bureaucratic usurpation of their educational role.

Is the University a Special Case?

Fred Baumann
Assistant Executive Secretary, UCRA

A misleading first impression of this conference would find that the most fundamental division was over the proper extent of government intervention in higher education. The panelists seemed to review many of the arguments used in the familiar debates over government intervention in the economy or federal intervention in state and local affairs. From that perspective, it might appear that conservatives such as Dr. Bork, Professor Shils, and Professor Bloom joined in opposing government intervention, while liberals such as Dr. Bonham and Dr. Tollett defended it and others, like President McGill and Professor Powell, occupied a middle ground. That viewpoint would also lead to the conclusion that the issues involved in the University's relations with the State do not have very much to do with the peculiar character of higher education, but have almost entirely to do with how one views government intervention into social institutions in general.

Dr. Bonham's view, a familiar liberal one, confirms the impression. He wishes in general to make "the kinds of sociopolitical arrangements which will more likely tend to the social priorities of this society," without "needlessly treading" on the rights and dignity of institutions. Among the rights Dr. Bonham allots to the university is defense of what he calls "the essential principles of its domain." But Dr. Bonham does not tell us what these principles are. He does say that the university can no longer claim to be a "special and unique preserve of Western culture or a special sanctuary," because its "basic social function" and the "external social environment" have changed. Indeed, the only difference Dr. Bonham sees between universities and most other institutions is that universities suffer the "particular cost quandaries of modern nonprofit institutions."

I think it is fair to say that if the "external social environment" and the "basic social function" of the university can determine whether it will be a special preserve of culture, then social environment and social function are the essential determinants of the university's character. Thus, for Dr. Bonham, universities are one more "sociopolitical arrangement" for tending to society's priorities. It is therefore easy to see why he is impatient with any principled objections to the imposition of other social priorities on the university and why he contents himself with criticizing excessive zeal and arbitrariness committed by "certain government bureaus" in implementing policy.

Dr. Bonham seems fortified in his view by the belief that society's priorities are both evident and evidently good. Thus he says that there is little dispute among academics about "the social intent of present-day legislation." And in case his meaning is unclear, he explains that there is a difference between "thoughtful and analytic intellectuals" and "our most vocal free enterprisers." Little wonder that Dr. Bonham seems undisturbed by his prediction that those whom he calls the "academic guild" will be met with the intolerance of the majority if they insist on claiming the university as a "special sanctuary." The majority will presumably be acting according to the consensus of reasonable academics in this, as in its other social priorities.

Against Dr. Bonham's trust in government as the twin repository of reason (as sanctioned by academic opinion) and authority (as sanctioned by democracy), Dr. Bork invokes a familiar conservative vision. Where Dr. Bonham argues the rightness of the content of government intervention, Dr. Bork argues the harmfulness of the form. In the delegation of more and more authority to the state, all other institutions will suffer a "twilight of authority." Citing Toqueville, Dr. Bork contends that without powerful and autonomous private institutions, among them universities, our liberties may be in danger.

As between these two views, each representative of a broad and familiar current in contemporary political argument, Dr. Bork's view has the merit of taking into account the structural effect of government action on private institutions and hence on society as an entity. Dr. Bonham's movement from faith in the intent of social legislation to faith in the result of its imposition (except for the excesses to which he objects) seems too rapid. Also, it is curious that Dr. Bonham so readily identifies the "social priorities of the society" with those he favors and with those of most academics. For example, according to all public opinion polls, including a Gallup Poll taken in Spring 1977, preferential treatment on the basis of race (which Dr. Bonham himself favors) is overwhelmingly opposed by the vast majority of Americans, including the majority of those groups supposed to benefit from preferential treatment. If by the priorities of society Dr. Bonham means the priorities of the whole of society, as measured by the existence of a strong consensus of the general public, and if he really means that our task is to implement those priorities by instituting proper sociopolitical arrangements, ought he not then to be looking for ways to end preferential treatment rather than for ways to extend it? And if, as I suspect, Dr. Bonham actually believes that preferential treatment is a sound policy which should be pressed whatever the majority of the American people may think, what becomes of the majoritarian relativism according to which institutions have their character determined not by their inner nature, but by society's understanding of their function? May one be allowed to defend preferential treatment without regard to the tolerance of "the majority of Americans," yet not be allowed to defend the university's status as a special sanctuary if the majority demurs?

Still, Dr. Bonham may be more consistent than he appears. Describing the consensus on the benign intent of government policy, he appeals not to the majority of Americans but to the common opinion of academics and "thoughtful and analytic intellectuals." If their view is taken as the true source of society's priorities, then the apparent contradiction disappears. But in that case it appears that the "academic guild" may not be as bereft of special privilege as it seemed. Rather than having lost the claim to the university as a special sanctuary, in this formulation the claim has merely been traded in; in return academics have received special privileges in the formulation of social policy.

The disagreement between Dr. Bonham and Dr. Bork, deep as it is on the content of overall social policy, yields to agreement on the special character of the university. Dr. Bork is at least as emphatic as Dr. Bonham in denying that "universities are so different and more subtly complex than other institutions that regulation is bound to be uniquely

239

destructive when applied to them," and in lamenting the professorial misconception that only the university is concerned with excellence in its appointments.

That agreement, however, reveals the truly central issue of this conference: the university's right to make any special claim for itself. But it is only possible to assert this if Dr. Bonham and Dr. Bork have more to contend with than the snobbery, blind traditionalism, and idealistic anachronism they appear to recognize as opposing them. In the papers of Professor Bloom and Professor Shils a serious case is made for the university as a special sanctuary, a case not dealt with by Dr. Bonham or Dr. Bork.

As Professor Shils formulates it, there are institutions, like government, which dwell in the realm of practice, and institutions, like churches and universities, which attempt "to find the meaning and laws of existence." Each kind of institution has its own concerns and character and should not be tyranically subsumed by the other. Professor Bloom makes the point more radically. It is not just that the active and contemplative lives each have their own character and institutions. The university differs from other institutions, private and public, in that it is "dedicated to the knowledge of the permanent concerns of man as man, not to the fragments of man that we find in this time, in this place." This means that the university, when it is doing its proper job, always and in principle challenges the basic beliefs of our society (and consequently, its social priorities).

The university thus has a human function that transcends its social function, but it has a social function as well. According to this view, though, its social function is not that of serving society along the lines society has selected for itself. Rather, it serves society by questioning, opposing, and humbling society. Professor Bloom is right, I think, in making a test of a society's decency its respect for such questioning and humbling.

If a university cannot and may not be harmonized with any society's particular purposes it then has a special position among social institutions. The argument for the autonomy of economic institutions such as the market is after all that their freedom is superlatively in harmony with society's purposes. Even churches which hold the morals of this world up to the searching light of the next can by that very division resolve the tension of their relation to the state. Various doctrines, from "inner emigration" to total obedience to secular authority, to the division of church and state, have sought with partial success to settle the position of a transcendental religion in civil society by a clear demarcation of claims. But the tension between a true university and a decent society cannot be resolved in this way.

The temptation to government to reduce the university to harmony will always be strong; the temptation to the university to enjoy the benefits of that harmony will, as Professor Bloom emphasized, be, if anything, especially strong in a liberal democracy. Yet the disharmony must be maintained both for the sake of the university and society. Therefore, special restraints are necessary to perpetuate that disharmony.

Yet this argument does not at first seem to have much to say to the reality of the American university. Molded by the Morrill Land Grant Act, by the post-Sputnik flood of socially directed largesse and in general by the pragmatic, material demands of a liberal society, the American university understands itself to serve society directly and not by opposition. One need only think of President McGill's listing of the practical achievements of American universities, Professor Powell's complex account of the interpenetration of government and academy at an institution whose very existence is predicated on the need for a direct social service, or of Dr. Finn's sober account of the federal government's funding of specific projects, to wonder what possible *use* the American university could make of the arguments raised by Professors Bloom and Shils. In its full form, as Professor Bloom presents it, it is only that "core" of the university, which treats of the permanent questions of human existence, that can claim the protection of special sanctuary, since whatever is directed to public utility, he contends, may properly be regulated by the society which it serves. Yet today, not only would it be unrealistic to expect the many relatively well-funded disciplines which pursue public utility to acknowledge the primacy of the few poverty-stricken disciplines which do not, but it would not even gain them the desired end of establishing a position which the state may not invade. Thus, are those not right who saw in the discussion between Professor Bloom and President McGill the conflict of an anachronistic idealism and contemporary pragmatic realism, when they dismiss the American university's claim to be fundamentally different from other social institutions?

I do not think so. While Dr. Bork is surely right that "excellence" is not the peculiar characteristic of the academy or of its hiring standards, the professors who make this common and inadequate claim nonetheless mean something by it that is not mere snobbery. The claim reveals a genuine perception which, however, academics find extremely difficult to articulate.

Dr. Powell's paper gives a set of clues both to what that perception is and why it is difficult to articulate. He tells of a school with an obvious, direct social purpose just as the understanding of that purpose underwent radical change. The change was not simply imposed from without; the institution itself had produced the theorists and advocates of change. But something happened to the institution's internal coherence. Outside funding transformed its mission, and by its magnitude weakened collegiality. Individuals pursued special projects without much regard to a common purpose. This effect was intensified by the fact that the change of mission involved less emphasis on teaching an acquired subject matter and more on discrete experiments in new styles of education. Dr. Powell is not opposed to the change in the school's mission, but he is clearly uneasy about the centrifugal effect it has had on the faculty of the school. Yet if the purpose of the Harvard School of Education were simply to serve society why should the loosening of collegial bonds be more than a minor annoyance?

Professor Shils offers some significant illumination in speaking of academic morale and ethos. Their essence, he seems to suggest, is "this interior life of the university, this devotion to knowledge as intrinsically valuable which sustains the pursuit of knowledge about things which are of practical importance." Is it not this "interior life" which makes institutional coherence so desirable? That is, however it may appear to society and society's political representatives, a healthy discipline must keep alive within itself argument, mutual criticism, experiment, and redefinition of questions. This may be true of even the most socially directed, practically useful disciplines, such as a school of education. Without that "interior life" the discipline will calcify and in the end not even be able to solve society's problems on society's own terms.

The nature of that "interior life" differs greatly according to the discipline. Those disciplines whose origins are defined by an external, social purpose will probably be dominated by the solution, on set lines, of practical problems, unlike disciplines where the most fundamental questions of the method, purpose, and character of the discipline remain permanently open. However, even the most externally directed discipline will, if it is alive, face crises in which its purposes and self-conception are radically challenged, not merely by changes in the external social environment or "basic social function" but by developments in the perpetual internal argument within the discipline. Dr. Powell's account is but one example of such a crisis that occurred, for external and internal reasons, in all the social sciences throughout the past decade.

But when such a crisis of definition arrives, the scholars of the discipline find that they must transcend the old categories and terms of reference of their discipline, if only to defend them from attack. At such moments, specialists have to leave behind their specialties and enter or at least approach the world of those disciplines in which the permanent questions of man as man are the permanent subject. Thus, for example, the choice faced in the Education School must, if approached rationally, lead to considerations about the kind of human being education ought to produce and about the fitness of certain kinds of education for certain kinds of societies, both philosophic questions which must be dealt with before instrumental strategies can be advocated.

Dr. Powell's paper also reveals the excessive simplicity of the view of even the most socially directed part of the university as an instrument of society's priorities. For after all, in this case, society's priorities, as expressed by federal officials, were originally the priorities of a number of academic theorists. But for their belief in the value of experiential learning, the social priorities imposed on the Harvard Education School might have been quite different. Indeed, but for the inculcation in a generation of public officials by their teachers of the belief in social equality and the ability of government to create it, the social priorities imposed on the society as a whole might have been quite different. In a sense, far from the university being a sociopolitical arrangement tending to the social priorities of society, society is a sociopolitical arrangement tending to the social priorities of the university.

To recognize this is of course not to conclude that academics as a class have any special wisdom in formulating social policy or that they have any special right as a group to have their views taken more seriously than others. (Scholarly knowledge, when combined with good judgment, may of course give that authority to individuals.) Rather, this recognition is an acknowledgement of the seminal effect on society of developments in thought which are generated internally and which at their most interesting and crucial go beyond both the orthodoxies of the society and the discipline.

It is that perception of the actual autonomy of the university which is so difficult to express in the American university, and which takes the inadequate forms so justly criticized by Drs. Bork and Bonham. The university believes it is supported for the sake of the Nobel prizes, the medical and agricultural technology, the B.A.'s value in *embourgeoisement,* for the sake of everything but the intellectual occupation which creates the rest. As a consequence, its importance and centrality have become hidden to us. But the uneasiness found in Professor Powell's account, the sense expressed by many that the government does not understand the character of higher education, even perhaps the frequent attempt to substitute political power or prestige for academic freedom, all speak of the sense that something is missing in the account of the university as just one more institution with a social function to perform.

The argument for block grants is a case in point. Dr. Finn may well be right that the federal government is not likely to give them. However, they would enable a university to pursue its serious educational business without dressing up programs with a spurious originality designed to entice foundations and government agencies which tend to confuse colleges with novelty stores. As such, it is an argument for that "interior life" which is autonomous and cannot predict its results. Similarly, the argument against the imposition of the "industrial model" on faculty hiring procedures need not express indifference to discrimination outside the university. While the training of a bricklayer is indeed lengthy, the grades of skill in the craft many, and the difference between an excellent and a merely competent bricklayer large, at least there are set skills and job descriptions which unions and employers can agree on. Thus, one is either licensed to work in marble or one is not. But after the point is reached where an academic is entitled to teach graduate students, agreement about skills and job descriptions breaks down in many disciplines and the ebb and flow of the interior life begins to take over. Developments in the discipline itself determine what skills are required, and disagreement is far more widespread and lasts far longer than elsewhere.

Thus, the university's claim to autonomy is, though ancient, no anachronism. Though rarely fully stated, it reflects actuality. And though it does not exclude claims of autonomy by other institutions, it is not the same claim as theirs. Medieval guild privilege is not claimed. Recognition by the state of the primacy of the university's interior life is claimed. It is claimed for the sake of the university but should be granted for the sake of the state, since in even the middle run, society will receive little of genuine benefit from a university conceived as its instrument.

A Minority Report

Eli Spark
Catholic University of America

Let me record a few only seemingly random reflections during the conference, which time did not allow to be expressed from the floor. Some, I am certain, will call them jaundiced or cynical, and try to shrug them off; others, I think, will agree deep within that they are realistic; still others, I hope, will at least think about the problems of the university and the state in light of them, perhaps for the first time, and suffer some shock. This may be a minority report, but it should be recorded.

There were many, and generous, allocations of blame for the troubles in our paradise, to the bureaucrats, the Congress, the executive, the judiciary, the foundations, the philanthropists and others—but, in our righteous self-esteem, not to the universities themselves, and their faculties, administrators, and students. Haven't we overlooked the very heart of the matter? Should not our analysis, like charity, begin at home? We assume, and preach, our own sanctity. Our deeds, however, tell others that we are sanctimonious, and that we mainly wish to make the universities our own private sanctuaries.

I was intrigued by one speaker's characterization of the bureaucracy as being not simply "mediocrity," but "mediocrity in depth." As a lifelong observer of higher education, from both within and without, may I suggest (with only a soupçon of hyperbole to enhance the flavor) that "mediocrity in depth" has become a pretty fair characterization of the great mass of our colleges and universities, and of all their constituent elements of faculty, administration, and students?

Our conference heard frequently the term "the Academy" as a general referent to our multitude of multitudinous modern universities and colleges. I suggest it is a misuse. How little relation they bear, in purpose, form, method, orientation, content, and results, to the real "Academy" of the Greek philosophers, or to the medieval universities and the great teachers whose clusters of following students established them! Using the labels of worthiness and learning, and even wearing the mantles of worthiness and learning, do not magically create either worthiness or learning. Ready capitulation by faculties and administrations to student "demands," their readiness to hand their responsibilities over to those who have not yet learned how to be responsible, professors' treating the university activity as only one of several (some of the others often being the more financially profitable), have been poor auguries indeed for the transmittal of standards of judgment or morality by our universities. One thinks of Charles Homer Haskin's phrase about the "outside activities which are the chief excuse for inside inactivity in the American college."

For most of my life, I had observed that the least educated, though perhaps the most humane, group among what used to be referred to as "educated" Americans were the medical practitioners. Long before they had become the merely adept, strictly specialized, laboratory and computer technicians and surgical repairmen of today, the doctors had no time for learning or living our inherited culture and wisdom. Now I sadly find that I have had to conclude, after a half-century spent in the study, practice, and teaching of law, that all branches of the present legal profession have overtaken physicians—that lawyers (the hordes unwisely added to the profession in recent years should perhaps be called "pseudolawyers"), judges, legislators, government officials, and new-style law professors now are the champions. And close behind them, I think, come the crowds of production-line Ph.D.'s of the past twenty-five years or so, who constitute the bulk of the alleged faculties of our alleged universities. Lawyers and teachers—technicians, perhaps; but educators only very occasionally.

In many areas discussed, it seems to me that not nearly enough blame was laid on our modern courts and judges for their endless willingness to entertain lawsuits on any and every subject, and from any

246

and every source, however inappropriate a means they may be to deal with essentially policy and legislative matters, and in which they distort and pervert the proper judicial function of courts when they proceed to act on them, usually creating turmoil and new problems in the process. They ought to call vague statutes and unwarranted regulations under them invalid and void, for example, and not proceed to legislate or regulate by acting allegedly as courts; nor should they appoint themselves superintendents of schools, or welfare administrators. They refuse to heed the late Justice Frankfurter's teachings about the importance of judicial restraint. Excited by the opportunity to try their hands at all sorts of social, political, and economic surgery with the penknife of a judicial decree, they use neither antisepsis nor anesthesia, but hack away *ad libitum*. Meanwhile, the *proper* business of the courts languishes everywhere!

The appearance and views of President McGill of Columbia recalled to me the splendid and imposing dignity of his predecessor of my era, Nicholas "Miraculous" Butler. In the Butler years of the "tiny" budgets which President McGill looks back at so longingly, there was no modern university president, but an educational giant. President Butler, a worldrenowned figure, was a classically trained philosopher and self-trained statesman, whose views on every subject were sought and respected throughout the world, a perennial American presidential possibility, and a national leadership resource. For all his small budgets and low faculty pay, but with the enormous dedication of all to the university enterprise, he made of Columbia one of the world's great centers of learning and scholarship in all the areas of humanities and the sciences and the social sciences, with its Nobel laureates including Butler himself. I keep finding enduring truth in the old adage that a university consists of a student at one end of a log and Mark Hopkins at the other.

And how tiresome it became to keep hearing the term "discrimination" over and over again, and all its variants, from a group of presumably highly literate people. To discriminate is precisely to note distinctions, to evaluate differences, to reach sound preferences, to make suitable choices. That is the very business of the cultivated and educated mind, and it should be the principal business of the university—unfortunately not practiced enough!—and one of the principal results of a university education. Instead of talking about "invidious discrimination," "willfull discrimination," "ill-motivated discrimination," "politically motivated discrimination," just garden variety "discrimination," and even the perfectly obvious "reverse discrimination," would we not put the substance of the matter into wider and sharper and better focus if we dropped the by now merely talismanic phrases and talked instead of steps "to overcome prejudice," where demonstrably unfair and harmful prejudgment is involved, which is based on whims or ideology but not facts—and only then?

The Alienated Intellectual and Government Bureaucracy

David S. Lichtenstein

I

Robert Nisbet recently declared, "Our clerisy's cant notwithstanding, today's 'democratic' state is in fact a vastly more powerful structure, more penetrating of the lives and minds of its citizens than any seventeenth century Divine-Right monarchy ever was. But try to argue this truth, this platitude in the halls of the universities, or within ear-shot of most of our intellectuals!"[1] He added,

> Freedom can die. As Goethe once wrote: "Lawgivers or revolutionaries who promise equality and liberty at the same time are either utopian dreamers or charlatans. . . " But if the process is gradual enough, as it is likely to be in the free West, I am not sure very many people will even notice when the final line between a relatively free order and a collectivist servitude has been crossed. A few more years of egalitarian and redistributionist rhetoric, a few hundred more "entitlements," another million or so members of the centralised bureaucracy pledged to achievement of equal rations, equal housing, equal social esteem, equal strength and beauty, and how would one possibly know of the transition?

Lest Nisbet's indictment of bureaucracy be considered as a bit of hyperbole, I invite the reader's attention to some recent samples of an overzealous bureaucracy engaged in the extension of authority beyond rational purpose and reckless of the consequences. On February 5th, the Tennessee Valley Authority was enjoined from further construction of an almost completed dam costing about $110 million, on the ground that the completion of the project would destroy the habitat of a three-inch long fish, the snail darter (which feeds on snails on the river bottom). It appears that the snail darter falls into the category of an "endangered species" under the Endangered Species Act. The TVA board members issued a statement that said,

> We are, of course, extremely disappointed, and regret that it comes at a time when the nation is experiencing severe energy problems, when completion of the project would add approximately 200 billion kilowatt hours of electricity to the energy supply for a year. That's enough to heat about 20,000 homes in the TVA region with electricity. Or, to put it another way, it would take about 14 million gallons of oil to generate that much electricity.

Another example: On May 1, 1976, some of the most distinguished scientists in the U.S. issued a statement on the safety of nuclear energy which challenged the alarms and distortions of scientific data by Nader and his allies.

> All too often, arguments have been supported by quotations taken out of context, untested assumptions, and emotional rhetoric; scientific data have been stretched far beyond their area of reliability. In defense of their pre-conceived stands, some participants in the debate have even raised improbable scenarios of the future, which can lead only to confusion and irrational fear.[2]

The statement by the scientists noted that:

> . . . without an adequate energy supply for the next century, the world will be unable to solve its pressing human problems. For the first time in history we have the capacity to abolish poverty, hunger, disease and illiteracy. But in order to achieve these goals, we must

250

squarely face the continuous need for increased energy production. Against the background of continuing human need in this country and abroad, there is no reasonable alternative to increased reliance on nuclear power to satisfy our energy needs. The use of nuclear power offers a temporary easing of this world wide need for power, and time to seek more effective and permanent solutions through sources beyond those mentioned above.[2]

The committee's final conclusion was:

We therefore endorse the responsible use of nuclear energy, subject to all appropriate safeguards. But we oppose regulations directed at curtailing and ultimately banning the use and development of nuclear power. In the long run, improvement can not be achieved by moratoria and bans but only by creativity and search.[2]

Despite all evidence as to the safety of operating reactors, the executive director of the Union of Concerned Scientists was happy to point out in a recent round table on nuclear power safety that the majority of the nuclear power plant projects in the United States were cancelled or postponed last year.[3] The Friends of the Earth, in a suit filed on May 31, 1973, sought to close down twenty of the thirty-two nuclear power plants then in operation, because of alleged deficiencies in the emergency core cooler system.[4]

It would not be too difficult to convince a man from Mars, divorced from our cultural presuppositions, that he was visiting a society bent upon self-destruction. He would find its material achievements held in question by a new class risen to enormous power and prestige, known as the intelligentsia. A nonplussed Martian might ask some very simple but mind-blowing questions. Although impressed by the material achievements wrought upon this planet, he might ask why so intelligent a people as the Americans have been brought to a dead halt in the construction of atomic energy plants, and face an energy crisis without being able to take advantage of its own technology. He might ask with increasing wonder why a country would furnish billions of dollars of wheat, without the exaction of any quid pro quo, to feed an enemy dedicated to its destruction; an enemy, indeed, which proclaims the superiority of its own

251

system, but cannot provide food for its own people, or will not, since it allocates so much of its resources to the relentless expansion of its ideology.[5]

Mr. Bork in his paper suggests that universities are natural targets for those riding a new surge of egalitarianism and populism. I am more inclined to agree with Schumpeter that the paradigm of the "enemy" for the disaffected intelligentsia is the system of private enterprise itself, a target which can most effectively be undermined by a moral crusade. Because of the increasing politicalization of universities, their cooperation and acceptance of the same goals as proponents of welfare programs, environmental restrictions, and affirmative action programs is taken for granted.[6] Indeed, intellectuals in bureaucracy must be rather astonished by any claim for exemption from such programs by those whom they consider natural allies. In short, universities are *not* the prime target of deliberate hostility on the part of government regulatory agencies which have proliferated in the last few years; they are just incidental victims.[7]

I do agree with Mr. Bork that universities make an effort to understand the nature of bureaucratic government. Consequently, I should like to address myself to the problem of (a) the current climate which has swept universities into the vortex of employment opportunity legislation and (b) an evaluation of the possibility of extricating higher education from public policies which are ill-designed and counter-productive insofar as they impair the integrity and goals of universities. It is my central thesis that Mr. Bork is essentially correct in pointing out that the autonomy and self-governing capacities of universities depend upon the public's perception of their pursuit of scholarly ideals and disinterested learning. To the extent that faculties engage in ideological warfare under the guise of scholarship and are perceived as another politicized element of society, universities will damage their image and undermine any plea for exemption from public policies applicable to other enterprises.

I should like first to take a brief look at the social and political factors which have given rise to the avalanche of regulations which constitutes a radical departure from the "old line" administrative agencies, such as the SEC, FCC, ICC, FTC, NLRB, and CAB, some of which antedate the New Deal. These agencies were an almost inevitable development in a complex industrial society, since neither the traditional judicial process nor legislative statute could cope with problems of broad economic and social policies and their application to particular cases. The excesses and indeed reckless irresponsibility in some areas of private enterprise, as for example, on the part of public utility holding companies, was revealed in a series of Congressional investigations. These abuses clearly called for remedial legislation and resulted in the Public Utility Holding Company Act of 1936. The so-called independent regulatory agencies now exercise control over a wide range of business activites including motor carriers, railroads, airlines, and broadcasters. Suffice it to say that administrative law has had a similar development in England, at least up to about ten years ago. At that point, the U.S., having achieved a welfare capitalism, turned away from a primary concern with the regulation of business enterprise, as such, and moved towards the employment of the regulatory agency as a device for attempting to achieve a solution of moral issues, egalitarian ideals, and quality of environment. The public interest which called forth the "old line" regulatory agencies (ICC, etc.) arose out of the necessity for restraint of economic power. Indeed, this period might be called the Era of Economic Regulation. Whereas the Europeans opted for government ownership and operation of "natural monopolies" such as railroads, telephone, electricity, gas, or broadcasting, we chose to leave these enterprises in the hands of private companies, but subject to regulatory commissions operating under broad delegations of authority.

In the last few years, however, we have witnessed what Theodore Caplow aptly calls the Era of Protest.[8] Irving Kristol suggests that the impetus for this new wave of regulation (including water pollution, air pollution, traffic pollution, etc.) derives from a "new class consisting of scientists, lawyers, city planners, social workers, educators, criminologists, sociologists, public health doctors, etc.—a substantial number of whom find their careers in the expanding public sector rather than the private. The public sector, indeed is where they prefer to be. They are, as one says, 'idealistic'—i.e., far less interested in individual financial rewards than in the corporate power of their class. Though they continue to speak the language of 'Progressive-reform,' in actuality they are acting upon a hidden agenda; to propel the nation from that modified version of capitalism we call 'the welfare state' toward an economic system so stringently regulated in detail as to fulfill many of the traditional anti-capitalist aspirations of the Left."[9]

Peregrine Worsthorne (oddly enough writing about England) states that

what we are witnessing in this country is the emergence of a new challenge to democratic order—a challenge that comes from a novel claim to privilege which is challenging democracy more brazenly than any aristocracy or plutocracy of old. It is a privileged minority that rests its claim to power not on property or lineage but on a qualification far more formidable and overwhelming: moral superiority. It does not demand that the wealth of the country should be organized to suit its interests. It demands that its will should prevail in matters of morals, that the quality of society should be determined by its values and according to its tastes.

But in an affluent society more and more of the burning political issues are matters of morals. Nuclear weapons, race, permissiveness, and so on—these are the genuinely divisive issues. How can the majority will prevail in these fields against a minority that claims divine sanction for its views? Democracy is faced today by a new version of the divine right of kings and of the prescriptive right of aristocracies. It is the divine and prescriptive right of the progressive establishment to impose its moral patterns regardless of the majority will. And because this claim is essentially moral it is infinitely less open to democratic compromise than earlier disputes centring on the class struggle.

The class struggle was about wealth, about the distribution of property, about the share-out of the national cake. By its very nature it was susceptible to democratic compromise, since the argument was essentially quantitative not qualitative, about good rather than the Good, about money not morals. The class war, therefore, by its very nature was susceptible to arbitration to the democratic process of give and take.[10]

I entirely agree with the main thrust of Worsthorne's analysis—i.e., that material disputes over distribution of the national income (in a democratic society) are soluble through compromise, and ultimately through political intervention in the market place to redress the balance of private economic power. The National Labor Relations Act which threw the weight of government behind the efforts of labor to organise is as good an illustration as any. But the new moralism of the sixties, cloaked in the rhetoric of egalitarianism "and the belief that law can effectively guarantee fairness in every relationship" constitutes a crusade without rational limits, reckless of the consequences (since attempts to implement moral criteria incorporated in a statute will frequently conflict with other moral values), and wilfully blind to alternative methods of social control.[11]

As Edward Shils indicates, referring to the decade of the 1960s, "Discontent had indeed come to be regarded as the only allowable attitude of an intellectual. Many persons who had not previously placed themselves in the category of intellectual now did so and being an intellectual entailed the obligation of outraged discontent. Anger became a virtue when it was directed against authority."[12] The philosophical orientation of the crusading intellectuals is difficult to fathom. One might say that they are idealists of a Utopian hue driven by a passion for egalitarianism, or some millenarian urge to turn our industrial society into an environmental Garden of Eden. But the nagging question then remains as to why their efforts flow only in certain directions. Why do some crusades capture their imagination at certain junctures in history and others fade away? Is it merely fashionable to be an environmentalist? I think not. I believe that a key to an understanding of the alienated intellectual, is the lack of a sense of responsibility for the *consequences* of forcing environmental and egalitarian mandates beyond any rational cost-benefit measure, and an indifference to alternative solutions. Rational calculation in the formation of public policy requires freedom from the hostility, hatred, and vengeance which attributes social evil to the deliberate design of "malignant interests." Such attribution confuses alleged motives as causes of action with rational grounds for action, and ignores the likely consequences of feasible alternatives of policy.

One of the most baneful legacies of orthodox Marxism is the concept of "exploitation," which necessarily implies that all social relations can be explained in terms of exploiters and exploited. The concept of exploitation is psychologically crucial to a sense of moral indignation. The attempt to force the concept of "exploitation" into sociological explanations of the causes of crime, poverty, discrimination, etc., results, for example, in identifying the urban problem as white racism, to which was ascribed the poverty of the black inner city population. The Community Action Program "specified the social problem as being exploitation, rather than racism, and proposed as a desired end-condition the partition of urban territory into autonomous white and black zones controlled by their respective residents, each zone running its own schools, police, public services, social agencies, churches, banks, and retail establishments."[13] Furthermore, the emotional drive of the term "exploitation" touches a responsive chord in American culture, due partly to the ease with which guilt feelings can be aroused in an affluent society, and partly to economic and historical illiteracy, which enables proponents of superficial explanations of complex social phenomena to substitute rhetoric for analysis.[14] Similarly, the excesses of affirmative action programs arise out of an assumed need for reparation of past exploitation. "To most people legitimate equality is epitomized by equality of opportunity for the great diversity of tastes, talents, strengths, and aspirations to be found in a population. But to a rising number of intellectuals this is the worst kind of inequality, for it produces, it is said, a meritocracy, which is in its own way as evil as any of the historic forms of aristocratic privilege."[15]

There is another emotion that seems to animate antinuclear plant construction and environmental groups. I refer to the combat mentality of a small band of dedicated warriors battling "the entrenched interests." Heretofore, the axis of division between the "vested interests" and groups which sought to transform the capitalist system could be drawn along a liberal/conservative line. On such causes as the minimum wage, right to work laws, or progressive taxation it would be safe to say that there was a conservative and a liberal position.[16] But there is no a priori reason why passion should be aroused and embattled forces lined up on pollution, equal employment opportunity, freedom of information, etc. After all, it could reasonably be anticipated that employers would resist social control over the wages they pay employees, but there is a universal appeal in programs for clean air, clean water, and similar goals; why should a conservative be less interested in clean air than a "liberal"?

I suspect the crusading zeal for a score of antipollution statutes falls along one side of the liberal-conservative spectrum for the following reasons:

(a) The momentum for "economic regulation" reaches a point of diminishing returns. It is difficult to sustain a crescendo of mounting enthusiasm for "wars against poverty" where victory is elusive and the dry statistics of actual achievement appear due more to forces of a productive economy than to some final battle for redistribution of income.

(b) The momentum for social transformation inspired by socialist dreams of a "planned economy" or nationalization of "the key sectors of the economy" which aroused considerable enthusiasm during the depression can no longer be kept alive. It was the moral appeal of socialism which commanded the loyalty of its followers. In mid-nineteenth century, socialism arose as a *cri de coeur* against the bitter price of child labor and slums which were the accompaniment of the industrial revolution. Attempts to implement socialism programatically came a cropper when it was discovered from experience that nationalization of industry proved to be no panacea for ailing sectors of the economy. However, socialism was a myth which served a useful purpose. As a rallying cry it aroused the conscience of mankind to care about the innocent victims of a rapid industrial transformation. The term "collectivism" which was once considered as pointing to the golden grail of socialism has turned into a warning signpost of a nightmarish Soviet communism. It proved to be a misleading abstraction, but in all fairness I believe that to most socialists the term collectivism was merely a symbol, an emotionally charged term that spoke more to the idea of community and the brotherhood of man than to some institutional arrangement that could ever be put into practice. In short, collectivism was at best a utopian idea, perhaps like an Israeli commune, and at worst, a conception in which there lurked the seeds of totalitarianism.

(c) Perhaps the most effective way of illuminating a "mental set" is to examine the way in which ideology and a passion for social transformation influence different approaches to a solution of social problems. Attitude surveys can tell you that professors of sociology are more "radical" than professors of law or business administration—which is, so far as it goes, worth knowing, and incidentally gives employment to a lot of graduate students who run the data through IBM machines. But such surveys tell you nothing about the etiology of attitude formation and why attitudes are impervious to rational discourse and empirical evidence.[17]

Perhaps redistribution of income and the pursuit of equality are the two most crucial areas of domestic policy where ideology has supplanted intelligent social criticism.[18] Since I am not prepared to debate the economic merits of various schemes for redistribution, whether through taxation, transfer payments, or otherwise (and in any event it would be beyond the scope of this paper), I shall confine myself to the psychology of the disaffected intellectual. Let us assume for the sake of argument that current distribution of income takes the form of a bell-shaped curve and that such a distribution equates with the random distribution of merit and talent. In my opinion no argument could ever convince a radical redistributionist that a skewed distribution of income reflects the ineluctable fact of diversity of human talent in any social system and that beyond a certain point (as the Swedes have discovered) no economic system can function without differential rewards.

The very thought of the intransigence of human nature to his utopian scheme tends to leave the idealistic intellectual frustrated. He is reluctant to accept the fact that there are inherent limits to redistribution of wealth and income, beyond which a social system may break down, or become recalcitrant to transformation short of totalitarian control. A conservative social critic can accept limits with psychological tranquility; he will not allow achieving the best to interfere with achieving the better. The radical critic, on the other hand, judging by his rhetoric, seems to be engaged in a battle which demands the personification of evil, since his élan and momentum would be dissipated if there were no enemy to be overcome, fought against, regulated, controlled, and finally subdued. As Murray Weidenbaum points out, "The promulgation by the government of rules and regulations restricting or prescribing private activity is not the only means of accomplishing public objectives."[19] He adds that ". . . Government itself has available to it various powers other than the powers of regulation. Through its taxing authority the government can provide strong signals to the market. Rather than promulgating detailed regulations governing allowable discharges into the nation's waterways, the government could levy substantial taxes on those discharges." But it is doubtful that the use of taxation to control pollution would satisfy the craving of intellectuals for combat against malefactors; and indeed, the entire crusade might collapse if some neutral instrument like taxation proved more effective than bureaucratic regulation to eliminate evils.

The motivation which would lead a handful of "concerned scientists" to attempt to brainwash the American public about the safety of nuclear reactors in the face of overwhelming evidence to the contrary, lies at the heart of moral crusading. There is more at stake here than just a desire for jobs in the bureaucracy. There is a profound malaise and alienation from society which is at work among intellectuals. Certainly this does not affect the vast majority of the members of the Sierra Club, who are sincerely concerned with clear streams and the dangers of environmental congestion. But the minority of intellectuals who have capitalized on this desire are a different breed. Their "moral crusading" is insatiable and each triumph is but a prelude to a further demand that society be moulded into their image. Although the majority of the public might be more concerned with jobs than aesthetics, or with consumer goods than with parks, they must be forced to accept the superior wisdom of an intellectual elite, who know what is necessary for a good society.

On the face of it, the goals of (a) equal employment opportunity, (b) improvement of environmental quality, and (c) the public's right to know (Freedom of Information Act) can scarcely be assailed when couched in abstract moral terms. Unlike social welfare programs, however, more problems are generated than can be solved under the "moral type" programs because their implementation through rigid rules and regulations frequently results in conflicts with other moral values. The univocal pursuit of one value such as environmental quality to the exclusion of others equally valid morally, is truly the definition of fanaticism.[20] Likewise, under the rhetoric of "secrecy in government," the Freedom of Information Act has been deployed as a weapon of ideological warfare to undermine the confidence of the public in national security agencies. The conflict between confidentiality of the internal decision-making process of government and the public's "right to know" can be extremely dangerous in compelling disclosure prior to international negotiation. This is especially true in cases where the demand for confidential documents is actually designed to undermine confidence in the agency. Under the guise of environmental concern the public has been completely misled about the dangers of nuclear reactors, and environmental legislation has enabled small groups to close down construction of energy-generating plants. Under the guise of equal employment opportunity the integrity of university faculties is seriously threatened.[21] In each case, however, any potential victim who resists further extension of government control is at a serious disadvantage in defying moral crusaders.

II

We live in an age of ideological conflict, and every institution, including private enterprise, universities, churches, etc., has to make choices in the interest of preserving autonomy—in some cases resistance to the power of the state may be justified in order to avoid destruction. This is not to suggest that universities, as such, should launch themselves into political warfare, or enlist their resources on one side or the other of ideological struggles; quite to the contrary, this would be the death warrant to their independence. They must capitalise on the one legitimate claim they have to resist against any interference by the state with their internal jurisdiction—and that is the importance to a democratic society of preserving the integrity of scholarship and freedom to pursue truth. In the long run, the gravest danger to universities is the damage they have done and continue to do to their own image, as Mr. Bork incisively points out. The claim to integrity of scholarship will ring hollow when propaganda is presented by distinguished professors as impartial research. What respect will the public accord to the tradition of impartial scholarship when historians violate every canon of objective historical research and regard for evidence, to produce so-called "revisionist accounts" of the cold war?[22] True it is that history is constantly being rewritten; and it is the glory of historians that they can develop greater depths of insight into the multiple causation of such crucial events as the French revolution or the English Civil War of the seventeenth century. The work of scholars who have dedicated their lives to the intensive study of medieval history, for example, is wholly admirable because the revisions flow from the discoveries of scholarship rather than from the imperatives of ideology. Willful distortion and manipulation of historical evidence as a weapon in ideological warfare on the part of politicised scholars will inevitably jeopardise and ultimately undermine the public respect which is indispensable to the preservation of their independence[23]

There is much more to be said (and it is of great urgency that it be said) about the teaching and writing in such fields as contemporary international politics, where prescriptions of policy and empirical investigation are almost inextricably interwoven.[24]

In a day and age when university professors are writing for the mass media on political issues, and appear as leaders of antiwar or prowar sit-ins, there are baffling problems of where to draw the line between the rights of the teacher as a citizen, and his duties to his students and colleagues as well as to the ethics of his profession.[25] However, the limits of this essay do not allow of any further exploration of these issues. I merely want to underline Mr. Bork's comments. I would only suggest that once upon a time there were guilds which set internal standards of excellence and quality of performance by their members—shoddy material was instantly condemned. If constant surveillance of their own output by the academic community is not exercised in order to protect the public from political seduction in the guise of scholarship, then the moral case for independence from government interference will, as Mr. Bork indicates, be badly damaged.[26]

As one who is outside the academic world, I applaud the vigilance and courage of the members of the UCRA. Tragically, this is only one of many battles that will have to be fought to preserve academic integrity. I am told that Israeli soldiers take an oath to dedicate their lives to prevent another Masada. Perhaps a similar oath by teachers to fight *à outrance* all attempts to deploy scholarship in the interest of ideology would not be amiss.

NOTES

1. Robert Nisbet, "The Fatal Ambivalence," *Encounter,* December, 1976.

2. Scientists and Engineers for Secure Energy, "Scientists' Statement on Safety of Nuclear Energy," May 1, 1976. This group consists of more than 100 distinguished scientists and engineers, including five Nobel Prize winners.

3. American Enterprise Institute, "Is Nuclear Power Safe?" (A Round Table sponsored by the American Enterprise Institute for Public Policy Research, Washington, D.C., May 15, 1975.)

4. For the activities of Nader and his followers, see Andrew S. McFarland, *Public Interest Lobbies* (Washington, D. C.: American Enterprise Institute, n.d.), ch. 5. McFarland concludes that "the energy stands of Nader organizations add up to a low-energy-growth position" (p. 77).

5. See "Will U.S. Bail Out Russia?", *U.S. News and World Report,* August 25, 1975, p. 16.

6. "Thus, from the university system comes a certain measure of institutional inter-connectedness of the whole intellectual stratum." Edward Shils, "Intellectuals," in *The International Encyclopedia of the Social Sciences,* ed. D. E. Sills (New York: Macmillan, 1969), p. 402.

7. Jacques Barzun refers to government contracts and grants for research in science which have transformed academic administration, and notes that "critics have seen in this transformation the danger of government control. If by this is meant political or personal interference with what a scientist or a private university chooses to study or to think, the fear is unfounded. Government officials are more afraid than anybody else of doing something construable as meddling." *The American University: How It Runs, Where It Is Going* (New York: Harper & Row, 1968), p. 142. Mr. Barzun's remarks do not cover affirmative action programs.

8. Theodore Caplow says ". . . in the Era of Protest, there was only a peripheral concern with economic institutions, and no important changes were made with respect to business management, government regulation of the economy, the operation of securities markets, methods of investment, tax structure, or labor-management relations. The Era of Protest was concerned with stratification rather than economics. It challenged authority but not property, and even though status rights and property rights might seem inextricably related, the sociological common sense of the public was able to draw a fairly sharp distinction between them." (p. 151). He later continues "One reason why so many of the social projects of the Era of Protest achieved disastrous or ironical results was that, under cover of the prevailing rhetoric of social improvement, they were launched without definite end-conditions in view, and in some instances, with a firm commitment to mutually incompatible goals." *Toward Social Hope* (New York: Basic Books, 1975), p. 152.

9. Irving Kristol, "On Corporate Capitalism in America," *The Public Interest,* no. 41 (Fall, 1975), p. 134.

10. Peregrine Worsthorne, *The Socialist Myth* (London: Cassell, n.d.), p. 207.

11. Murray Weidenbaum says, in his article "Reducing Inflationary Pressures by Reforming Government": ". . . Each of these regulatory agencies (EPA, OSHA, etc.) was created to further one specific objective—a cleaner environment, healthier working

261

conditions, safer products, and so on—and they were created at different times under different circumstances. Legislative mandate in hand, each agency pursues its individual tasks as it sees them. Yet increasingly the achievement of one agency's objective may frustrate another'' (p. 288).

"To an economist, government regulation should be carried to the point where the incremental benefits equal the incremental costs, and no further. (Indeed, this is the basic criterion that is generally used to screen proposed government investments in physical resources.) Overregulation—which can be defined as regulation of which the costs exceed the benefits—should be avoided. But if policy makers tend to ignore or downplay the costs of regulation, we are bound to overregulate—as, indeed, we do today'' (p. 286).

"The use of taxation [to control pollution] would not be meant to punish polluters, or even to give them a 'license' to pollute. Rather it would be meant to make use of the price system by encouraging producers and consumers to shift to less polluting ways of producing and consuming goods and services. The basic point is simple: Most people do not pollute because they get positive pleasure from dirtying the environment. Rather they pollute because it often is easier or cheaper than not polluting. If the government were to change basic incentives through the tax-price mechanism, individuals and organizations (both public and private) would be encouraged voluntarily to alter their economic behavior so as to make it more in keeping with the goals of the society. Perhaps most important would be the shift to public-private relationships from the current adversary position to a more neutral and efficient mode of conduct." *AEI Studies on Contemporary Economic Problems* (Washington, D. C.: American Enterprise Institute, n.d.), p. 292.

12. Edward Shils, "Intellectuals and Their Discontents," *The American Scholar,* Spring, 1976, p. 200.

13. Caplow, *Toward Social Hope,* p. 63.

14. Thus, backwardness of development in so-called underdeveloped areas is allegedly due to rapacious exploitation by Western industrial societies. Cf. P. T. Bauer, *Dissent on Development: Studies and Debates in Development Economics* (Cambridge: Harvard University Press, 1972). See also, Lipset: "In the United States the characteristic stance of the intellectuals and the educated strata which support them, has been moralism. They have scorned society for failing to fulfill agreed-upon liberal values. They have repeatedly challenged those running the nation with the crime of heresy, with betraying the American Creed." "The Paradox of American Politics," *Public Interest,* Fall, 1976, p. 161.

15. Robert Nisbet, "The Pursuit of Equality," *The Public Interest,* Spring, 1974, p. 106. Cf. Irving Kristol, "Taxes, Poverty and Equality," *The Public Interest,* Fall, 1974.

16. This is apart from whether such a division on public policy is rational; i.e., rationally each proposal should be tested on its merits and not whether it is labelled liberal or conservative.

17. "It is an elementary truth of the psychology of perception that what a man sees depends often upon his beliefs and expectations. The stronger the beliefs the more they function like a priori notions whose validity is beyond the tests of experience. Hopes can be so all-consuming that they affect even the range and quality of feeling. The consequence is that the shocks of reality, in terms of which the natural pragmatism of the human mind experiences actuality, lose their educational office. To say that a man is seized and transformed by an abstraction is a metaphor but it expresses the empirical fact that an

idea-system, instead of functioning as a guide to conduct, can operate in such a way as to transform habits, feelings, and perceptions of the individual to a point where marked changes of personality are noticeable." Sidney Hook, *Political Power and Personal Freedom: Critical Studies in Democracy, Communism and Civil Rights* (New York: Macmillan, 1962), p. 175.

18. See Robert Nisbet, "The Pursuit of Equality," *Public Interest,* Spring, 1974; also, Charles Frankel, "The New Egalitarianism and the Old," *Commentary,* September, 1973.

19. Murray Weidenbaum, "Reducing Inflationary Pressures," in *Contemporary Economic Problems,* pp. 291–292.

20. Thus, the failure of the TVA to complete the Tellico dam, as a result of environmental lawsuits, will probably result in unemployment for thousands of workers in the Tennessee valley. It may be that the beauty of the Hudson River valley will be marred by a Con Ed generating plant, but in a time of energy shortage, a choice will have to be made between aesthetics and jobs for the unemployed. Fanatics must be forced to make choices between competing values in the court of public opinion—as well as in the federal courts.

21. "Affirmative action practices ignore both choice and career characteristics by the simple process of putting the burden of proof on academic institutions to explain why their percentages of minority and female faculty do not match the kinds of proportions preconceived by governmental authorities. Career characteristics have been 'validated'—which is virtually impossible. The statistical 'validation' process, as developed for written tests in education, involves prediction for a very short span of time on a very limited number of variables, such as grades and graduation. To extend the 'validation' concept to the whole hiring process for complex professions with many dimensions is to demand mathematical certainty in areas where good judgment is the most that can be expected. In such circumstances, where 'validation' amounts to convincing government officials, it means convincing people whose own career variables—appropriations, staff, and power—depend upon not believing those attempting to convince them. General findings of reasonable hiring decisions would be a general sentence of death for the agency itself. More basically, this situation replaces the principle of prescriptive laws with ex post administrative determination of what should have happened, combined with never-ending burdens of proof as to why it did not." Thomas Sowell, *Affirmative Action Reconsidered: Was It Necessary in Academia?* Evaluative Studies (Washington, D.C.: American Enterprise Institute, 1975), p. 37.

22. See Robert James Maddox, "Cold War Revisionism: Abusing History," *Freedom at Issue,* Sept.–Oct. 1972; also, Oscar Handlin, "The Failure of the Historians," *Freedom at Issue,* Sept.–Oct. 1975.

23. ". . . the university is that institution in the society endowed with the special function (and the extraordinary immunity) of searching for truth and evaluating the culture of its times. In this sense, it is free to question everything—in theory. If it is to be true to its purpose, nothing is exempt from its scrutiny. But if it is to have the immunity from reprisal that goes with this power, it must obey the self-denying ordinance of remaining at the level of theory, of speculative discourse. The question whether anything is to be put into practice is a question, not for the university, but for the society. In this model, the university stands outside the society, and contains within itself all varieties of creeds and beliefs, and all kinds of persons, subject to the one qualification of competence in the world of learning and

scholarship. These qualified individuals, scholars are free to explore any question, and test all areas of human experience—in theory.'' Daniel Bell, ''Quo Warranto—Notes on the Governance of Universities in the 1970's,'' *Public Interest,* Spring, 1970.

24. See Charles Frankel, ''The Difference Between Being In and Being Out,'' *Public Interest,* Fall, 1969; Colin Gray, ''The Practice of Theory in International Relations,'' *Political studies,* June, 1974; Charles Frankel, ''The Scribblers and International Relations,'' *Foreign Affairs,* October, 1965; Carol H. Weiss, ''Policy Research in the University: Practical Aid or Academic Exercise?'' *Policy Studies Journal,* Spring, 1976; and Robert K. Merton, ''Role of the Intellectual in Public Bureaucracy,'' *Social Forces,* May, 1945.

25. See Sidney Hook, *Academic Freedom and Academic Anarchy* (New York: Dell, 1971), p. 163.

26. As Midge Decter has said, ''When a historian like Staughton Lynd proclaims Hanoi to be the model for the achievement of freedom by small nations, he is perverting both the use of his intellectual discipline and his mandate as a thinking man. . . .

When Susan Sontag, wishing to express her horror at the fruits of modern technology, launches an attack upon the Faustian spirit of the whole of Western civilization ending with the observation that 'the white race . . . [is] the cancer of humanity,' she undermines the very ground on which she herself is entitled to speak or write. . . .

When Robert Brustein, dean of the Yale drama school, indiscriminately and in a tone of deepest self-gratulation lends his sponsorship to any and all works of art whose intention is subversive, he is in fact subverting nothing so much as that artistic integrity to which he professes devotion.

The examples could multiply. They abound in the liberal weeklies, in the highly influential *New York Review of Books,* in some of the quarterlies, and are to be heard from the platform of every forum, symposium, teach-in, and round table on peace.'' ''Anti-Americanism in America,'' *The Radical Left: The Abuse of Discontent,* W. P. Geberding and D. E. Smith, eds. (Boston: Houghton Mifflin, 1970), pp. 154-155; see also, David S. Lichtenstein, ''The Radical Intellectual and U.S. Foreign Policy,'' *Ideas* 3, no. 1, (1971).

Would a Reorganized Federal Department of Education Mean Better Higher Education?

Miro M. Todorovich
Bronx Community College, CUNY
Executive Secretary, UCRA

In the United States reorganization is often viewed as a cure for many problems. During the era of rampant political interference with civil service appointment, the federal government created the Federal Civil Service Commission. The Commission was supposed to stamp out the evils of political patronage. (At this time, for different reasons, the CSC seems to be on its way out.) In the late sixties New York City installed a network of Local School Boards as a cure-all for that school system's ills. In less than a decade the Atomic Energy Commission became the Energy Research and Development Agency only to find itself reorganized into the Department of Energy. Whenever there appears a new problem or crisis, one sees the establishment of a study group or commission to suggest change and reform.

Reorganization may have merits particularly in the administrative domain. To begin with, certain operating structures may have serious flaws and are in need of change or improvement. The old League of Nations with the rule of absolute equality among member states was essentially doomed to inaction from the very start. Its organizational form was just too much out of step with the international political reality. Its successor, the United Nations Organization with its narrower yet quite powerful Security Council, is somewhat closer to a viable enterprise. Its effectiveness still depends upon an agreement between the big powers; its operation is however more in tune with the living rules of international diplomacy.

Changes in organizational structures may also facilitate the rejuvenation of personnel. Any enterprise of some longevity accumulates a network of executives and employees who, after a while, reflect not only the requirements of specific tasks or decision making for which they have been hired, but also an intricate cross-relationship of human sympathies and antipathies, fraternizations, and supportive alliances. One encounters ties based on loyalties or biases which have little relevance to the specific job at hand. Personnel turnover becomes slow even if there are obvious shortcomings in operation. A "healthy" reorganization then introduces a wind of change that weeds out incompetence and gives the "new blood" a try. In noncivil service levels of government administrations such sweeps come quite naturally with every new election. However, the entrenched "tenured" bureaucratic infrastructures, in and out of government, resist such natural cycles, and reorganization often remains the only weapon for institutional transfusion.

Akin to this aging of personnel is programmatic inertia. Ideas, plans, and programs are the product of human imagination that, even if initially creative, does in the course of events gradually develop the "best possible world" attitude. Where people may initially have noticed causes for improvement, they later discover compelling reasons for a status quo. This leads to an organizational stalemate that can be broken by reforms based on new and innovative solutions. As a side effect, reforms often generate renewed public support for a variety of programs. Newsmen love to report "dramatic developments," and media exposure never harms the movement of progressive causes.

On balance, therefore, there are numerous situations when reorganization and reforms may be desirable and beneficial. Operational structures become better adapted to tasks, personnel gets regenerated, programs appear refreshed, and funding becomes more plentiful. Many difficulties however may be of such an essential nature that they defy efforts at reorganizational cosmetics. For example, the life of the New York Rheingold brewery was extended several times by well-intended efforts of mediators and planners. The same treatment is now applied to New York's Radio City Music Hall. The brewery finally succumbed to unsurmountable financial woes, and the Music Hall may have to follow suit. Reorganizational virtuosity obviously cannot compensate for the lack of economic *raison d'être*. Other types of proposed reorganizations may again be only retreats in disguise. A typical case of this kind is found in the treatment of mental patients. Initially, people with mental problems were moved away from society into large-scale centralized mental institutions where "highly specialized and trained care could be available." After a number of scandals and television *exposés* of retarded childrens' centers, many mental patients are now in the name of innovation sent back into the same old neighborhoods to live a "fuller life." Such searches for new and improved solutions all too often resemble the promotion of "new and improved" commercial products which happen to be more new than improved.

When it comes to higher education, innovators and reformers are, so to speak, in their natural habitat. Colleges and universities have been, after all, constantly in the forefront of the search for the new and the modern interpretation of the old, and one can expect that what is taught to others will also be applied to the institutions themselves. Thus on the general educational level, suggestions for reform seem to be as numerous as there are reformers. From Mexico we heard suggestions to deschool society; in Britain they pioneered universities without walls; France attempted to adjust curricula to the wishes of future employers; and in the United States not so long ago the university was likened to a service station. During the recent turmoil over a span of only a few short years, some universities abolished curricula, others abolished grades, many dropped dormitory regulations, while some experimental colleges abolished almost everything (except the salaries). Some administrators still try to compact four years of undergraduate work into three, and others like to see their students "study while they work." Some schools offer easy education ("life experience credited") while others advertise lifelong education. There is modular learning and media teaching. The list of proposals and facts seems almost unending.

In the area of relations between the universities and the federal government several study groups have tried, through suitable reorganizations of the federal government, to improve the latter's interaction with institutions of higher education. An interesting entry among the recent efforts in this direction is a proposal for the "reorganization of the Federal government in the areas of education and support for scholarship," prepared by the Carnegie Council on Policy Studies in Higher

Education. Noting that the item for education (outlays $7.8 billion, 3,500 of full-time personnel)[1] is literally buried in the overall Department of Health, Education and Welfare (outlays $128.8 billion, 136,460 full-time personnel),[2] the Carnegie Council proposes a splitting of HEW and the establishment of the following alternative scheme:

1. Development of a Department of Health, Education, and Science organized around the theme of growth;
2. Development of a Department of Labor and Human Resources, absorbing the welfare responsibilities of the present HEW, organized around their work;
3. Establishment of an Undersecretary (or Secretary on the DOD model) of Education, Research, and Advanced Studies, within the Department of Health, Education, and Science, while elevating the status and redefining the functional responsibilities of the bureau chiefs within the present Office of Education; and
4. Assignment to this Undersecretary (or Secretary), among other duties, of coordinating responsibilities through federal agencies for:
   Educational programs, through a Council on Educational Programs,
   Basic research and scholarship, through a Council of Institutes of Research and Advanced Studies, while preserving the essential independence of the individual institutes, and
   Student financial aid, through a Council on Student Aid.

It is clearly the implicit hope of the Carnegie Council that by concentrating the federal educational policy—putting it into a federal department of manageable size—there could emerge at least a beginning of a rational federal policy towards higher education, something that according to many analyses has not existed in the past.

While such hopes may be partially justified and reorganizations may lead to some improvement in the university-state relations in the United States, some of the important faculty unions have very much disagreed with the merits of this proposal. On the one side, the National Education Association has gone even a step further and is on record as favoring the establishment of an outright Federal Department of Education. At the opposite pole is the American Federation of Teachers which finds little if any value in such a plan. Health and welfare should not be separated from the education of citizens according to the AFT. Both sides have advanced persuasive arguments in favor of their respective positions, but the very possibility for such fundamental disagreement raises doubts about the value of administrative reshuffling in this rather critical field. Such doubts are even more compelling if one recognizes the intricacies of the history of university-government dealings which brought about the present state and the sensitive problems of understanding, which seem to be at the root of some of the difficulties.

The present-day dependence of American "houses of intellect" on the federal government did not materialize overnight. There was indeed a time when American institutions of higher learning could exist and flourish in a truly autonomous way. As America grew to maturity, colleges and universities developed into a pluralistic system comprising an amazing variety of institutions of varying size, differing styles of teaching, and complementary curricular programs. Of course, like all things in life, American colleges and universities had to contend with the predictable amount of headaches and difficulties. One encountered all along confrontations between faculties and individual trustees, boards of regents, or other governing bodies over matters involving educational policies and topics for scholarly research. Political pressures from different quarters did appear with worrisome regularity. There were also recurring tug-of-wars between the faculties and administrators who, unlike their European counterparts, did not necessarily emerge from the scholarly ranks of the institutions.[3] Finally, always present was the endemic financial toothache—the fact that there was never enough money for what scholars and educators would like to accomplish. Still, over and above what one could call the "normal difficulties," until the middle of this century, colleges and universities of the United States were, as a group, able to decide in an autonomous and self-consistent way matters affecting their intellectual and academic existence.

At first even after some gradual yet significant changes were introduced into the financing of universities, the basic ways in which things were run remained essentially unaltered. Initially, the government financing was simply a matter of convenience. For example, the American government during World War II needed certain goods and services and was willing to pay the universities to do the urgent job. The universities, on the other hand, liked the idea of being able, on government expense, to expand their laboratories, staff, and graduate student body. This symbiosis worked so well in wartime that it was continued into the postwar years and was even extended to fields far removed from the initial technological and other war-related areas. During subsequent years, however, the character of this governmental subsidy changed from an option into something a college or university could not do without. The cost of running a university increased markedly and could not be sustained further by tuition, endowment moneys, or state and city funds. These increases in costs were partly unavoidable because, among other things, schools turned out to be very labor-intensive enterprises and thus were extremely sensitive to raises in salaries, social security payments and pensions, and other fringe benefits. Also, the style of the administrative operation changed to accommodate the changed practices in the surrounding society. Schools opened public relations offices and planning departments, hired lobbyists and now some even pay for liquor served at student parties. This further escalated the already inflated budgets. Not all of these moves were absolutely necessary, and schools could have avoided, at least partially, some hikes in expenses. Still, throughout the fifties and sixties, the budgets of even the traditionally frugal institutions continued to escalate. This made the majority of the colleges and universities in one way or another critically dependent on government support.

The previously described change in the financial situations was matched by a corresponding change in the character of the government bureaucrats. The innocent customers of the war years became shrewd buyers: they not only wanted to get the goods for which they were paying, but they insisted also in telling the producer (university) how to make the product. It is well known that when a governmental administrator wants to tell someone how to do something, he gathers a committee and writes a regulation. In addition, such a regulation, if appropriately written, need not cost the government a penny—the whole burden of compliance may be put on the shoulders of the supplier (college). Furthermore, from the point of view of the government, the fact that a regulation is *gratis* removes all practical constraints from the rulewriter, and he can easily begin to overregulate. This seems to have happened at the American state-university interface, leading to a proliferation of regulations and a proliferation of reasons for regulating. Subsequently, mounting regulatory pressures dislocated the universities in many ways, and these episodes are very vividly described in the issues of the *Chronicle of Higher Education, Change Magazine, Measure,* and other educational publications.

A particular set of complaints relates to the haphazardness with which the federal government decides to purchase goods from a contracting university. The Congress or the administration first decides to allocate funds for a variety of goods ranging from the very substantive (e.g., improvement in the laboratory teaching of science), to the socially desirable (e.g., increase in the number of general medical practitioners in certain rural areas of the country). These programs are ordinarily time-limited and may be continued, expanded, or cancelled depending on the momentary prevailing judgment of the decision-makers in Washington.

At the receiving end of this governmental largesse are university administrators who, while interested in change and innovation, must nevertheless view as their primary concern the continuing and orderly perpetuation of their home institution. While congressmen vote millions of dollars for vocational education or the increased participation of minorities in scientific education, university administrators must secure funds for faculty salaries, the operation of libraries, building and ground maintenance and other mundane tasks which are clearly alien to congressional rhetoric but are the unavoidable realities for the planners of university budgets. There is here a serious mismatch between the certifiable daily needs of the schools and the funds allocated by way of some 400 different program-oriented federal channels.

To overcome this incongruity, school officials and faculty are ever more regularly spending large amounts of time and effort learning about the available opportunities and trying somehow to match these with the capabilities and needs of their institutions. By now, administrators have developed a reasonably skillful art of packaging by which they assemble a workable school budget from the many diverse and elusive components reported in the Federal Register and in the reports of the various granting agencies. Often this involves initiating subtle or not so subtle modifications of the overall programs offered by their institution in order to qualify for the federal dollar. Sometimes this means altering student admissions policies—as in the recent case of some medical schools which must comply with provisions of the law in order not to lose *all* their federal moneys. In many cases this implies going to court to fight regulations attached to appropriations when the cost of compliance seems to exceed the benefits of the federal grants.[4] In all cases, the question can be raised whether the enormous amount of time spent in administrative deliberations by everyone in a university—from the president down

271

through the departmental chairmen to the lowest faculty member—would not be better spent on substantive educational matters. The *raison d'étre* of academic institutions is being wasted instead on the juggling of budgeting figures—an unproductive endeavor but justifiable because of the sheer necessity for survival.

There are members of the academy who have well adapted to the present state of affairs, and who may take issue with the conclusions of this paper. They point with pride to the successes of the past and insist that circumstances have not yet reached an unbearable state. They plead for continuing accommodation and suggest that certain undeniable excesses are of temporary nature.

However, a growing segment of academic opinion is beginning to see the dangers inherent in the present trends for both the economic stability and educational integrity of their institutions. One reads in a recent issue of the *Chronicle of Higher Education* that, according to a national survey, "Colleges Prefer Corporate Gifts over Government Support—[because] campus officials say private grants have fewer strings attached." The American press has also just reported that several well-known medical colleges have decided to give up all their federal support rather than yield to bureaucratic pressure and change their admission and curricular policies.

The crisis in university-state relations seems to be coming to a head, and the need is evident to explore alternative avenues by which such problems could possibly be resolved.

Mindful of the crisis some academic groups have invested time and effort to design and apply palliatives. Administrators have, for example, acquired the habit of regularly reading the Federal Register, monitoring proposed new regulations and commenting on them within the mandated 30-day period. Academic presidents are willing, with increasing frequency, to sit on various governmental advisory panels in the hope that they can affect at the very time of conception some of the rules under which they will have to live. Organizations like the American Association of University Professors and the American Council on Education have developed well-staffed Washington offices which exist only to monitor events on and off Capitol Hill, and try to provide an academic input into various congressional and agency hearings. The philosophy behind these actions can be simply summarized as a belief that a more direct and intimate contact with governmental bureaucrats should result in a better break for the universities. This *rapprochement* from the university side should, in the opinion of reform-minded study groups, be further matched by corresponding moves in the quarters of the government. "A Department of Education with a clearly defined constituency would do a good job" says the NEA. "More responsive officials in *all* Departments *and* the White House would do a better job" says the AFT. "Growth should be the main theme around which to reorganize the administration" suggests the Carnegie Council. These proposed solutions differ widely, but they all have in common the American belief that appropriate restructuring of organizational forms would bring with it the solution of the problem.

There are other students of the academic scene like Robert Nisbet, Edward Shils and Allan Bloom who have come to the conclusion that the underlying problems lie much deeper and cannot be resolved by simple administrative manipulation. According to them, there are difficulties with the ways in which each partner in the university-state interaction perceives the other and even with the perception each partner has of itself. In particular, one real difficulty stems from a fundamental lack of understanding, on the part of modern egalitarian societies, about the intrinsic life of the intellect and the role of institutions of higher learning. The government looks at the university just as if it were another enterprise which can be contracted to provide a particular service. These services may be of many kinds, from training of manpower to the study of international trade policies, but in all cases the purchaser wants the best product for the least money and expects that the enterprise abides by all rules and regulations applicable to any other industrial or commercial outfit. Such imponderabilia like the role of universities as trustees of the intellectual and cultural heritage, the support for "ivory tower" thinking not yielding obvious immediate results, or the subtle differences in the internal scholarly climate of different departments and schools are rarely, if ever, reflected in the contractual language of agreements between the government and the universities. Colleges and universities are required to pay Social Security, obey all safety rules, fulfill every Equal Employment regulation, and help the handicapped by special subsidy if necessary; the government in return does *not* show concern for the depletion of the intellectual capital, for the need for pure disinterested scholarship, for the peculiar professional hierarchies needed for the validation and advancement of knowledge, or for the special corporate relationship found within the quasi-monastic departments of some of our best and most renowned schools. Such considerations and a related understanding are foreign to the pages of the Federal Register. No wonder that we encounter persistent and growing tensions between a government trying to act as patron and the recipient profession, which continuously feels misunderstood. *There is here a basic asymmetry between the demand of the government that the university obey all of its rules and the almost total unwillingness of the same government to adjust its actions to the intrinsic life-rules of the university.*

According to this analysis a great deal must be done—in addition to and beyond the simple administrative reorganization—to bridge the large gulf of misunderstanding that exists between the university and the state. According to this view, academies must first persuade the democratic audience that the modern university at its best is not only consistent with, but also essential to the fulfillment of the highest ideals of democracy. Furthermore, only after articulating a well-reasoned and credible case for being considered *different* from ordinary enterprises, will the university be able to delineate its many functions and negotiate for its support in toto through a well-balanced financial diet, rather than the current chaotic funding on which it now bases its financial health. To do this, the academic negotiators would also have to study in depth the ways of the government before undertaking such an educational campaign for converting the tight-fisted legislators and bureaucrats. Finally, the success of such encounters would greatly depend on the degree of conviction with which the academic leadership pleads the special nature of their case.

While the above program has all the virtues of simplicity, its realization faces numerous obstacles. Foremost among them is the divergence of opinion within the academy itself concerning the mission of the university. For example, the purists may wish to suggest a sharp and elegant intellectual agenda only to be denounced by those who prefer broad meadows to restricted ideologically tainted gardens. Conversely, those who give academic freedom a most liberal interpretation find themselves accused of defining the university by whatever happens to be taught at a university—a weak definition of a mission indeed! This gap between the two main camps seems quite wide and a credible formulation of the university's mission—as distinct from the intuitive feeling of many members of the academy—may have to await such time when a more general and therefore more acceptable constitutional formulation can be agreed upon. This fact will by necessity delay the implementation of a serious university-state negotiating gambit. Indeed, without a credible conviction on the part of academic negotiators, there can be no effective academic posture.

No matter what the immediate difficulties, however, the question will have to be resolved within a not too distant future. There are periods when limited adjustments and finer tuning can smooth out temporary rough spots. Our era is not of this kind. At the present time university-state confrontations seem to affect the very foundations of our intellectual life and the bases of our earlier successes. Future progress will therefore depend on how well we describe and justify our past performance. The message of the Conference seems to be that the earlier we approach this task, the better the chance for success.

Administrative reforms can at best buy us some time.

NOTES

1. Carnegie Council on Policy Studies and Higher Education, data for the year 1976.
2. Ibid.
3. One often finds business management overtones in the running of American institutions of higher learning.
4. One should note that in most situations ordinary business contractors can pass along to the consumer the increased cost of regulation; universities cannot.

"New Class," using the term coined by Milovan Djilas in his well-known book. The term refers to the many, mostly self-appointed, guardians of social morality and welfare who, presumably in possession of higher wisdom and virtues, seek to control our daily life. The third and last group involves the tangibly productive segment of the society, the individuals who bake the bread, build the houses, fight the wars, pay for higher education, and, yes, try to keep the streets clean. One recalls the remark by another participant of the conference who, to emphasize the unique qualities—and prerogatives—of his fellow scholars, contrasted the faculty chairmen with the "garbage collectors."

It is then proposed that the present condition and travail of the institutions of higher learning may be profitably viewed in terms of frequent struggles for power between these three interest groups: the mostly but not entirely scholarship-oriented academics, the power-seeking, ascending New Class, and the general working population whose moral health and working habits the New Class seeks to control.

*　　　*　　　*

Few would disagree that one of the most important recent political developments has been the enormous increase in governmental power. An increasingly autonomous administrative New Class has come to dominate public life. In the name of populism, democracy, and higher virtues, the traditional autonomy of individuals and institutions alike are being challenged and abolished as the New Class consolidates its hold. Constitutional guarantees which were previously regarded as barriers against governmental encroachment are now reinterpreted to justify governmental intervention. New moral imperatives—presumably implied by Constitutional articles—are discovered and formulated by activist judges and passed on to the New Class bureaucracy which then proceeds to work out and to enforce specific guidelines and regulations.

In the name of a higher morality democratic consensus is being ignored or even suppressed. The continual "discovery" of new social shortcomings and the moral failings of the electorate have become necessary in order to justify the existence and the activities of the economically largely parasitic New Class members. The destruction of consensual society has become a logical objective of the New Class, at least until a majority agrees to its leadership, lest its members become superfluous and its bureaucrats unemployed. For example, few knowledgeable persons doubt that a single free, public referendum on the question of forced busing of schoolchildren would free many thousands of planners, supervisors, statisticians, and bus drivers for more productive work. Incidentally, the entire system is financed by increasingly large amounts of money, much of it extorted with questionable constitutional legitimacy from the public.

Another important and in many ways remarkable development has been the rapid growth and expansion of higher education. By any measure, higher education has become big business. Professors Shils and Finn have informed us that $15 billion in federal funds are poured each year into the system, $1,500 for every college student and nearly $24,000 for every faculty member in the land. Although generally deplored in academic circles because of the usual strings attached, federal money has rarely been turned down.

Academic prosperity had, of course, its own consequences and two will be singled out here. First, rather paradoxically, it seems that with increased riches the individual importance of faculty members has actually declined. As a group, academics may have well increased their total social weight but only at the cost of losing some of their individual importance. The number of communicants has explosively increased, and the demand for meaningful academic communication has probably remained the same. If such is the case, one would expect an increase in academics' competitiveness and frustration. The other, and related, consequence has been the concomitant social elevation of university administrators who are viewed as the true representatives of the academic enterprise regardless of their academic talents or distinctions

The growing affluence and complexity of the university, and its dependence on state and federal financing, have increased the gap between the faculty and the administration. Academics have always viewed the campus bureaucrats with a measure of suspicion (and received a somewhat patronizing attention in return). But new factors and tendencies have now entered the equation. On the one hand, many successful academics have become skillful organizers and grant-finders—one is tempted to say entrepreneurs—jealously guarding their empires against encroachment by university officials. On the other hand, by negotiating, distributing, and supervising the spending of state and federal funds in progressively increasing quantities, many university officials have become a part of the ruling New Class machine itself.

Formally, the top administrators still continue to raise funds, calculate cost-benefit ratios, and review academic regulations. But the difference now is that, to raise funds, they must please the federal bureaucrats, which means they must optimize the ratios according to New Class criteria and enforce regulations which are determined less and less by those who must live by them. University administrators at the very summit of the system now have no more in common with their academic employees than the executives of the General Motors Corporation have with their assembly plant workers.

In fact, the multiversity officials now frequently act as campus representatives of the government and its agencies. They are the local enforcers of governmental regulations and protectors of New Class interests. Looking over the earlier remarks by Columbia's President McGill, there is little in them which contradicts my theses. If anything, he sounded more like a chairman of the board than an academician. He dwelt on financial matters, governmental regulations, and he pleaded for circumspect action. He cited adverse experiences of AT&T which went into court over the administration of affirmative action only to regret this step later on. When faculty members discussed principles, President McGill advocated corporate prudence. He gave the bureaucratically sound but academically dubious warning that he who asks too many questions receives too many answers.

"Do not accept your own wisdom as to constitutional questions because it may not work out that way," he cautioned the faculty members present, adding that "one needs, at all cost, to preserve the essential character of the functioning of our institutions so that we can do our work." He did not explain what character and what work.

Professor Bloom's reference to President McGill as "Professor Bill" may have won Bloom a friend but certainly confused the issue. "Chairman Bill" might have been more appropriate. In any case, a skillful administrator is no more a professor than the president of the Ford Corporation is a car mechanic or the Soviet premier and party secretary is a proletarian. It is of course difficult to argue practical wisdom when someone proposes expediency. But it is then equally difficult to take seriously the many academic voices demanding social reforms for others but claiming special exemptions for themselves.

When weighing the actions of federal and campus bureaucrats, one should note that, in many cases, the circumstances that would weaken an individual's position produce the exact opposite when a bureaucrat is involved. For instance, when one borrows money, one's financial strength and independence generally suffer. If a government borrows money, however, its autonomy and financial muscle generally become stronger. The hundreds of billions of dollars of the national debt have not weakened the central government; they only increased the federal bureaucracy and made it less responsive.

In a similar manner, an increase in externally imposed rules and regulations does not generally weaken campus officials. It may weaken the faculty and threaten the autonomy of the institution, but it will strengthen the administration. New and restrictive federal regulations, and even court proceedings against the university, will in most cases only increase the importance of its officials. With more rules to enforce, and more lawsuits to litigate, their staff and their budget will grow, as will their salary and social status.

It is by now an observable fact that every time the New Class authoritarians discover another social need and another moral principle, they increase their prestige, wealth, and power. They receive yet more funds and they write yet more rules into the Federal Register. And, every time the new directives are passed on to the campus administration for enforcement, the campus bureaucrats increase their prestige and power. They tighten their control over faculty and academic matters; they hire more aides and consultants; they make more headlines, and then they go on another lucrative tour of the lecture circuit. It is their academic employees—and the institution as a whole—who lose in the process.

*   *   *

One can of course only view the collaboration between the campus officials and the Washington bureaucrats with alarm since it portends the ultimate demise of academic freedom. The latter may fade away just as surely as the autonomy and independence of neighborhood schools did. But the academic scene is only a part of a more general and equally worrisome picture. The great push is on for a total cultural homogenization, and for a progressive elimination of the individual autonomy and freedoms which were supposed to be guaranteed by the Constitution. Using moralistic slogans and coercive judicial and governmental interventions, the New Class is invading all phases of our personal and public life. Cultural and educational pluralism is celebrated in words but destroyed in fact. Unimportant decisions are left to local groups; the controlling power is transferred to Washington.

Even President McGill spoke about "the remarkable recent growth of federal initiatives in regulation" and agreed that, "University people accustomed to thinking in terms of constitutional protection find the Federal Register to be quite a revelation. . . . One of the major features of the regulatory process is that regulations are typically cast in such a way as to place the burden of proof of good behavior on the defendant institution, reversing the ordinary requirements of legal procedure." And yet, he concluded that federal regulation was not a threat to academic freedom "in principle, and certainly not yet." He suggested that the major problem was "not in the area of academic freedom, but in the rigidity of the regulations themselves." "During the last fifty years," he reflected contentedly, "we have entered into a remarkable partnership with the federal government. In so doing we and government have managed to create an extraordinary educational enterprise contributing greatly to the advancement of our nation." President McGill then listed various achievements and proposed that, "our technology continues to be the marvel of the rest of the world." He concluded that "Our country and our educational system" have been projected "into positions of world leadership" and "the evidence of success is clear as the Nobel Prizes begin to roll in."

In fact, Dr. McGill even indicated that federal regulations might actually be welcome. "No experienced university president," he said in a guarded way, "would think of criticizing a process that has liberated America's minorities, protected our consumers, and provided a standard of living for American workers unequalled elsewhere in the world."

One shakes one's head over this sweeping statement. Can anyone, even a university president, really believe it was the federal bureaucrats who provided us with our present high standard of living? The quoted statement becomes yet more puzzling, when taken in the context of the bulging Federal Register. President McGill himself admits that federal regulations "sponsored a formidable bureaucracy in Washington" and elsewhere, and resulted in a "stupendous" paper flow. But yet, he still views the New Class bureaucrats as protectors and liberators.

To protect the consumer, the federal regulators now impose some 5,600 regulations by twenty-seven different agencies on the steel industry. The General Motors Corporation estimates that the documents it has to file in connection with the certification of its cars for sale in a single year would make a stack fifteen stories high. OSHA has even issued twenty-one pages of fine-print regulations on ladder design including how much to indent the screws. To cope with this flood of requirements and ordinances, universities and colleges were compelled to hire virtually hundreds of lawyers and to establish entire legal departments in order to handle the problem.

To help liberate America's minorities, the Los Angeles City school system distributed to all of the districts a set of requirements ("Memorandum 10"). Teachers who wish to change their previously stated racial identity must now present not only their birth certificates, but also *verification of racial ancestry back to their grandparents.* One presumes the European immigrants may use the birth certificates of the three ancestral generations which they had to obtain under the Nazi occupation to show they were not Jewish.

*   *   *

Last school year, Henry Kissinger, the former Secretary of State, was offered a teaching position at Columbia University, of which Dr. McGill is the president. In response, Professor Kesselman, a New Leftist in the department of Political Science, circulated petitions, created a lot of adverse publicity, and otherwise agitated in the usual hard left terms in an attempt to block the appointment. Although the overwhelming majority of Columbia's faculty and students apparently favored the appointment, and although Kissinger was obviously eminently qualified for the position, Dr. McGill was not quoted in the media as condemning Kesselman's totalitarian ploy. Nor has he used the occasion for a principled defense of academic freedom. Dr. Kissinger, of course, looked for employment elsewhere.

Present inaction can be compared to the well-publicized actions in a similar incident which occurred several years ago and which Dr. McGill himself mentioned in his presentation. While chancellor of the University of California, San Diego, he vigorously defended the academic freedom, and the right to an academic position, of Herbert Marcuse, the leftist totalitarian who was urging the imposition of Lenin's brutal "first phase" on the American society. At the time, Dr. McGill did not hesitate to condemn in the sharpest terms those who advocated that Marcuse not be reappointed. If anything, he showed a complete indifference to those elements of San Diego's working people who opposed Marcuse's reappointment, who sensed that Marcuse's totalitarianism, his openly proclaimed policy of "repressive tolerance" threatened their freedoms and democratic mode of life. Presumably, what is suitable for the academics is not suitable for the garbage collectors. *Quod licet Jovi, non licet bovi.*

The irony is that in real and objective terms it was San Diego's workers who, however clumsily, tried to defend the freedom of speech which Marcuse has labored all these years to abolish. And it is equally ironic that it should be primarily those who are highly educated who seem to fall for the Marcusian sophisticated nonsense. Is it possible that those San Diego legionnaires with whom McGill had to "joust" displayed an instinct for survival which college administrators have outgrown?

"I found it very hard," Dr. McGill noted in his earlier remarks, "to see [Herbert Marcuse] as a threat to any government, but that perhaps does not reflect on the power of his ideas. In that vehicle, whatever he believes to be true is my obligation to defend." One wonders whether the freedoms of so-called "right wingers," the Shockleys, the Jensens, the scientific hereditarians, would be defended with equal ardor when their meetings are disrupted and they are prevented from speaking. In effect, for many years on many Amercian campuses, no one could speak up for American policy without risking assault from the totalitarian left which operated with almost complete impunity.

Witnessing "Senator Joseph McCarthy's merciless public handling of a fellow graduate student whose crime happened to be that he believed in Marxism" caused Dr. McGill to experience a "chill," still "very difficult to deal with" in San Diego a decade and a half later. This is to his credit.

On the other hand, one can only wish that President McGill were equally alert to abuses from the so-called political left. Was he similarly agonized by the actions of the leftist bully boys (at the same university, Harvard) when, a few years ago, they demanded the right to run university affairs and to disallow speakers with whom they disagreed—including lawfully and democratically elected public officials—from addressing the student body? This is however a "familiar litany" since everyone knows that, relatively speaking, there is much less willingness on the part of "university people" to view the excesses on the so-called Left in the same light as the excesses on the so-called Right.

Just a few years ago, there were elements on the campuses who rooted openly for the victory of the Communist "reformers" in Southeast Asia. When the U.S. finally moved to neutralize the Cambodian military sanctuaries, many acted as if the very future of mankind were at stake. Riots were staged and instruction was brought to a standstill on behalf of human freedom and dignity. Now that the U.S. has withdrawn from Southeast Asia, all is quiet on the campus fronts. Few care that millions are being tortured and killed all over Cambodia, Laos, and South Vietnam. After the Khmer Rouge moved into Phnom Penh, the Cambodian capital, its members drove millions, including the bedridden in the hospitals, into the countryside, many of them to die. Those unable to walk were thrown out of the windows. Over the succeeding months, people from those regions tried to flee to freedom by any means available. Other hundreds of thousands are still held in "reeducation" camps of the Indo-Chinese Gulag. Nevertheless, there are no campus freedom fighters to be seen now. One can easily imagine what would happen on our campuses today if a similar savagery was perpetrated by the governments of South Africa or Chile. Can it be that many of our "university people" truly accept Marcuse's liberating doctrine of "repressive tolerance" which he spells out as meaning "intolerance against movements from the Right, and toleration of movements from the Left?"

Should the Patron Be the Master?: The Autonomy of Public Universities and Colleges

Paul Kurtz
Professor of Philosophy
SUNY at Buffalo

Most of the papers in this volume focus on the role of the federal government in higher education. They are concerned with the vast increase in federal regulations, and the consequent undermining of the autonomy of institutions of higher education. Unfortunately, very few of the contributors have addressed themselves to still another serious danger to the independence of higher education. I refer here to the role of state governments and localities in funding and regulating of colleges and universities.

This problem is especially crucial for state-supported universities, but also for the many community colleges funded by county and municipal governments. In an effort to provide expanded educational opportunities for larger sectors of the citizenry, state and local governments have entered into the university and college business on a massive scale. Many states are also playing an increased role in regulating private institutions that clamor for public funds. State and local government officials very often have a more parochial or pragmatic attitude toward higher education than do officials on the national scene; as a result, the vitality of the institutions under their jurisdiction may suffer. Professorial staffs that teach at such institutions will readily attest to these facts. Indeed, the most persistent problem for public institutions is what is increasingly viewed as the onerous role of governmental interference in the academic process itself. Controllers of the public purse strings have often felt it their duty to intervene into the governance of universities on budgetary grounds—insisting, for example, on productivity criteria for faculty, often on a strictly quantitative student-faculty load basis—and they have cut academic programs of high quality on purely utilitarian grounds.

My own direct experience is with the State University of New York, the largest in the nation, but this can no doubt be generalized to other institutions of the land. Increasingly, what is at stake is the viability of these institutions in the face of narrow-minded legislatures or budget bureaus.

I am surely not denying the need for responsible scrutiny of public institutions. On the other hand, our commitment to a basic principle, the need for the autonomy of the university, increasingly is being eroded—this time not by McCarthyisms of the right or the left, self-proclaimed vigilantes or ideologues, the advocates of student power, the Babbitts of virtue and religion, or powerful vested interests, but by political powers charged with the overall responsibility for institutions of higher learning.

In a period of inflationary pressures, when demands for tax cuts are strong, educational quality often has to suffer at the hands of political expediency. As a result, many faculty and administrators feel that they no longer run their institutions, but that the state capital, Albany or Sacramento, is in charge—and usually it is some powerful legislative committee or some anonymous bureaucrat in the governor's office who calls the shots. One is constantly asked to justify the expenditure of funds, the addition of faculty, the introduction of new programs, the retention of old ones. Where there are expanding educational horizons and a rapid growth of institutions, prosperity is in evidence and some autonomy is tolerated; where there is stability or retrenchment, indiscriminate budget cutting threatens.

This problem has been all the more exacerbated by the growth of collective bargaining. Some states require that the faculty be represented by a bargaining unit. In New York State, the Taylor Law mandated that the faculty organize and be represented by some agent—the AFL-CIO, AAUP, National Education Association, the Civil Services Employees Association, or some other group. Often this process places the faculty in an adversary relationship with the government about wages, working conditions, productivity, and effort. In the process the spirit of collegiality is sacrificed.

No doubt, some of this is inevitable. Big education, demanding public funds, must be regulated by those charged with fiscal responsibility. But as a result the university often suffers; it is constantly being placed at the mercy of whatever political vicissitudes arise. Whether the party in power will cut taxes and spending, stabilize the level of expenditures in the face of inflation (which is a *de facto* cut in budget), or increase funding for the university is always uncertain. Neither the president nor the chancellor is his own master; how his institution fares depends, in the end, upon political considerations far beyond his control or that of his faculty.

Today all too many universities have to contend with bureaucratic or legislative insensitivity to the needs of higher education, and extraneous standards are used to evaluate academic programs simply in terms of their "cash value." Granted, often there is fat that can be cut, but just as often budget cutting may go right to the bone and marrow of qualitative education. Sometimes there is a bartering between upstate and downstate interests: a battle for support between urban universities and suburban or rural interests.

We in the university are no doubt responsible in good measure for the problem: many of our colleagues have actively sought increased governmental spending for higher education. In addition, parents, wanting to see their children educated, have voted to support such programs. A case can be made, however, that an overinvestment in *public* education is unwise. I am surely not objecting to the founding of land grant colleges nor to the growth and vitality of state and municipal universities and colleges, but I think there may be dangers that these and others will be swallowed up by the bureaucratic-political maze, and fidelity to the principles of academic freedom and integrity will be compromised. I think that it is a profound mistake to politicize all of the institutions of society. Our churches have remained strong without direct governmental aid, due of course to the constitutional principle of the separation of church and state. Although many churches claim to have financial difficulties, they have managed to survive, and some have even prospered. Similarly, until very recently the arts have flourished without financial support. I am in no way objecting to some governmental support of the arts, but we must be careful that in the process the arts are not politicized or qualitatively impoverished. Some former liberal supporters of govern-

289

ment grants have expressed considerable disquietude that this is already occurring. The publishing industry, which is strong and vigorous, is still largely free of government support. It is regrettable that the case has to be made again for the need to preserve free, voluntary institutions in a pluralistic democracy, institutions outside of the realm of political control.

I think it would be a profound tragedy if all of our institutions of higher education were nationalized, yet this in effect may be slowly happening. In spite of ourselves, both on the federal and state level, there is mounting evidence of increased *de jure* regulation and *de facto* control. The private sector in education is steadily being absorbed or outdistanced by the public sector. I realize that our elementary and secondary schools, in order to be viable, need to depend primarily upon public support. I am prepared to defend this support without qualification. (I believe also that private schools have a *raison d'etre* in a pluralistic framework.) Our institutions of higher learning, however, seem to me to be of a different order because of the creative character of research and the pursuit of knowledge. Granted that some governmental role is inevitable, indeed desirable—in granting tax-exemptions to nonprofit institutions, in the accreditation of degree-granting institutions, in support of research and student scholarships, etc. But we must be careful that we do not barter away our birthright for the promise of largesse: the patron should not become the master. I would hope, therefore, that public universities would actively seek to develop supplementary funds from endowments (for those that do not have them), alumni giving, increased fees, etc., in order to retain some measure of independence.

Publicly supported institutions have an especially compelling need to resist political control and to make the case for their autonomy in relative, if not absolute, terms—for no principle is absolute. This can best be done if at least three conditions are fulfilled: First, there is the need to develop an enlightened public that appreciates the proper role of higher education in American life. I fear that public trust has eroded in the minds of many citizens. Much of this is a fall-out from the intemperate behavior of faculties, administrators, and students during the late sixties. We must strive to reestablish an understanding of our vital function in society and our need for internal authority over our own educative affairs. Second, we should seek to encourage the emergence of enlightened public officials who have some appreciation for cultural values and some sense of the intrinsic worth of learning and research. And third, but not least, we need to cultivate the development of a responsible faculty, keenly cognizant of its moral obligation to use public monies wisely. Unfortunately, there has been an erosion of faculty responsibility during the days when the university succumbed to ideological fervor. Since then, institutional loyalties have declined and been replaced by primary career commitments. Professors need to have their sense of mission reawakened, both in fulfilling the immediate goals of their institutions in educating and servicing students, and in their long-range enduring contributions to the arts and sciences of human civilization. In my view, the first order on the agenda, as always, is the imperative to clarify for all concerned that universities have a purpose that transcends the reigning political, ideological, economic, or religious forces of the day. If we are to keep alive the free pursuit of knowledge, we can only do so where academic freedom and autonomy are preserved.

Contributors

Robert C. Andringa
Dr. Andringa was the former Minority Staff Director of the Committee on Education and Labor of the U.S. House of Representatives. He is currently campaign manager for Congressman Quie.

Fred Baumann
Dr. Baumann was the Assistant Executive Secretary of the University Centers for Rational Alternatives. He is currently a National Fellow at the Hoover Institution on War, Revolution and Peace at Stanford University.

Charles Bazerman
Dr. Bazerman teaches English at Baruch College–CUNY. He has written on literature and the teaching of writing.

Allan Bloom
Dr. Bloom is Professor of Political Economics at the University of Toronto.

George Bonham
Dr. Bonham is Editor-In-Chief of *Change* Magazine.

Robert H. Bork

Dr. Bork was former Solicitor General of the United States, a Consultant for the Cabinet Committee on Education and Professor of Law at Yale University.

Charles M. Chambers

Dr. Chambers was a former Associate Dean of Planning and Development at George Washington University. Presently, he is Staff Associate and Legal Advisor for the Council on Postsecondary Education.

Chester E. Finn, Jr.

Dr. Finn was a former Research Associate in Governmental Studies at The Brookings Institution. He is currently legislative assistant to Senator Daniel P. Moynihan.

Robert Goldwin

Dr. Goldwin was Special Consultant on Education to the President of the United States. Currently, he is Director of Seminar Programs at the American Enterprise Institute.

Sidney Hook

Dr. Hook is Emeritus Professor of Philosophy from the New York University. Currently, he is a Fellow at The Hoover Institution at Stanford University.

Donald Hornig

Dr. Hornig was the former President of Brown University, former Chairman of the Federal Council on Science and Technology and an Honorary Research Associate in Applied Physics at Harvard University.

Martin Kramer

Martin Kramer is former Director for Higher Education Planning, HEW. He is currently serving as a Senior Fellow at the Carnegie Council on Policy Studies in Higher Education.

Paul Kurtz

Dr. Kurtz is Professor of Philosophy at the State University of New York at Buffalo and Editor of *The Humanist*.

Richard Lester

Dr. Lester is Emeritus Professor of Economics from Princeton University and author of *Anti-Bias Regulation of Universities*.

David S. Lichtenstein

Dr. Lichtenstein is a former government attorney and former Branch Chief of the International Satellite and Communication Division of the Federal Communications Commission.

William J. McGill

Dr. McGill is currently President of Columbia University.

James A. Norton

Dr. Norton is Chancellor of the Ohio Board of Regents.

Henry R. Novotny

Dr. Novotny was Associate Professor of Psychology at California State at Bakersfield and a psychological consultant to the California Correctional Institution at Tehachapi. He is currently the Director of The Center for Psychological Therapy—A Psychological Corporation.

Arthur G. Powell

Dr. Powell is a Lecturer on Education at the Harvard Graduate School of Education.

Robert Sasseen

Dr. Sasseen is Dean of the Faculty at California State University at San Jose.

John R. Searle

Dr. Searle is Professor of Philosophy at the University of California at Berkeley. He was a lecturer at Christ Church, Oxford, and a visiting professor at Brasenose College, Oxford. Author of *The Campus War,* Dr. Searle served as a consultant to the President's Commission on Student Unrest (the Scranton Commission).

Edward Shils

Dr. Shils is Professor of Social Thought and Sociology at the University of Chicago, a Fellow of Peterhouse College at Cambridge University and the Editor of *Minerva*.

Eli Spark

Dr. Spark is on the faculty of The Catholic University of America in Washington, D.C.

Miro Todorovich

Dr. Todorovich teaches Physics at Bronx Community College of the City University of New York and is the Executive Secretary of the University Centers for Rational Alternatives, and the Coordinator of the Committee on Academic Nondiscrimination and Integrity.

Kenneth S. Tollett

Dr. Tollett is the Director of the Institute for the Study of Educational Policy at Howard University

Carol van Alstyne

Dr. van Alstyne is the chief economist at the American Council of Education. She is coauthor of *The Costs of Implementing Federally Mandated Social Programs at Colleges and University*.